"You could call this 'Europe on 35 Laughs a Day.'"—*Hartford Courant*

"A funny, lighthearted book by two guys who just want you to have fun in Europe."—*Playboy*

Let's Blow thru Europe

is the most hilarious travel guide you'll ever read. Here's why:

No other guidebook is so relentlessly sophomoric.

We make fun of everything all the other guides hold dear, from British beer, to the Arc de Triomphe, to the gondolas in Venice.

LET'S BLOW researchers wear those wacky Groucho Marx nose-and-glasses everywhere they go.

They're always good for a laugh.

LET'S BLOW has been Revised! and Expanded!

We didn't just renew our passports, we actually *went* to Europe again and looked around. If a charming restaurant we recommended in the first edition has become an overpriced tourist trap, we make them pay us big bucks.

No other guidebook shows you how to do a dozen European cities in just two weeks:

We'll show you how easy it is to blow through all the famous sites like Westminster Abbey and the Louvre, so you can spend all your time drinking beer, cruising the clubs, and meeting other libidinous youth "on the road." Admit it—after three or four 15th-century cathedrals, they all look alike, right? Be honest.

LET'S BLOW is your passport to a helluva good time in Europe.

Disclaimer

All the prices, addresses, and phone numbers were absolutely, 100% correct when we wrote this book. Trust us. Not a single mistake.

Sometimes, though, stuff happens. Like, you get to Paris and some restaurant has moved from #35 to #53 *on the same street.* Or you discover the phone number has changed from 567-1989 to 567-1988. Look, they do this *all the time* in Europe. Hell if we know why. Maybe to avoid taxes or *Let's Go*'ers or something.

Our advice is, don't sweat the little stuff.

On the other hand, if you find really major changes—such as London is now in Germany, or the Swiss have a sense of humor—let us know, because that counts as Big Stuff, and we might want to put it in the next edition. Plus, someone should tell the Swiss.

You can write to us in care of Mustang Publishing, P.O. Box 3004, Memphis, TN 38173, USA.

Revised! & Expanded!

LET'S BLOW

Thru

EUROPE

Thomas Neenan & Greg Hancock

Mustang Publishing Co.
Memphis, TN

Helping Let's Blow

If you have suggestions, corrections, or a very pretty sister, send us her picture. We read every piece of correspondence, especially when it contains a check. All checks will be cashed. Please note that mail received after Wednesday will be ignored. Make checks payable to Mustang Publishing, Inc. Address mail to *Let's Blow thru Europe*, **Mustang Publishing Co., Inc., P.O. Box 3004, Memphis, TN 38173 USA.**

In addition to the bomb threats and terrible grammar our readers send us, many beg for a job as a researcher or editor. Unfortunately, the charter of Mustang Publishing Company, Inc. enables us to employ only your very pretty sister.

Distributed to the trade in the U.S.A. by National Book Network, Lanham, Maryland and in England and Europe by Gazelle Book Services, Lancaster, England. For information on distribution in other areas, please contact Mustang Publishing.

Much of this book is intended as satire. For you humorless, politically correct types who get offended, just lighten up.

Library of Congress Cataloging in Publication Data:

Neenan, Thomas, 1958-
    Let's blow thru Europe / Thomas Neenan and Greg
Hancock. —Rev. and expanded ed.
        p.   cm.
    ISBN 0-914457-46-2 (alk. paper) : $10.95
    1. Europe—Guidebooks.   I. Hancock, Greg, 1956-   . II. Title.
D909.N38 1992
914.04'558--dc20   91-50886
                                                                        CIP

Printed on acid-free paper. ∞

10   9   8   7   6   5   4   3   2

Dedications

To dedicate a book like this to people you love is only slightly less romantic than naming a sewage treatment plant or a prison annex after them. (After you finish the book, you may feel we're doing the prison annex a disservice.)

Despite this difficulty, Thomas dedicates the even-numbered pages, half the maps, and the back cover to Gretchen, whose love, devotion, and smiles make his life so happy.

That leaves Greg the odd pages, the front cover, and the rest of the maps to dedicate to his mother, who suggested the title *Laughing All the Way* for this book; to his father, who himself survived a whirlwind two-week tour when he was supposed to be enjoying his retirement; to his sister Carol, who could fill 16 volumes of travel humor; and to Pamela, whose encouragement, laughter, and love prove endless. Please don't take offense to the odd-page idea, though—it really has nothing to do with your personalities.

Acknowledgments

This is a book for *all* travellers, not just those travelling on the interest from their trust funds.

We certainly could not have brought this opus to fruition without the dedication of our researchers and writers.

Many readers inquire about our methods of choosing correspondents. Indeed, some readers even apply for a position themselves—when they didn't even apply to an Ivy League school! (Amusing notion, eh?) Of course, our criteria for writers is most strict. First, they must attend *our* school, regarded as the finest institution of higher learning in the land. (But, 'tis true—we suck at sports.) However, as proof we have the common touch, several of our researchers did attend *public* high school. Second, each writer must have a suitably pretentious name to embellish the credits page.

Let us first toast the efforts of Chloe Dunster Remington, who rambled through London, the Gateway to Europe ("*Porta, porta, portam*," to quote a *mot juste* from my days at Choate.) Her pungent, crisp prose was a pleasure—nay, a joy—to edit. Bravo, Chloe!

And who could read R.Z. Benjamin Rosenkrantz's exquisitely crafted descriptions of the aromas, the sights, and the sounds of Paris without blinking a surreptitious tear from an eye? Huzzah, R.Z.!

No pale words of mine can ever thank Portia Cabot Harkness for her fecund, feral characterizations of Dublin, the city of Joyce, Yeats, and my own favorite minor poet, Aoghan Liam MacMurthy O'Suiacain. "Erin go Bragh, Portia go Bragh."

Many a glad hosanna rent the air when FedEx delivered the latest missive from Wentworth St. John d'Courcy. Germany in all its Gothic glory sprang from his pages into our very own *Lebensraum.*

We received much copy written in an elemental, earthy style from Simon DuPont Hiltonsmith. Simon is a terrific chap, just mad for lacrosse and games of all sorts. Unfortunately, because of a snafu, Simon was writing from Equatorial Guinea, and there's the rub. Try as we might, in all conscience we could not squeeze his material into a book on European travel. I could have made a darn good case for British Guinea or even the Belgian Congo, but Equatorial Guinea was, as the state school students say, "too far-out, man."

Back home in old Thatcher Hall, our spirited crew had scant contact with Morpheus, "sweet father o' soft rest." Like the doomed characters in Schowlenskiratsky's *Die Erinnerügen,* we toiled day and night to separate the gilded prose from the dross. Our only respite came at 3:00 each afternoon, when I indulged editorial privilege and insisted my merry band break for tea and thinly sliced cucumber sandwiches.

Finalement, my heartfelt thanks to Crispin Trevor Holmes, the bard of our happy gang, who brightened many a long night by playing Early English folk songs on his lute. Crispin, we are forever in your thrall.

These few simple words are my swan song, my *chant du cygne.* Though they be played *larghetto,* they are also played *con anima.* Before I bow and leave the darkened stage, it behooves me to thank my father, Jefferson FitzWalter Adams. What a year for the Adams clan! Imagine—I become editor of *Let's Blow* the same year my dear pater donates a new library to the College. What a year, indeed!

Humbly, I lay this opus at the feet of my dearest, beloved Athena, my precious songbird, she of "th' glad smile ere the dewy grass shall caress her pearly-toed pieds" (to quote one of my own sonnets).

In closing, allow me also to thank thee, Dear and Gentle Reader, for shelling out the bucks for this rag so I'll have something on resumé when I apply to law school.

Ciao,
Horace Jefferson FitzWalter Adams

(Acknowledgments for the normal peoples' edition:)

Acknowledgments

But seriously folks, we could not have perpetrated this book without the help of many friends scattered around Europe. Most will never speak to us again once they see how we trashed their cities, ridiculed their customs, and generally abused their hospitality, but hey—what are friends for?

For much help on the Dublin chapter and for testing pints of Guinness in many pubs, we thank Frank Neenan and Aine O'Neill. And thanks to Paul Neenan, whose special brand of cynicism could fill a book in itself, and to Mom and Dad Neenan for making all the Neenans such compulsive travelers.

On the London chapter, we owe a great deal to Keith Waterton for letting us stay at his flat and to Michele Neenan, who persuaded him (against his better judgment) to do so. Keith recommended many of the restaurants in the London chapter, so if you have a terrible experience, write us and we'll send you his phone number.

Unfortunately for you, the best food in Paris is not available to the public but is made by our friend Helene Guineaudeau at her great apartment, where we have had the pleasure of staying too many times. We know this book will only confirm Helene's opinion that we are "teepical stupeed Americaines," but we hope she'll allow us to visit in the future.

We want to thank our many German friends, including Jurgen Dahmer and the beautiful Rita, Peter and Chris Berneth and their two *kinder* Johannes and Matthias, who knew long before their parents that we couldn't be trusted. We also kept trying to mooch off our friends Uli and Suzie, but they were always wise enough to be out of town when we appeared.

We owe a lot to Rollin Riggs, our editor and publisher. The lot we owe is next to a crack house in the Bronx, and you may pick it up any time, Rollin.

Among other friends who helped by laughing at our poor jokes or suggesting their own were Giselle Weiss, T. Randy Lee, Marifaith Hackett, Tish Dunne, Dick Gold (who actually endured a boat trip on the Rhine), Jack Moore (who believes you *can* judge a book by its cover), Dima Kaminsky and his lovely wife Lena (who provided warmth in Moscow), and Maureen Kalasa (the first person to show us how to cut *Let's Go* down to a useful size). A special thanks to Pamela Hancock, who was willing to risk a high profile, fast track, high yield, power lunch position on Wall Street to help when the going got tough.

Finally, we must thank the three blond and very drunk young women from U. Missouri (Rolla), whom we met at the Milkweg in Amsterdam. Their knowledge of and attitude toward Europe ("Egypt is, like, the *neatest* place in Europe!") convinced us *Let's Blow* had a market.

Maps by
Candace F. Rechsteiner
and Pamela Hancock.

Note: Maps are not drawn to scale.

Preface
to the Revised!
Expanded! Edition

It's been three years since the first edition of *Let's Blow thru Europe* soiled the shelves of your local bookstore. We, the authors, got rich and fat on the money we wrenched from the wallets of gullible travelers. Now, jaded by the constant round of New York literary parties and celebrity bashes on the West Coast, we decided it was time to squeeze back into our Levis, tug our college sweatshirts over our bulging guts, place our international stock funds in a blind trust, and head off to rediscover ourselves and Europe. The result: this Revised! Expanded! Edition.

We won't bore you with all the usual tripe about how good it was to be "on the road" again, with the smell of clean air in our noses and only our wits to put a roof over our heads. Actually, it was hell. The problem, as Tom Clancy warned us, is that success makes you soft, and you lose your artistic edge. It's difficult to explain to a non-artist like you the titanic struggle that goes into creating an epic terrific enough to be the *ABC Movie of the Week*, the soul-wrenching effort required to endorse GMC trucks and Maxipads in countless commercials. When we first wrote *Let's Blow*, we never imagined how easy it would be to lose touch with the little people, like you. So doing this Revised! Expanded! thing was no piece of cake, believe us.

Consider Paris. The Concord gets you there the same time you were in the shower at Clancy's place that morning. You take your limo into the city, throw your bags in your suite at the George VI, and off you go on the old grim routine. Check out the Eiffel Tower. Yeah, still there. Why in God's name can't they tear down the old stuff like they do in the States and put up something *new* for tourists to gawk at? Back to the hotel to change before dinner. Sift through a pile of faxes. Do we want to debate Judith Krantz on "Afrocentric Themes in *I'll Take Manhattan*" at NYU? Do we want to play Jay McInerny and John Updike in the Miller ProAm Literary Invitational at Lake Tahoe? (*Miller*, for chrissake!) Plus, the usual crop of endorsement offers: Would we consider a *Let's Blow* cologne? A *Let's Blow* action figure? A fax from our movie producer: Cher won't play the coed in the shopping scene in our new Cancun chapter (too demanding), so would we prefer Meryl Streep or Julia Roberts?

On to dinner with French glitterati. All they want to talk about is whether Jerry Lewis or Mickey Rourke will be in the *Let's Blow* movie. Maybe, but only if they can play a coed... Two weeks later, there's a 12-page piece in the French film magazine *L'Affront* called *Jerry Lewis et Mickey Rourke: Cross-dressing ou Non?*

Of course, we have to go to one of the crummy restaurants in the first edition of the book, now renamed *Let's Blow Ciao* in our honor. Police barricades everywhere, flashbulbs popping. Only Robin Leach stands between us and the door. Inside, the walls are hung with mementos from our original trips. By the Men's Room is Greg's truss. In the Ladies' Room, a collection of Amex receipts and airline barf bags. We both have to slow dance with Max, the owner. The editor of *L'Affront* scribbles notes furiously. Everyone who's anyone is there: Bianca Jagger, the Aga Khan, Norm Schwarzkopf, Andy Warhol—hmmmm, thought he was dead.

Back to the hotel in the wee hours. Have to take a call from Tokyo. Our Japanese editors are having trouble with the concept of a two-week tour of Europe. Most Japanese tourists can only take one week. Could we make the book a little less comprehensive? We suggest they hire the editor of *USA Today* on a freelance basis.

Up next day at the crack of noon. Deal with the overnight mail. The City of Zurich, represented by the New York law firm of Post, Hoc, Ergo, Propter, & Hoc, is suing to be included in the book. Martha Stewart has invented a new money belt made of used toilet rolls and old panty hose. She wants a plug in the new edition. ABC wants to send Sam Donaldson and a camera crew to spend the night with us in one of the quaint hotels we recommend. Send the camera crew and a rabid pit bull and it's a deal, we tell them.

Spend the day exploring the smelly old Latin Quarter, accompanied by crews from a French network and folks filming an Amex commercial in which Sean Connery plays a pickpocket. Watch for it during the Superbowl. The whole city appears overrun with college kids. What a drag. Everywhere we turn we're up to our nipples in fresh-faced dweebs from Iowa clutching the competition, *Let's Go Europe*, like a five-pound chastity belt. Of course, with the cameras running for *Nightline*, we have no choice but to slip on the Ohio State/Wisconsin/Texas A&M (insert your own diploma factory here) sweatshirt and mug for the cameras like retarded hyenas.

Our last night in Paris, and we have to attend some charity affair at the U.S. Embassy. Luckily, there's plenty of wine—they're serving a Californian vintage, and the French guests confine themselves to taking one sip and then spitting it into a plant.

Finally, back to the States, to hole-up in our slope-side condo in Telluride, where we've suffered days of tortured, artistic solitude—foregoing perfect powder *and* a reception for the Playmate of the Year—to pound-out this Revised! Expanded! edition for you.

So here it is, our meticulously re-researched guide to everything that's anything in Europe. It only remains for us to scribble all the usual nonsense about hoping you have as much fun reading this as we had writing it . . . blah, blah, blah . . . the best years of your lives . . . yak, yak, yak . . . going to discover Europe but discovering yourself instead . . . You know the drill. Fill in the gaps on your own time, would you? We gotta run—Madonna's on line 2.

Thomas "T.N." Neenan
Greg "The Greg" Hancock
Bayonne, N.J. (near Bruce's house)

Contents

# *Introduction*

There's an empty time in a young person's life, after high school and before going for it in the Real World, when questions of identity and belonging arise. It's a time of private search and personal growth, a time to assess where you've been and where you're going, a time to blow a lot cash before you have to worry about stuff like IRAs, SEPs, ARMs, and KIDs. Though many young Americans seek professional counseling, most try college.

In this book, we will discuss a crucial aspect of that personal growth experience, The Trip To Europe—a journey that has become a rite of passage as important as the first sexual experience, the first keg party, and the first exam in Chem Lab.

There is a plethora of well-meaning, do-goody books about traveling in Europe. Most fall into the *Europe-on-$XX+tips-a-Day* and *How to Immerse Yourself in All the Glorious Culture of Europe and Also Get Good Souvenirs* categories and are aimed primarily at the blue-rinse/polyester-golf-pants brigade. The practical information in these books is organized along the lines of "Yes, Conrad Hilton *does* serve prune juice at his hotel in Geneva" and "When you're in Albania, be sure to spend a day at the marvelous Kitchen Utensils Museum in Tirane" and "If you plan a few years ahead, a private audience with the Pope is easy to arrange."

Meanwhile, the books aimed at a younger traveler fall into two categories. First, there are the *You Can Travel around Europe on $5 a Month* guides ("Because, like, you can hitchhike and eat wild plants"), encouraging you to crash on European dudes' floors and maybe bike to Nepal later. This type of guidebook is aimed mainly at people who spend winters in Cuba picking coffee, freeloading off the socialist paradise, and summers in Cambridge or Georgetown, freeloading off friends and telling them how refusing to get a real job is a protest against The System.

The second and more popular youth-oriented guide is 900-pages thick, has an orange cover, and is memorized by big-boned, crew-cut boys named Bob from Stevens Point, Wisconsin, and frat boys from Rutgers who "don't want to get ripped-off, man." This guidebook can be very pious, emphasizing your role as an Ambassador Of Your Country. It lists hundreds of boring museums in towns you'll never get near in countries you've never even heard of. It provides you with glossaries of foreign words that enable Ambassador Bob to charm a Greek peasant with an opening line of "YES! ME HELLO! NINE-EIGHT ROOM PLEASE STUFFED GRAPE LEAVES."

The problem with this book is that it's written by teams of Harvard Art History majors who were all bigtime nerds in high school. Their idea of a great put-down is to say, "You have Van Gogh's ear for music." Let's get real here. If people were really interested in an old castle in some backwater Bulgarian town, they would have turned it into condos by now.

As an alternative, we proudly offer *Let's Blow thru Europe* as a game plan for a continental blitzkrieg. Since going to Europe is an essential part of a young person's life these days, we figure you should at least have a few laughs while you're over there. And if the laughs come at the expense of some of the world's greatest cities and sights, well, hey, if they can't take a joke . . .

We're offering no less than a radical new approach to European travel: We will guide you through *everything* in Europe that any normal, educated person has ever heard of, and we'll do it even if you've got only two weeks.

For example, did you know you can easily see Rome in one evening? Or do the much-heralded Rhine River Tour without ever getting on a boat? We'll tell you where to buy postcards and t-shirts, how to behave towards fellow travelers, how to handle all those foreigners, where to find American Express offices,

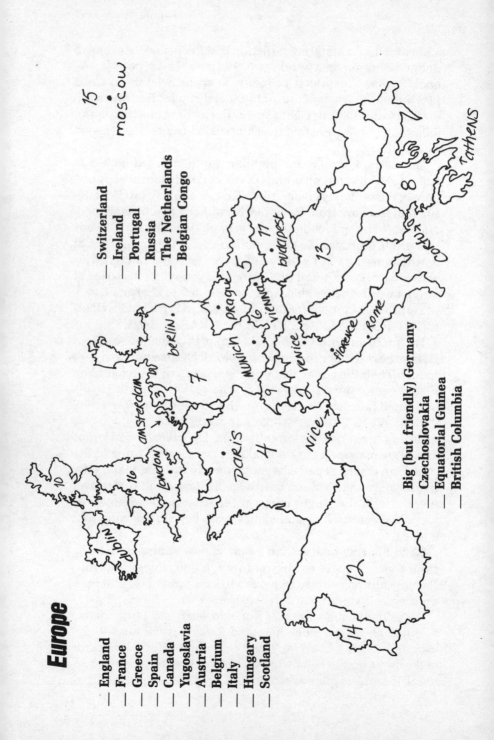

Europe

— England
— France
— Greece
— Spain
— Canada
— Yugoslavia
— Austria
— Belgium
— Italy
— Hungary
— Scotland

— Switzerland
— Ireland
— Portugal
— Russia
— The Netherlands
— Belgian Congo

— Big (but friendly) Germany
— Czechoslovakia
— Equatorial Guinea
— British Columbia

etc. As a bonus, we'll even throw in Cancun at no charge, in case you want to take a real vacation.

With this book as your guide, you can assimilate all you need to know in less time than you spent studying for your last psychology final! What's more, the book is written in plain, simple language that anyone can understand. We have intentionally avoided words like *escargot*, *art nouvelle*, and *menage a trois*. More conventional guidebooks will limit your possibilities by overwhelming you with details that have little to do with vacation travel. (Why, after all, do you think Daytona Beach and Palm Springs are rapidly displacing Europe as key destinations for young travelers today?) It's time to bring things back to perspective, and that's what we're going to do.

Getting Oriented

First, look at the little map on the other page. It shows the cities we'll be discussing on our two-week jaunt. We begin in London, England. By day four, we're in Amsterdam. From there we dash to France, where we visit Paris, followed by a few magical, bare-nippled days in Nice. Next we'll hit Munich and hit it hard, this city best known for its Oktoberfest, beer, and Hofbräuhaus t-shirts. Then it's down to Italy, blowing through Florence and Venice to Rome, the city of a thousand lights—in one night. From Rome, we'll show how simple it is to see Greece in two days. After a busy day in balmy Athens, it's *arivederchi* and *adieu* Europe, hello U.S. of A.!

And in case you have a few days more than the standard 14-day tour, we've even included insightful coverage of cities a little off the beaten path, like Prague, Berlin, Budapest, Vienna, Dublin, and Moscow. And, of course, Cancun.

Cancun? Isn't That in New Mexico?

Well, no, actually it's in Mexico, which is a big country south of Texas, which is a big country south of the United States. But still, you ask, why should Cancun be in a book about *Europe*?

Mostly, because we thought it would be funny, that's why.

Pop Quiz!

Before we proceed, it's imperative that you can at least identify on a map the countries you'll be visiting. Use the map on page 16 and match the number in the country with the list prepared as an answer sheet. Use a #2 pencil and be sure to fill in your answer completely. There are more countries listed than appear on the map, and you may use an answer only once.

The solution appears on page 33. You may grade your quiz yourself, or send it to Mustang Publishing for professional evaluation. Be sure to provide the last four digits of your Social Security number and a check for $25.00.

Timetable

The timetable outlined below will allow you to see everything in Europe in two weeks. Remember, this schedule is only a guideline. It does not have to be followed with the same rigor as your oral contraceptive prescription.

Day 0: Catch your flight to London.

Day 1: Arrive in London.

Day 2: Bloody well spend it in London, mate.

Day 3: London. Take overnight boat/train to Amsterdam.

Day 4: Amsterdam. Drink Heineken. Ogle prostitutes.

Day 5: Take train to Paris.

Day 6: See Paris. Drink wine. Fall in love. She breaks your heart, so go to Nice.

Day 7: Nice. Very Nice. Take overnight train to Munich.

Day 8: You vill drinken lots of bier.

Day 9: Travel to Rome. You willa drinka lotsa wine.

Day 10: More Rome. More wine.

Day 11: Take train to Brindisi, then take ferry to Corfu.

Day 12: Corfu. Crash a moped.

Day 13: Head for Athens.

Day 14: Athens. Buy a Greek fisherman's cap for an uncle you don't like very much.

Day 15: Head for home. Read a book about Europe on the plane so you can say something intelligent to your parents at the airport.

You'll notice that this timetable allows little opportunity to sleep. Hey, we're not completely dumb, you know. You see, by not letting you sleep, we didn't have to spend months schlepping around Europe, checking out every ratbag hotel so we could warn you about them.

Besides, you're not on a vacation, you're on a Mission. What do you want, *Let's Snooze thru Europe*?! No chance, lightweight. We recommend that you build up resistance by pulling several all-nighters before departure. During this training period, you should eat only cold pizza, Fluffernutter, Doritos, and onion dip. This diet will protect you from any intestinal bug in Europe, since your bowels will be in total chaos before you ever set foot on the plane. Remember, too, that sleep deprivation can do interesting things to the brain. If you start to imagine you are either Boris Becker, Boris Yeltsin, or Lt. Worf, relax. It's a normal, mind-expanding aspect of international travel.

Of course, it's possible to sleep en route to the next city, and most of the naps you'll take on this adventure will be snatched on moving trains.

Guidebooks

One of the serious questions you'll face when packing for the trip is what books to take. First, you'll of course need three copies of this book. (If you're a cheapskate reading this book while standing in the store's travel section, we hope you catch something itchy from a toilet seat in Hungary.) Another useful book to take along is the *Thomas Cook European Timetable*, which looks as entertaining as the circuit diagram for a 500 MHz Fourier Transform Magnetic Resonance Imager. Once you get used to it, however, it will prove invaluable.

Our close personal friends, the *Let's Go* series, can also be useful. The big problem with *Let's Go* is that God or somebody once called it "The Bible of Budget Travel," and it takes itself a tad too seriously for our tastes. Don't these people go to Europe to have *fun*? Of course, what can you expect when you send a Harvard history major to Paris to write about the hot spots in town? To him, all the hot spots have been museums for 200 years.

If you're really on a tight budget, or if you just love a bargain, check out *Europe for Free*, with thousands of free things to do and see all over Europe. It's published by the same company that issues this fine product, and there's ordering info on page 256 (convenient, eh?).

Finally, there's a book that's even more useless than ours, but it's almost as funny—*Dave Barry's Only Travel Guide You'll Ever Need*. We taught Dave everything he knows about humor-writing, and we're so proud of the progress he's made. Keep it up, Dave!

Countries

Now let's have a word about **countries**.

There are lots of different countries in Europe. Many of them don't really matter because nobody you know has ever been there (sort of like South Dakota). European countries are like our states except for a few differences. The biggest difference is that Europeans, through no fault of their own, speak all sorts of crazy languages. Not just the ones you've heard of like French, German, and Spanish, but also Dutch, Swedish, and Serbo-Croatian for chrissake!

You've probably taken German I or maybe even French II. Our advice is: forget you ever did. Europeans get kind of weird when they hear you mangle their language. Just speak English louder than normal. If they don't understand, simplify things by using only nouns like "t-shirt," "sleep," "food." Gestures are also good. (Watch *Sesame Street* before you leave to brush up on non-verbal communication.)

As we went to press, the number of countries in Europe was something of a moving target, rather like the number of Elizabeth Taylor's husbands. We lost East Germany, which was eaten by Big Germany, and all the Communists who lived there have disappeared. Ditto for that old evil empire, the Soviet Union. Yugoslavia is currently trying to become 23 million little countries, one for each Yugoslavian.

Also, several new countries have appeared, like Estonia, Latvia, and Lithuania. Though nobody we know has ever been to them, apparently they're for real. In fact, an intrepid team from *Let's Go Europe* is in Latvia even as we write, compiling breathless lists of dusty museums, 12th-century monasteries, and Viking ruins that will be next year's "must see" items. Plus, a two-man (excuse us, two-*person*) team of Harvard linguistics majors are in Estonia, working on a glossary of useful Estonian phrases, like *"Harvé gyrdden 'Roseanne' wherthen dö?"* ("Do you guys get 'Roseanne' here?").

Regarding these historic changes, senior management at

Mustang Publishing—*au contraire*—is taking a wait-and-see attitude. Mustang editors are Long View, Big Picture kind of guys. After all, who's to say what next year will bring? Maybe Big Germany gets even bigger by a nostalgic acquisition of, say, Poland? Perhaps Moscow, attempting to lure foreign investment, changes its name to Vegas-on-the-Moskva? Or maybe the French decide to try to *win* a war for a change? Naaah, let's be realistic here.

Getting Ready

While many travel books will suggest every item you'll need down to how many pairs of socks to pack, we've narrowed the checklist to eight essential items:

1. Passport
2. Eurailpass
3. Travelers checks and cash
4. VISA or American Express card
5. Money belt
6. Day pack
7. Duffle bag
8. This book (three copies)

To further simplify things, pack items #1-4 in item #5. Pack #6 in #7 until you hit the dusty trail. Keep this book handy in case the plane runs out of toilet paper over the Atlantic.

What else you pack is your own business. We figure you're old enough to make your own sock decisions. Plus, if you find you need something later, you can buy it with items #3 and #4. For example, if you forget your toothbrush, you won't have to borrow someone else's, just buy one—unless you're visiting Albania or unless you really *want* to (as a gesture of *glasnost*). Similarly, condoms are an international commodity, though the ones sold in less-developed countries have all the sensitivity of a heat-shielding tile on the Space Shuttle.

It's important to keep things like your passport, Eurailpass, money, credit cards, return airline tickets, diaphragm, etc. in a safe place. A nylon, zippered money belt (which can double as a hernia truss, just in case) gets our vote. Don't be ashamed to wear it. You can always recognize fellow American travelers by the conspicuous bulge under their shirts above the waistline. (Italian men, by contrast, prefer to display their bulge *below* the waistline.)

Bring a duffle bag as well as a day pack, because most train stations have coin-operated lockers where you can throw your duffle bag full of moldy clothes when you get off the train. Use your day pack to carry this book, your diary, your camera, and anything else you may need for the day. When you're in the locker areas, take note of all the tourists sleeping on the dirty floors. These people have taken the advice of another travel book that describes the train station as "a safe place to sleep." Hah.

Passports and Visas

There are two things you cannot buy in Europe: a passport and a Eurailpass. You'll definitely need a passport and, for some countries, a visa. This may become confusing, so let's simplify things a bit.

A **passport** is like your student ID. It lets people know you're a red-blooded American, with an inalienable right to sneer at funny-looking food, wear obnoxious t-shirts, and sing the theme song to *Gilligan's Island* anywhere. A **visa**, on the other hand, is more like being granted guest privileges at a fraternity. It lets you into the action for a few weeks, at least. Not many places require visas from Americans anymore, though you will need one if you decide to try Moscow, for example.

You need a passport before they'll let you on the plane, let alone on foreign soil. Consider getting it about two months before you plan to leave. The best way is to compile the following four items and visit the Post Office or local Hall of Records:

1. A certified birth certificate (a hospital copy won't work, even if those really *are* your tiny footprints). You usually get this from your State Representative.

2. Two photographs of yourself. Go to a place that advertises "Passport Photos While-U-Wait," like Kinko's or a photo store. The Polaroids your roommate took when you were passed out with underwear on your head won't do.

3. A photo ID to prove you're the same person you claim to be on your birth certificate. (Note to teens: You can use your

real driver's license here, since you don't have to be 21 to order a passport.)
4. Cash or a check for $42.00.

It will take four to six weeks to receive your passport in the mail. The good news is, it's valid for ten years. By that time, you're certain to have foreign travel completely out of your system, and you'll be content to spend your vacations at the Jersey shore or fixing the gutters on your house.

Let's be practical, though. Not all of us are organized enough to order a passport within six weeks of departure. Maybe you're leaving next Wednesday and didn't realize you needed a passport. Don't despair, because you can have the Passport Office send it by Express Mail. If you're leaving tomorrow, you can go to a Passport Agency, located only in big cities like New York and Washington, DC. There, for an even larger fee, you can get a passport while-u-wait. Try to avoid this at all costs, since these places have limited hours and unlimited lines. For complete information, call 202-647-0518, or write to the Passport Office at 1425 K St. N.W., Washington, DC 20522.

When you get your passport, take time to reflect on what it represents. Be damn proud. It identifies you as a red-blooded American, born to run, born to be wild. Protect it like your family jewels. (In fact, the crotch region in your money belt is a good place to keep it.) Lots of foreigners out there will stop at nothing to get their hands on an American passport, and if you lose it overseas, well, we've all seen *Midnight Express* and *The Killing Fields*. . .

ID Cards

Though many of you may fear getting carded, it can actually be a good thing in Europe, since you'll save money if you have the right ID. Students can get an **International Student Identity Card (ISIC)**, which costs $14. It provides the only recognized proof that you are a student and allows discounts on things like theater tickets, local transportation, museums, and airfare. It also provides some accident and sickness insurance. Order one from the student affairs office on campus before you leave and especially before you graduate, since you must prove you're a full-time student to get it. (Non-students under age 26 can get an **International Youth Card**, which offers many of the same discounts as the ISIC card.)

For more information on both cards, contact **Council on International Educational Exchange (CIEE)**, 205 E. 42nd St., New York, NY 10017 (phone 800-438-2643 toll free, or 212-661-1414).

Your card identifying you as a member of the Justice League of America that you got by sending two boxtops from Frosted Flakes will be of little use in Europe.

Eurailpass

Next, you'll need a **Eurailpass**. These suckers are really neat. They allow you to get on almost any train in Europe at almost any time and go almost anywhere (except in England, for some reason). Blowing through Europe demands efficient use of the train network, so the Eurailpass can be a lifesaver. If you're under 26, get the **Youthpass** (about $450), since that's what everybody else will have.

"Hold on!" you yelp. "A Youthpass has a 30-day minimum, and the *Let's Blow* tour is for only 14 days." Well, you can't get anything past you young people these days. You're absolutely right—you'll have about two weeks left over on your ticket. Well, you could visit John on his junior year in Strasbourg (France) or Karen on her exchange program at Frankfurt (Germany). Or, you can investigate your roots by going to the small village in Poland that your great-great-grandfather left 200 years ago, hoping there's a great-great-granddaughter (once removed) there who happens to be cute and thinks you are, too.

In any case, we'll discuss cities a little off the main *Let's Blow* route later, which you can explore at your own discretion. The important thing is that we do the Big One, and anything else is just icing on the cake. (Sorry, the Eurailpass isn't worth diddly in Cancun.)

The trains you'll ride on the Eurailpass are going to provide much more than transportation through Europe. They will serve as your picnic table, social club, and on occasion, your overnight lodging. They will be a point of contact for meeting others also trying to Discover Themselves. You'll be amazed how quickly even the shyest person can strike up a conversation about trite travel themes.

The one-price/unlimited-travel concept of the Eurailpass eliminates anxieties about getting on the wrong train or falling asleep and missing your stop. You can always get off and get back on in the other direction. If you are robbed by gypsies in Rome or get blotto and misplace your money belt at the Hofbräuhaus in Munich, your Eurailpass grants instant solvency. No embarrassment, no awkward explanations, no standing in ticket lines.

Here's a little trick you can try with this magic carpet of a ticket: Say you're on your way to Munich, tanned and rested after your respite in Nice. A cute Chi O. from UCSB happens to be sharing your compartment, and, naturally, you begin talking about travel. Be sure to ask her first where she's heading, and then it's easy to respond with "Oh, wow—I'm heading to Lucerne, too! I hear it's a really awesome place." Forget Munich for now—we can catch up later. Simply consult the little map that comes with your Eurailpass to figure out where Lucerne is, and you're on your way—with a new friend, no less.

The point is, the Eurailpass allows you to be spontaneous and flexible. Neat, huh?

Train Story

It was a warm and sultry evening, and the cafe at the corner of rue La Fayette and rue d'Hauteville was filled with a mix of travelers and locals, all drawn to this waiting place in the shadows of the great railway stations of Paris. There were lovers and losers, old and young, rich and poor. There were passionate Italians and stolid Germans, grimy railway workers and pretty American coeds. And on this evening, as on every other evening for the past 30 years, Blind Maurice played his mandolin in the corner.

Ernest ("but my friends call me Bud") Wills finished his beer and hoisted his backpack onto his shoulder. He headed out into the warmth of the evening and toward the massive depot. Bud was feeling a little down. Sure, it was neat to be in Europe and to be, like, seeing old stuff and all, but sometimes a guy can get a little blue, what with trying to figure

A variation on the Eurailpass is the **Flexipass**, which is for those of you who may want stay in one place for a few days. With the Flexipass, you have options like nine days of travel within a 21-day period, or five days within a 15-day period.

For more info on Eurailpasses, Youthpasses, Flexipasses, and Backstagepasses for Guns N' Roses, contact CIEE, your travel agent, or Rail Europe (230 Westchester Ave., White Plains, NY 10604; phone 800-345-1990 toll free, or 914-682-5172.)

Alternative Ways To Travel

"What about **bicycling**?" you ask. "Some travel books say biking is a cool way to see the back roads of Europe." Forget it. The best analogy we can conjure is: having a bike with you is like carrying an anvil in your backpack. Actually, carrying an anvil is a lot safer. Because of World War II or something, Europeans never got to buy those excellent '59 Caddies that were wide enough to host a family reunion (including all your cousins from back east), so most roads are only big enough to fit those dumb mini-cars that Shriners drive in parades. And while it may be true that some trains allow you to carry your bike in

out the language and the money and stuff. Anyway, how was he supposed to know the girl at the bar wasn't just lonely, too? Alright, so she *was* wearing at lot of black lace, but hey, so does Madonna.

Bud trudged up the dirty steps into the main hallway of Gare de 'Est. All around him hummed the hustle and bustle of this crossroads of Europe. The air reeked with the smell of a hundred brands of cigarettes, of strong espresso, of sweat and cheap perfume. The night had a hint of mystery and promise, a foretaste of broken dreams, tearful reunions, and rides to nowhere.

In the distance, the trains waited, with only an occasional puff of steam to betray the animal strength chained beneath their metal skins. They stood silent, like a pride of lions waiting to begin their powerful glide forward on haunches of burnished steel. They yearned to leave, to gather speed, to feel the urgent call of the open track ahead, the night air swooshing a special car, what will you do when your hotel room is a 10th-floor walk-up?

"Could I **hitchhike** then, to save money and, like, meet cool people?" Forget that one, too, unless you're the type who also thinks it's perfectly safe to arrange a side trip to Baghdad or skip the condoms in Haiti.

American Embassy vs. American Express
One thing to remember when you travel is that in all the big cities you'll find both an **American Embassy** and an **American Express**. People say they're different, but in effect they're the same thing. Think of both as kind of alumni clubs of your college in foreign cities.

Where To Stay
1. Hotels and/or bed-and-breakfasts.
2. Youth hostels.
3. The train.
4. Other peoples' rooms.

over their loins as they reached the open fields, anticipating the moment when, in full cry, their whistles would scream at curves, their fiery hearts would pound "Shusa-BOOM, Shusa-BOOM," their carriages would repeat countless unholy couplings and decouplings, as the great trains bellow through the black countryside, bound for the unknown.

Most of this excessive imagery was lost on Bud. He just thought it would be cool to find a compartment all to himself. He climbed aboard the 11:35pm to Munich and walked slowly through the train until he found an empty cubicle. After stowing his pack in the overhead bin, he settled onto the hard leather seat. *This time tomorrow I'll be in Munich*, he thought to himself. *Man, I can't wait to hitch up with Rich and Scooter. I'm in the mood for some serious partying.*

He pulled out the copy of *War and Peace* he had brought from Northwestern, intending to read it on his trip. He had figured it would be easier to read *War*

How To Get Over There

Fly, dummy. If money is no problem but exactly when you leave is, contact a travel agent and say you want a one-way ticket to London and a return flight from Athens. On the other hand, if you're concerned about cost but flexible about dates, try a charter airline booking agency. Read the Sunday paper's travel section or the *Village Voice* for current fares and special deals. Some good possibilities for cheap flights include **Access** (800-333-7280), **Airhitch** (212-864-2000), **Council Travel** (800-223-7400), **STA Travel** (800-777-0112), and **Travac** (800-872-8800).

For a real adventure in flying, try **Virgin Atlantic Airlines** (800-862-8621). They show MTV videos of their own record company's artists, plus cartoons. A lot of rock musicians use Virgin, so you might get to sit with a British metal band that just completed a U.S. tour—a perfect way to start your trip.

Another airline famous for inexpensive flights to Europe is **Icelandair** (800-223-5500), but the cheap flights land in Luxembourg, where the biggest thing going is the new McDonald's.

---

and Peace while he was in Europe because, you know, he would be in the place where it was set and stuff. So far, he wasn't having much luck. Those old timers' names were real jawbreakers, and all the Russian places made him confused.

He tossed the book aside with a sigh and pushed back the curls on his forehead. (Some of the little sisters back at the frat said he looked just like Johnny Depp when he did that, so he did it a lot.) *Gee*, he thought to himself (remember, he's from the midwest), *I wish the door would open and . . .*

The door opened and a beautiful young woman stood there shyly. "Scuzi," she whispered. "May ich (*she poked herself gently above her firm breasts*) share your seat?" Her accent was of the Iowa plains, fragrant with fresh-shucked corn. Her smile was expensive California orthodontist. Bud jumped up so fast that he almost forgot to push back his curls, but he did, and Cindy (U. Cal. Riverside) was instantly

Other Practical Tips

Songs to Know Before You Leave:
1. Homeward Bound
2. Born in the USA
3. The City of New Orleans
4. The Boxer
5. God Bless the USA

Useless Currency Information:
1 North Korean *won* is equivalent to the following:
4.5 Moroccan *dirhams*
73.4 Mongolian *tugriks*
450 Albanian *leks*
32 Cape Verde Islands *escudos*
3.9 Burmese *kyats*
17 Laotian *kips*
77.7 Ethiopian *birrs*
.5 Angolan *kwanzas*
112 Bhutanese *ngultrums*
a herring sandwich in Holland

smitten. She thought he looked just like Johnny Depp when he did that.

The conversation was a little stilted at first, each beginning to talk at once and then both stopping with a nervous laugh. Gradually, however, they established common ground. They both thought London was neat, they both loved Diet Pepsi, and they both knew someone in L.A. They kissed for the first time in the lovely village Rouvain in the French Alps. (It wasn't as romantic as it sounds. The train was doing 60 through an industrial development at the time.)

They necked all through Switzerland.

Soon they succumbed to passion. clutch-

ing, grasping bodies heaved w~ ~ey smiled

guiltily as the German b~ ~g as they hunted

and asked for thei~ ~ally, they slept in

through thei~ ~sunny August morning.

each ot~ the train pulled into

Münch~

Useless Current Information:
Europe uses 220 volts AC current, which is twice the U.S. standard of 110 volts. This means you must be sure the appliances you take—hair driers, alarm clocks, Salad Shooters, etc.—have a dual voltage option. Note to non-technical types: Your hair will not dry twice as fast with 220 volts.

Shopping

Buying stuff is one of the really great things to do in Europe. In each chapter, we will recommend things to buy, but let's get a few points established.

The first real European experience most of you will have is changing money. Don't get all hung up with the complexity of this. First-timers to Europe get obsessed with the fact that First National Farmers' Bank of Warsaw gives 11,452 *zlotys* to the dollar but charges 2% commission, when the cab driver offered 11,200 *zlotys* and no commission. Most of you won't have calculators along with enough floating point accuracy to figure the exact difference.

We have two pieces of advice. First, don't sweat the last three

It would be wonderful to say this story has a happy ending, but it doesn't. As Bud and Cindy skipped from the train hand-in-hand, they were greeted by Rich and Scooter—and Janice, Bud's girlfriend from Illinois. Her parents had given her a ticket to Europe for making the Dean's List. She hooked up with Scooter and Rich in Munich, and she planned to really surprise Bud when he got off the train. Boy, did she!

Janice and Scooter are married now. She's an Account Manager with Citibank and Scooter sells bonds on W Street. Cindy was really stressed from all the stuff th ppened. She and Bud dated for a while, but thos work out, istance relationships never really And Bud he now sells real estate in L.A. school some e heard, Bud was in grad he never did fin dwest. The funny thing is, ce.

significant digits. Usually, you're stewing about a few bucks at most, and life is short. Second, don't change all your dollars into British Sterling (which is money, not an aftershave) when you land in London.

In our experience, U.S. dollars go pretty fast in Europe. Once you hand 'em over and get, say, Italian *lire*, you're stuck with a bunch of smelly old bills that have more zeroes than your average Burger King Trainee Program. Even worse, everything in Italy costs millions of *lire*. Imagine: you order a pizza and a few brews, and the next thing you know you've handed over so many bills you think they're going to throw in a condo on the Riviera.

In our opinion, the best defense is a good offense. When you go into a restaurant, tell the waiter you'll be paying in dollars (it's often good to flash some $20's to give the guy the general idea). If there's any argument, remember that America stands for freedom of choice. If they don't like your greenbacks, walk down the street to another restaurant.

The other big thing to remember in Europe is to bargain like crazy. Foreigners just love to haggle. If you see a bikini in a department store in Paris that is "just so cute," don't just plunk down the sticker price. Europeans *live* to bargain, so you can really ruin their whole day and actually insult them by paying the retail price.

The best thing to do is slap down a $5 bill and smile a lot. If the clerk seems outraged, don't be fazed. See, it's just a game you're both playing. Have some singles handy and lay 'em down—but slowly. You don't want to appear too eager. You'll get the hang of things very fast.

Note: Please write and tell us if these techniques worked for you. Include your IQ and Alma Mater.

Benetton Stores

There are a gezillion Benetton stores in Europe, and they are spreading like one of those computer viruses. Pretty soon, all of Europe will be one huge Benetton store, with London where the sweaters are and Athens behind Better Sportswear.

Postcards

It's very important to send lots of postcards from Europe. But the problem is, you can spend a lot of time and energy haggling for them in each city along the way. The best solution: buy 'em all at once!

If you fly into London, blow $20 and buy about three dozen. After all, there are only three kinds of postcards sold in Europe: pictures of churches, pictures of castles, and pictures of street scenes taken from a jumbo jet late at night from 38,000 feet. Let's be frank here. Most old, historic churches look pretty much the same. Ditto for castles. And, honestly, could you tell the difference between Toledo, Ohio and Toledo, Spain from 38,000 feet at night?

So, buy all your cards at once and then just mail them home gradually. Remember, though, you will need foreign stamps. This can be a real pain in the butt. How do you ask "Where can I buy postcard stamps?" in Greek? We sure don't know. And if you mime licking a stamp and putting it on a letter, you could get arrested. So, we suggest you bum stamps off the guys at the American Express office.

In some cities in Europe, you can also buy "art" postcards. Most of these consist of black and white photos of naked people doing things with food and bicycles. Well, if you have friends who like that sort of thing. . .

Public Transportation

Most big cities in Europe have a bus and/or subway system, because, oddly enough, not everybody has a car. On many of these buses and subways, the locals buy funny little tickets and cards. Though we won't be using much public transport in this book, we'll discuss the basics.

First, don't bother buying tickets or one-week passes or stuff like that. Since you'll be in each city for a few days at most, just get on the subway and go. It's unlikely you'll be caught, and if you are, just pretend to be a dumb American and smile a lot. If that doesn't work, slip the guy $5. Remember the Marshall Plan? Your grandfather's taxes built most of their subway systems, anyway. You're entitled.

Okay, so you get on and start moving. How do you know when to get off? Well, you need to ask someone. Below is an actual conversation we overheard on a tram in Amsterdam:

Bob: "Hey you guys, where are we going?"

Debbie: "Let's go to that neat square with all the street musicians. I wanna take some pictures."

Craig: "Yeah, maybe we can get some more hash cakes there. Do you remember how to get there?"

Bob: "Let's ask this old dude in the K-Mart suit." (*He points to an elderly man sitting two feet away.*)

Debbie: "Okay, you try him, Craig. You took German, didn't you?"

Craig: "Scuzi, doos yugen (*prods elderly man in chest*) knowen (*taps his own head*) strass where music?" (*He cuts a riff on his air guitar.*)

Elderly Man: "You will need to alight from the train at the next station. From there, it is a five-minute stroll to the square. In fact, you will pass a wonderful 14th-century church along the way. I'm certain you would enjoy its lovely frescoes."

Bob: "Thanks, man, but we don't do churches. Hey, you speak good American."

Craig: "Screw his American, man! What about my German?! Was I awesome or what?"

Debbie: "Come on, you guys, let's get off the train. Thanks, mister."

Bob: "Yeah, chow for now, old timer." (*He tries to high-five the elderly man, who retreats quickly.*)

Answers to Pop Quiz

1. Ireland
2. Italy
3. The Netherlands
4. France
5. Czechoslovakia
6. Austria
7. Big (but friendly) Germany
8. Greece
9. Switzerland
10. Scotland
11. Hungary
12. Spain
13. Yugoslavia (maybe)
14. Portugal
15. Russia
16. England

Note: **Belgian Congo** is actually a dance they do in Brussels.
British Columbia is a type of coffee served in Canada.

Meeting People

Meeting other Americans is a heck of a lot easier than trying to make time with foreigners. French 101 or Intro to Languages won't give you the proper colloquial techniques necessary to, er, achieve your mission in the three days you have in France. You already know the language necessary, and luckily, it's English.

In fact, it's much easier in Europe to master those otherwise difficult opening lines. You know how it is: When you meet that girl from Bio Lab at a party, you immediately have a subject to talk about. But back in lab, you can dissect an entire fetal pig with her and have absolutely nothing to say. Well, meeting fellow Americans in Europe is like party conversation. Here are some examples:

"Where are you from? New York! Wow, I know some guy from New York. His name's John. I'm not sure what his last name is, but man can that guy sock away the brew!"

"Where have you been so far? Hey, you should check out Munich if you really wanna party!"

"Where are you staying?" (You can get a lot of mileage out of this one if used correctly. Follow by saying you were planning to stay at the same place, or ask if there's room on the floor.)

Sensible People

Above all, on this trip you want to avoid **Sensible People**. They can be a real drag and will certainly cramp your style. Therefore, avoid traveling with anybody in ROTC, with people who have joined/are going to join/are thinking about joining the Peace Corps, guys named Stanley, women named Ethel, and anyone carrying a notebook computer.

For example, suppose you're walking down the corridor of a train, and you see two attractive gals sitting in a carriage by themselves. You and your buddy Joe think Hey, hey—Party time!, so you open the door and ask in your politest voice, "Are these seats taken?". . .

Trish: "Bonjour! Guten Tag! Mia casa es su casa. We would be really happy for you to join us."

Joe (thinking: *Talk about the hens inviting the fox! Now let's see how long it takes to get them wasted.*): "That's really nice of you to invite us in. Can I offer you ladies a shot of this really lethal Polish schnapps?"

Gretchen: "Thanks for the offer, but we brought our own spring water. We find that drinking spring water helps us keep clear heads."

Ron: "Clear heads, huh?"

Trish: "Yes, Gretch and I had a little too much wine in Paris, and we missed some of the museums as a result."

Joe: "Oh, are there museums in Paris?"

Gretchen: "Several. Trish and I did a lot of reading before our trip, and we assigned each city a score from 1 to 10 depending on how many 'must see' items it contained. We're plotting a curve of cumulative scores for sights seen versus contact days per city. We can then do an estimate of points scored per amount of money spent in each city and come up with a cost/sight dollar value for each city. So far we've shown a positive variance!"

Joe: "Oh. Great, I guess."

Trish: "It really pays to be organized. One of my jobs is to keep our database of people to whom we must send postcards. Our laptop computer really comes in handy."

Ron: "You brought a computer on your vacation?!"

Gretchen: "We thought everyone did nowadays. I don't see how you could manage otherwise. How do you boys figure out your currency futures or keep track of your vitamin supplement program?"

Joe: "Well, we manage. But you are having *fun* on this trip, right?"

Trish: "We decided on a strategy of 40% enjoyment and 60% education before we left. We primarily envisaged this trip as an integral part of our MBA programs. We discussed at some length the globalization of commerce, and we wanted to investigate cultural and business opportunities in the emerging East European markets, especially since most trade barriers have been removed."

Gretchen: "And have fun while doing it, of course."

Joe (*muttering*): "It doesn't sound like you left any time to *do it*."

Trish: "Excuse me?"

Joe: "Uh, nothing. Well, we'll take off and let you guys get back to work. We have to, uh, plan our strategy to invest in German brew . . . I mean, eh, liquidities."

Ron (*moving quickly toward the door*): "Yeah, nice meeting you."

Gretchen: "Would you like to take this copy of the *International Herald Tribune*? We've already prepared a summary sheet of the day's news and . . ."

Canadians

One of the more peculiar sights you'll see on your travels is groups of regular-looking Americans wearing backpacks and covered from head to sneakers with little red maple leaves. These folks are from **Canada**, and they are called **Canadians**.

Despite the fact that 83% of American high school students think Canada is part of Maine, it is, in fact, a whole country north of us. (That "north of us" thing is really going to bother the other 17% of American high school students, who think Canada is south of us.)

Most of the Canadians we've encountered on our trips were normal, but some of them can get a little peeved about questions like "So, what part of the States are you from?" or "So, what do you miss most about the States?" We realize that telling you this is like giving Jodie Foster's home phone number to John Hinckley, but we know you'll handle this delicate issue of international relations with maturity and restraint.

So if you end up sharing a room with a Canadian, don't be insensitive as he pulls off his maple leaf pajamas, hums *Oh Canada* as he showers with his maple-scented soap, puts on his maple leaf overalls, his t-shirt with the maple leaf back and front, his baseball cap ditto, hefts a backpack so covered with maple leaves that acres of Manitoba were clear-cut to supply the foliage, and, satisfied that nobody will ever confuse him for one of those barbarians from south of the border, heads downstairs for a well-deserved breakfast of Canadian bacon and pancakes with maple syrup.

To Do or Not To Do

Now we need to discuss in some detail a potentially difficult
area. Perhaps a realistic example is best:

Debbie is an attractive junior from Tulane, and she's On The
Road, a 90's Kerouac (except Kerouac was a guy—but it's the
90's, and we're an equal opportunity travel guide. . .). Before
she left the U.S., she had a wonderful night with her boyfriend
Dave. They talked about how much they were in love and how
they could get engaged next Christmas. Debbie promised to
write or call every day.

Now, Debbie has been on the road 11 days. Each day she is
confronted by new sights, new sounds, new smells. Each day
she meets fellow travelers—some are tired and lonely, also missing their loved ones; others seem content, savoring each moment. On the train from Munich to Rome, she meets Doug from
Penn State. He's tired and missing Laurie, also from Penn State.
They talk. There's a certain quoi* between them. They feel
drawn to each other. But, confused by their loyalty and longing
for Dave and Laurie, they become shy. What should they do?

Our advice: go ahead and Just Do It®. *Carpe diem!* Gather
ye rosebuds! Go for it! Tell yourself and each other that you have
only this one night, so spend it together and hold the memory
as a special warm reminder of a marvelous interlude. Believe
us, your hometown honey will understand. It's not like Doug
had a one-night stand on Homecoming Weekend while Laurie
was visiting her sick grandmother. Somehow, it's morally acceptable for travelers in foreign lands to seek companionship
from fellow travelers who might be "off limits" back home.

What To Wear

Packing for Europe can be a real pain. If you ever went to summer camp, you'll have it a little easier than most, since your
name is already sewn on the waistband of your underwear.

There are basically two ways to go on the issue of dress. You
can try to blend in with all the young Europeans you'll be
meeting (the "Euro Look"), or you can dress like a regular

---

*quoi=French word meaning a "spark" or "something in the air." May
also be expressed as "Hey, she was really coming on to me, man, and
I was pretty horny."

American. If you choose the latter, understand that you will stand out like someone in golf pants (your father, perhaps?) at a formal dinner.

Don't embarrass us all by wearing a "Gamma Theta Phi 1st Annual Pole-Sitting and Raw Pig-a-Thon (Sponsored by Zeff's Auto Parts and WXLR 91 FM Golden Oldies Tower of Power Blast from Your Past Hot Hits), Bloomsburg State College, Greek Week Monster Blow-Out Bash 1992" plastered across your chest. Shirts like that confuse people in this country, and, with any luck, get you arrested in others. However, a discreet message affirming your concern for Gay Rainforest Whales would not be amiss and may even score points with a Young Euro.

If you decide to go with the Euro Look, we have just one word to say: **BLACK**. Young Europeans wear more black than your average Orthodox rabbi. Basically, all you need is an assortment of plain black t-shirts and black parachute pants. BUT, there's a potentially huge cultural *faux-pas* here: You cannot go to Europe with a bunch of shiny *new* black clothes. First, only dyed cottons and wools will do. Second, try a little trick we learned on our first trip:

Gather all the clothes for the trip and tie them up in one big, black ball. That's right—the t-shirts, pants, undies, and giant wool sweaters all together in one big ball. Now dump the ball in a big washing machine and wash at the highest temperature. Add a few tablespoons of hickory-flavored barbecue sauce to the final rinse cycle. (Most of the sauce will wash out and the clothes will be left with a nice, smokey aroma.) Take the ball out (watch your back, because the sucker will weigh more than 14 accounting textbooks) and let it sit for a few days in some cold, dank place (any frat house will do).

Finally, dry everything, and, lo and behold, you'll have authentic Euro clothes—slightly mildewy and smelling of cigarettes. With these clothes, you can get into any rad music club in Europe.

And don't forget shoes. Of course, they must be black, but they may be either Adidas or Puma. Reeboks are out. If you've just bought a pair of $80 'Boks, save them for that aerobicize class you were going to take in the fall.

Money

As with love, you can never have enough money, so our advice is to bring lots. The best way to bring it is in traveler's checks, and we recommend **American Express**. (No, we're not getting paid to say that.)

Two reasons: First, American Express has offices in most European cities, and sometimes they'll give you a better exchange rate than the local bank. The second and more compelling reason is that Amex is pretty darn good about shelling out the bucks if you get mugged or if you drop your checks down the toilet while ralphing after a night of revelry in Paris. We've been mugged twice on our trips around Europe (who says travel writers have it easy?), and Amex came through like champs.

So, while you may want to use traveler's checks issued by the First Kentucky County Bank and Muffler Shop because Uncle Hal works there, you might have trouble finding a financial institution in Austria to cash them for you.

For information on American Express, call 800-221-7282. Their booklet, *Traveler's Companion*, lists all their European offices and other info.

You've probably agonized for weeks over whether to buy some foreign currency before you leave the States. Unless you're going to make major purchases in Europe—a château, for example, or maybe a nice museum—it's not really worth it. Just get your traveler's checks in dollars and bring a few hundred bucks in cash for emergencies.

Some of you may be anxious about running out of money in Europe. Well, there are several solutions. You might be able to get an odd job here and there, cleaning a hotel, babysitting, picking grapes, etc. You could sell blood, or maybe a kidney. And in an emergency, you can get money wired via **Western Union** (800-225-5227) or **American Express** (800-926-9400).

But with a little resourcefulness, you may not need any of that. Here are two good schemes to mooch a meal and a room for the night, and all it takes is a little planning:

Scheme #1: Before leaving home, buy the following four t-shirts: one Penn State, one Harvard, one UCLA, and one U. Illinois. If you find yourself in a crunch, wear one of these shirts, head for a big hotel, and just hang around the lobby. Wait until a bunch of elderly Americans return from their bus tour, then stand up and flash 'em the bait. Let's examine Bob in action:

Elderly American Tourist: "Whoa, Ethel, let me ask this young fellow here a question. Hi there, son. I couldn't help but notice your t-shirt. Are you a student at Penn State?"

Bob: "Yes sir, I am. Class of 1995."

Geezer: "You're not going to believe this, son, but you're looking at a soulmate! Fred Atherton's the name, Class of '49, Been with World Mutual Insurance for 40 years. This beautiful gal here is my wife Ethel, Class of '50. We're with our Flood, Fire, and Chainsaw Accident Group."

Ethel: "Don't forget Dismemberment, Fred. That nice couple from Houston is from Dismemberment."

Fred: "Absolutely right again, hon. This beautiful lady of mine is sharp as a tack. So how are things at Old Main?"

Bob: "Where? Oh, Old Main. Just fine, I guess."

Fred: "You live on campus, son?"

Bob: "Yessir. Uh, Smith Hall." (*Always go with something simple like Smith or Jones Hall. All schools have one. Don't get ambitious and go with Czernkowski Hall. It may backfire.*)

Fred: "Don't know that one. Must be after my time. So what are you studying, son?"

Bob: "Er, Communications. I worked my way over on a fishing boat, and now I'm just walking all around. I don't have enough money for a hotel because I spend it all on museums. But it's okay—I don't mind sleeping in the parks."

Fred and Ethel: "Sleeping in parks?!"

Bob: "Oh yeah, it's fine. I get lots of fresh air. If I could just stop blacking out from hunger, I could finish the epic symphonic poem about Penn State I'm writing."

Fred: "You hear that, Ethel? This fine young man is writing a symphony about Old State. Can I ask what it'll be called, son?"

Bob: "Eh, *Penn State Spiraling into the Future Like a Well-Thrown Football in P Flat Major Sharp.*"

Fred: "Hey! Son, you make me proud. What do you say to a steak dinner on World Mutual and maybe a few nights in the hotel here to help you get over the tricky parts in your symphony P Sharp thing?"

Bob: "Wow, that'd be great! Do you mind if I bring Julie along? We could just share a room."

Fred: "Who's Julie?"

Bob: "My girlfr, er, cousin, uh, I mean, my *lyricist*."

Way to go, Bob! He's home free for the night, and, if he really plays his cards right, he'll get an internship at World Mutual next summer.

Of course, for credibility, you must master some vocabulary for each school. Consider the following:

Harvard: Harvard Yard, Elliot House, The Game, Pater's Investment Firm, "My cousin Wentworth, who's a Yale man, I'm afraid."

Penn State: Joe Paterno, football, The Creamery, football, Rolling Rock, football.

UCLA: Mellow, freeway, hot tub, East L.A., "My girlfriend Kimberly."

U. Illinois: No special vocabulary needed. Just be as bland as possible and accent all your vowels hard.

Scheme #2: Here's another scam: If you're facing financial ruin, walk around the streets and find a stray mutt with big eyes. Take the red bandanna that you packed for this contingency, tie it around the dog's neck, and make a leash from your belt. Now for the trivial task of weaseling a room for the night.

Head for a place frequented by hundreds of college students. In London, try Leicester Square; in Paris, perhaps the pedestrian area in front of the Pompidou Centre; and in Munich, the narrow street outside the Hofbräuhaus is a sure bet. Once you sight a group of sorority sisters, unleash the dog and, with luck, he'll run over to them. (Important tip: Make sure you clean the mutt's paws first. Messing up Kristen's new skirt won't help this scheme one bit.) Wait for their squeals to drop below the 100-decibel level and then . . . Well, let's follow Ben as he ambles over, calling for the pup in mock exasperation:

Ben: "Churchill (or Nietzsche, or Axl)! Get over here, you dang
mutt. Oh, hi ladies, sorry about that. This little guy has a
mind of his own." (Ben winks at one of them like Tom
Cruise did in Top Gun where it paid off bigtime.)

Kim: "Ohmigod, is this dog yours?! He is just so cute!"

Marie: "He's just like my dog Boots back home. (She bends down
to pet the mutt.) You are so friendly. Are you from the
States, little guy?"

Ben: "No, he's just a little mutt I rescued from drowning in the
river a few days ago, and I guess we're stuck with each
other now. I had to miss my plane home because I
couldn't get his shots in time and 'cause he needs to
learn some English to get into the States." (Ben should
learn not to ruin a good thing by overdoing it.)

Joan: "I didn't know animals had to know English to get into
the U.S."

Ben: "Uh, sure they do. You don't think anyone would buy a
parrot that only speaks German, do you?"

Marie: "Well, I just think it's so neat of you to miss your plane
to save your dog. Where are you staying?"

Ben: "Oh, right now we're just sort of camping out. The little
guy eats so much that I can't really afford a hotel room.
It's okay, though—I can make do on one meal a day, and
I'm supposed to get money from home soon. Well, I've
got to get going. It might rain tonight, and we need to
find somewhere to crash where we won't get wet."

Joan, Kim, and Marie: "Oh."

Ben: "Well, it's been real nice talking to you. . ."

Kim: "Wait, I have an idea! Why don't you sleep on our floor?"

Marie: "Yeah, that's a great idea! We have this great suite that
overlooks the river, and we get room service every
morning."

Ben: "Gee, that's really nice, but I don't want to impose."

Kim: "No, really, it would be fun! We could help you pick out
a collar for Churchill this afternoon."

Ben: "For who? Oh, the dog. Well, it would be great of you
to take Churchill for the night, but I'll be fine in the
park."

Joan, Kim, and Marie: "No you won't!" "No way!" "Of course not!"

Ben: "Okay, ladies, we'll stay. But only for a week. We have our pride, you know."

Trains

Here are some tips on taking full advantage of your Eurailpass. Since train rides will consume a lot of your precious time abroad, these tips are quite valuable.

Overnight train travel will save money on hotels and time in transit. There are a number of overnight express trains that depart between 10:00pm and midnight from one major city and arrive the next morning in another. You should take advantage of them as often as you can, but be prepared so you'll be comfortable. Buy lots of beer, wine, and food to eat on the train—at the least the booze will put you to sleep. Also, pick up some fruit and juice for breakfast.

For maximum comfort, secure your own compartment. Here are some strategies for doing so:

1. Get on early, at least 30 minutes before departure.
2. Take the compartment in the middle of the carriage to encourage browsers to continue their search.
3. Pull the curtains closed, sprawl-out all over the seats, and pretend you're asleep.
4. If you're traveling with a special someone, put your hand in some part of his/her clothes to suggest to browsers that there's more going on in the compartment than they care to be part of.
5. Reserve the whole compartment ahead of time. Just flash your Eurailpass and get two seats, then go back a while later (or to another window) and reserve two more. It'll cost a few bucks, but it's still cheaper than a sleeper.
6. Get some ripe limburger cheese and spread it on the table and the seats.
7. Eat gas-producing food and fill the compartment with your own noxious deterrents. (Indian food works well.)
8. Don't shave, bathe, or comb your hair. Wear dark sunglasses and smelly clothes.

9. Put Public Enemy in your Walkman, crank it up, and sing along.

Poetry

While you're in Europe soaking up the atmosphere and feeling the cultural currents ebbing and flowing around you, how about writing some **poetry**? No, really, you can, and if there ever was a time to write poetry and get away with it, this is it.

We've got a few tips to help get you started. First, figure out what kind of poetry you want to write—the kind that rhymes or the kind that doesn't. Believe it or not, this is actually the biggest hurdle. Our advice: poetry that doesn't rhyme is probably the best bet for your first folio. (See—you're talking like a poet already!) On the other hand, if you're into Public Enemy or Dr. Seuss, go for the rhymes.

Okay, Lesson #2. How long should a good poem be? Well, it depends. Shakespeare wrote a lot of 14-liners called sonnets, but that was because he only had short notebooks. Actually, you can write an entire poem in just two lines. Don't believe it? How about this:

> The cat sat on the mat.
> He got fat, the poor rat.

So there. These two lines challenge us with an epigrammatic vision of a tortured feline wrestling with a twisted view of himself as a debased rodent, submerging his psychic confusion into obesity. The author's clever use of the word "mat" recalls the Finnish word *bflät*, which means "the sound your stomach makes after a large meal of millet." Altogether a fascinating little gem, pregnant with meaning.

Well, we won't suggest you attempt anything as broad in scope as the above example, at least not on your first try. In fact, we think your first effort should just be a stream-of-consciousness sort of thing, like the poem below that we wrote. We alternated writing each line and placed a time limit of one minute per line. We think you'll sense the taut urgency, the bitter angst, the total b.s. that permeates this piece. We cranked out this little beauty riding a train up the Irish coast when we were half crocked.

Exile Scream

The swans with their long necks reflecting in the half-
  silvered river, gaping, questing the sea.
The sheep graze quietly, framed by the opulent greens.
The Ugly Americans shout their stupidity among
  Norman ancestry.
Cold concrete greets the arrogant French tourist stepping
  ashore on the oft-imagined green sward, while the docile
  natives gaze, cow-like, on.

Hark! The stone-faced conductor casts a suspicious glance
  at the land's native son.
While in the fields, two hundred pounds of lamb chops
  ponder pensively their dewy pasture.

"No Budweiser here," a distant voice mutters.

Dogfish lay defiantly among the steadfast kelp, while crusty
  seamen span their seines through endless time.
The blond stranger stares vacantly at the fecund, seminal
  sod, while the telegraph wires, stretched tight as Zeus' bow,
  shriek some new atrocity into the distance.
Spotting a fawn in the forest's lush undergrowth, his
  thoughts turn to huntin' season in Virginia.

  Whoa! This one gets better every time we read it. Full of
"human condition" stuff, you know? It's bound to inspire your
first poems. Before you know it, you'll be wearing a beret,
smoking a pipe, grooving the jazz scene, and publishing in little-
known literary journals. And, man, will you be cool.

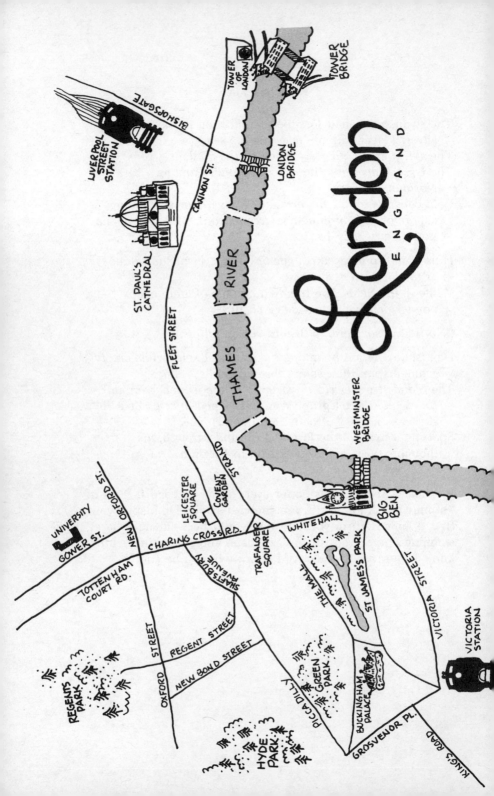

London

While the plane is making its final approach to Heathrow, get the address of the cute girl from Chicago sitting next to you, because you might, like, want to get together or something when you both get back home and compare notes on your Trip To Europe.

Once you've done that, it's time for action. As soon as the wheels hit the tarmac, stand up and get your daypack out of the overhead bin and dash to the front of the plane. Don't worry if the cabin staff yells at you. Remember, we have only two weeks for the Grand Tour, so it's crucial to hit the ground running and gain some quick yardage. Do you want all those other schmucks to reach Athens before you?

Once off the plane, you'll have to show your passport to a little geek with ketchup stains on his tie. After you blow him off, grab your backpack and get a bus to London.

Money

British money is confusing because an English *pound* is worth about $1.70. The thing to do is think of a pound as a "big dollar." This makes things seem a lot cheaper.

Now What?

Look at the neat little map we've drawn for you. It pretty much shows everything we'll be seeing in London.

From the airport, get a bus or train into **Victoria Station**. Once you get there, stand in the two-hour line to drop off your backpack. Big tip: If you talk to other Americans in the line (or *queue*, as we Anglophiles say), never say you've just arrived. It's better to say something like "Yeah, I've been touring England and Scotland for the last two months. It's a shame, you know, that all these tourists go to London and never see the *real* Britain."

Okay, we're in good shape now. You've dumped your backpack, and you just have your daypack with your passport, money, tickets, toiletries, sweatshirt, and contraceptives (hey, you never know). Next, leave the station and walk to the back of the building, where you'll find all sorts of cheap hotels and that peculiar British institution, the **bed-and-breakfast**.

You kids probably think a bed-and-breakfast is like the place on *Newhart*, right? It's run by a guy in a plaid shirt who was a tax lawyer in Boston and dropped out to write a soul-searching novel about a tax lawyer from Boston who drops out to write a soul-searching novel about a tax lawyer—ahem—and his gorgeous wife who has a Ph.D in English Lit and now makes goat cheese in the basement of their precious old house in Vermont, where you get to spend $110 a night to sleep in a room with no heat and no HBO. Well, kids, bed-and-breakfasts in London are a bit different.

In general, they consist of a big old house with a name like "Oceanview" (if it overlooks the railway yard) or "Oakhill" (if it's in the middle of a cluster of high rises). London B&B's are run either by loud women with huge breasts who call you "luv." or by small men from Pakistan who say "Yes, yes, yes" to every question. Either way, they tend to be pretty cheap (the prices, that is, and only sometimes the loud women, but let's not run before we walk, okay?).

By now, you probably feel like there's a small furry animal lying dead just south of your tongue, and your armpits, well, we won't even get into all that. This might be a good time for a shower and a power nap. Nothing much happens in England in the afternoon anyway, and there's nothing on TV.

When you wake up, climb back aboard your Reeboks and head out for the evening. When you get back to Victoria Station, you can head across the street to the **Burger King** for some late lunch/early dinner.

"But this is London!" some zucchini-head from Yale is going to whine. "I want to try some, you know, real *British* food." Okay, you asked for it. Walk past the Burger King (don't worry, you'll be back) to your First English Meal.

Food

It's probably true to say that the English have done for food what dioxin has done for the environment. Other guidebooks tell you the best English food is found in pubs. This is true, in the sense that the best sewage is found in toilets.

There are basically two kinds of British food. In the first kind, the chef takes gross parts like kidneys, tongues, livers, and tails of whatever animal happens to be the road-kill of the day, covers them with a batter made from sawdust and lint, and deep-fries them in brake fluid. These delicate morsels are then served with soggy, limp french fries.

The other thing cooks do is take the same body parts (adding extra goodies like cartilage and beaks), grind them into a paste, and cover them with a pastry crust with the texture of a car seat cover. This latter option, often given a quaint nom de guerre (oops, sorry, we said we wouldn't use words like that) like Country Pie, Shepherd's Pie, or Ploughman's Pie, also comes with those same moist-n-tender fries.

Luckily, there's a lot more to eat in London than British food. In the following section, we describe some restaurants that we really liked. We don't necessarily go for the cheapest places, because—let's face it—you get what you pay for. However, the following list includes places that we thought offered good value. In any case, you're on vacation, right?

Cranks (9-11 Tottenham St., W1; phone 071-631-3912) is a pseudo-vegetarian restaurant chain that has managed to stay in business since the mid-60's and is now growing fast thanks to the trend toward light, healthy food. It suffers a little from the British notion that cheese must be a vegetable because you can't fry it, and consequently, many of the dishes have more cheese on them than zits on a 14-year-old, but, all in all, it's a fun place to eat.

Veeraswamy (99-101 Regent St., phone 071-734-1401), the oldest Indian restaurant in continuous use in London, is rather expensive, but if you want to try first-rate Indian food, this is the place. If you have any nice clothes with you, wear them. If you've been carrying them around in a backpack for three weeks, check for mildew. You don't want other diners sending back their curry dansak because of the odd smell permeating the restaurant. Wouldn't do at all, old boy.

The only problem with Veeraswamy is that it's a bit too well-known by non-natives. Forget about meeting a retired major or two from the Gurkhas Rifles who will invite you for a weekend of pig-sticking or whatever. The diners at the next table are probably bankers from Chicago being wined and dined by their London branch and comparing the food to the great little Indian/Thai/Cantonese place near the mall back home.

Langam's Bar and Grill (Stratton St., Piccadilly; phone 493-6437). This is a great place to eat if you want to splurge a little for any reason (like, you called home and your mom said you made the Honor Roll; or, you just "found yourself" and decided to join the Peace Corps; or, you are/are not pregnant and are really excited/depressed). Actor Michael Caine is part owner of Langam's, and you can often see him sitting at the window table near the door during lunch. (You might ask him why he ever agreed to appear in something as awful as *Blame It on Rio*.)

Anyway, the food at Langam's is worth the trip. The menu is mostly classic French, so if you need to raise your cholesterol level, stop by. Langam's is also a great place to watch sleazy rich people fight it out with scornful waiters. You'll probably need a reservation in the summer.

School Dinners (34 Baker St., W1; phone 935-8262). This unique little eatery is our personal favorite. The format is as follows: the restaurant serves mostly terrible food dished out by young women tastefully dressed as schoolmarms. You must raise your hand and ask permission to leave the table from the maître d', who is dressed as a headmaster and wields a cane. If it's your birthday, you may request a "knee trembler," where you sit on a waitress' lap and get fed a whipped cream confection. This place can be a blast, though definitely weird.

The restaurant is actually a club, so there's a $10.00 membership fee for one-timers ($100 a year if you're going to make it a habit). The fun part is that you get put over the waitress' knee and spanked if you don't eat everything on your plate. We suggest you eat a really big meal before you go. It's not a restaurant for the timid.

Spaghetti House (20 Sicilian Ave., WC1A; phone 405-5215). As you could probably guess, this place does not feature *moo goo gai pan*. There are many good Italian restaurants in London, and we certainly didn't try them all. However, our friend Keith says the Spaghetti House "is the business, innit mate?" —and he should know because he bleedin' lives there, don' he? Figure about $10 for this one.

Other good places to check out are the reasonable **Soho Brasserie** (23-25 Old Compton St., W1; phone 439-3758) or the pricey **Le Caprice** (Arlington House, Arlington St., SW1; phone 629-2239) for French food. If you're yearning for the taste of real meat, consider **The Chicago Rib Shack** (1 Raphael St., Knightsbridge Green, SW7; phone 581-5595), where you can chow down for less than $20 (and that includes the wine). The best pizza in town is probably at **Grunts** near Covent Garden, which features pleasant Irish waitresses, great thick-crust pizza, and even a salad bar (about $7.00 per person, including beer).

Finally, despite what we said earlier, you really can find good food at pubs, particularly plates of cold meats and salads. Be cautious of the deadly mustard served in English pubs—it could do double duty as nerve gas.

British Beer

It is traditional to drink English beer with your meal, and there are basically two kinds of English beer: **lager** and **bitter.**

Lager is made in a time-honored manner as follows: an English brewer with a severe head cold gets a pint of Stroh's and, with a straw, blows air through the beer until all the carbonation is gone. He leaves the beer on a counter somewhere for eight days. Then, he sells it to you.

Bitter is made the same way, except the bartender adds two Rolaids tablets to each pint before serving it.

It's considered pretty cool to drink beer made by the smaller breweries. These beers generally have names like "Old Bartholomew's Dark North Country Royal Coalpit Christmas Ale" or "Honest William's Golden Red Scrumpy." In any case, they all taste equally bad. Fortunately, you can get Budweiser in England.

However, it is very important to pretend to *love* English beer when you get back home: "Oh, like, I just couldn't leave England until Mark and I had been to all 52 pubs in London serving Old Webster's Porridge-Mold Lager. It's so much better than bland American beer, you know."

Things To See

After lunch at Burger King (if you meet other Americans there, it's best to adopt the Nostalgia Defense: "You know, when you've been on the road *as long as I have*, you really get a craving for some good American junk food"), get some of the London sightseeing out of the way. Walk up Victoria Street to where it starts to curve towards the river. There you'll find your first **Important Old Thing**. At this point, it's crucial to stay calm and not get carried away by the moment.

(If it will help, think about the first time you played touch football for your dorm's intramural coed team. You're out there in midfield and a long pass comes sailing toward you, and you look over and there's Bob, that cute guy with the blondest hair. He's looking at you and suddenly you choke and you just *know* you're going to drop the ball! Well, *that* was a crucial time. The sight of this Old Thing is not.)

Relax! Sure, it would be easy to go beserk and start snapping pictures and buying postcards and running in and out of buildings and getting yourself all hot and bothered and finding that no, your deodorant does not work as hard as you do. Next thing you know, you've gone and broken a nail on some old doorway or something. No, we'll be calm and prudent. We'll talk ourselves through this monumental piece of history step by step.

Well, this first Important Old Thing is called **Westminster Abbey**. It's actually a big old church, and lots of important Brits are buried under the floor. You might want to go inside, but you'll probably be disappointed. For one thing, it's as dark inside as the New York subway during a power outage. (You'd think the Brits could have conquered one less country in Africa and instead spent some time inventing strip lighting, you know?)

Right behind the church is the **British House of Parliament**, which has **Big Ben** stuck on top so the politicians inside know when to go home. The British Parliament is sort of based on our Senate and Congress, and so the English are almost as free as we are, except they don't have The Weather Channel. Unless you're a history major, you don't need to spend any more time here.

The next thing to do is walk by **Buckingham Palace**, which is like our White House except the Queen doesn't pitch horseshoes in the backyard. Nonetheless, it's the place where the

Queen lives. Officially, you can't go in, but you could try chatting-up the soldiers at the gate, and maybe they'll let you in to use the bathroom or something.

This may be a good time to drop in and see your friends at **American Express** (6 Haymarket), just to let them know you've arrived and maybe bum a few stamps. Amex offices are great places to meet fellow travelers and hear familiar voices: "Actually, I've been in London since the spring, doing a book on Elvis as a cultural icon here. Book? Did I say book? Well, it's not actually a book yet. It's more of a term paper for my Modern American Culture class, but I have this friend who knows an editor at a publishing company, and he thinks . . . " "Hey, honey, this little gal behind the counter says that the Eiffel Tower is definitely in Paris and *not* in London. I guess your jackass brother screwed up again as usual . . . " "Whaddayamean you people don't take Visa?!"

After this breath of fresh cultural air from the homeland, you may want to head back to your quaint bed-and-breakfast and get cleaned up for the evening. Buy a pack of cigarettes on your way home. It's very important to smoke in Europe.

Nightlife

Most of the nightlife in England revolves around the **pub**. Though we've already discussed pubs a little, some further insights may be useful.

English pubs tend to have long names involving a) the royal family, b) adjectives, and c) animals and animal parts (e.g. "The Prince of Wales Jolly Green Swan's Head," "Merrie King George's Ass.") Head for the area around Covent Garden, which was once a popular fruit and flower market, but then they invented supermarkets.

Our advice is to try some pubs at random. The first curious thing you'll notice is that only Australians work in pubs in London (sometimes New Zealanders but, hey, same difference, right?). Nobody we talked to could explain this, just like nobody knows why all cheap motels on U.S. highways are run by families from India.

If you're traveling with some frat brothers, you can amuse yourselves by going up to the bartender and yelling in unison "USA #1!" or "Olivia Newton-John sucks!" Then, it's advisable to do your drinking next door.

After you've climbed inside two or three pints of that fine English beer, pass some time by engaging in small talk with the locals. Contrary to popular belief, the English do like to chat (see end of chapter), and when they discover you're an American it can be difficult to shut them up. Good topics of conversation with the English are 1) what a fox you think Princess Di is, 2) how much you enjoy English beer (so you have to lie a little), 3) the weather, and 4) the cultural superiority of the French.

New Non-Commercial Music

After a couple more pints of beer and some banter with your English buddies about whether Margaret Thatcher might run on the Republican ticket in 1996, it's time to get down to one of the most serious things you must accomplish in your days in London. This is, of course, your search for New Non-Commercial Music. Good clubs to begin your search are listed later, but you can't go until you're prepared.

At a proper New Non-Commercial Music club, you'll be greeted at the door by a bouncer with half his head shaved, the other half spiked and dyed taupe, an earring made from a beer can, and a t-shirt suggesting something anatomically impossible involving President Bush, Prince Charles, the Stealth bomber, and Vaseline. Try to buy his t-shirt.

Once inside, you get to stand in a wet, dark cellar while all around you people snort everything but Liquid Drano. After a few hours, a band dressed like actors from a 1920's Soviet movie will appear and sing a series of ditties describing suicide, drugs, unemployment, anarchy, revolution, murder, nuclear holocaust, and how my girlfriend left me. After these cheery little tunes, the performance may conclude with the band vomiting or tossing rat turds at the audience.

If all this sounds exotic and/or intolerable, just remember the last frat party you attended.

In any case, you're not necessarily there for a pleasant time. No, you're there so you can brag about the experience later: "Well, you know, the *real* London is about New Music. So, these really radical guys we met—one really gorgeous Australian guy—no, Joanie, I did *not* sleep with him—well, anyway, they took us to this club. It's kind of, like, an *underground* club, so it doesn't have a name or anything. And we saw this really cool political band. They did songs about, you know, U.S. missiles in Central America and stuff. At first, I felt a little weird, but then I told this guy that I thought U2 was pretty good. He said I was a 'real arsehull.' I think it means, like, an anarchist or something. That was really neat—you know, weird, but neat."

While at the club, buy t-shirts and tapes of the band. It doesn't matter if the tapes sound like two chainsaws inside a steel drum. The important thing is to have proof that you have been "into" the London club scene. Likewise, don't worry if you pay $15 for a t-shirt that shows an ugly man playing with himself and promoting a band called Anal Antics. People back in California will really flip when they see it. In any case, you're going to lie about how you got it: "Yeah, I saw this band in London. They were, like, totally wired, and the drummer just gave me his shirt. What a night, man! I can't even remember half the things we did." Uh-huh.

Clubs

Clubs in London run the gamut from punk palaces—where even the rats have bloodshot eyes—to places so exclusive they have no name, and everything in between. The best place to find out what's going on is *Time Out*, a weekly guide to what's happening in London and where to find it. What's hot changes with each passing season, of course, so the radical places we saw are by now probably as cool as Bart Simpson t-shirts, but some clubs you might check out are the following:

Le Beat Route (17 Greek St., W1V; phone 437-5782) Features (at least this week) lots of ska and also (periodically) New Wave. You know those people from school you hate because they're so cool and were in Europe last year? They spent a lot of time at this club. Black clothes are essential.

Zanzibar (30 Great Queen St., WC2B; phone 405-6153). More exclusive than Le Beat Route, but similar in style. Expect to pay a fairly heavy cover.

Limelight (136 Shaftesbury Ave., W1V; phone 434-1761). Currently one of the hot spots, it's a dance club with a rather yuppie crowd.

Ronnie Scott's (47 Frith St., W1V; phone 439-0747). Mecca for jazz fans in London. The quality varies, so call before you go.

Why does the audience in a jazz club always consist of depressed, Woody Allen look-alikes? I mean, does the music make them depressed, or do they go to the club depressed, hoping the music will cheer them up?

Stringfellows (16 Upper St., Martins Lane, WC2M; phone 240-5534) and **Studio Valbonne** (62 Kingly St., W1R; phone 439-3724) are two good dance clubs that feature new music by groups that neither you nor anyone else back home has ever heard of.

After the club closes, stroll back to Victoria Station with the other Americans you met there. This might be a good time to grab a late snack at Burger King and maybe write in your journal:

"I really think I've changed a lot on this trip. Since I've left the U.S., I'm really starting to deal with my feelings and stuff. It's just so neat to be in the same city and maybe to be sitting in the same Burger King where one of my ancestors sat hundreds of years ago. Like, I feel I'm sort of a bridge between the Old World here in Europe and my folks in Fresno. That's just really weird to think about. I guess I will go to law school after all. Now I just have to decide what to do about Mark . . . "

Shopping

London is a town where the patron saints of shopping, Imelda Marcos and Tammy Faye Bakker, would go wild. There are goodies galore, and you'll be glad you packed light.

You'll want to concentrate your assault in a few areas. First, check out the big department stores and schlocky shops on **Oxford Street** and **Tottenham Court Road**—good places to get ugly cheap gifts for your friends and family back home, like ashtrays with the picture of the royal family on them, mugs with the picture of the royal family on them, toilet seat covers with the picture of the royal family on them . . . well, you get the idea. Also, some of the department stores in this area offer good buys on cheap clothes, if you forgot to pack underwear.

The top of Oxford Street is key for any visiting American college student: the **Virgin Records Megahypercolossal Music Emporium**. Check it out. It's a great place to buy albums that no one—and we mean *no one*—back home has ever heard of. If you're from the midwest and think Michael Jackson is quite racy enough, thank you, then skip this stop and go to the zoo or something.

Virgin is also a great place to do some people-watching and test the patience of the sales help: "Hi, I'm looking for an early release by Ma Borisa and the Armenian Banjo Boys. I think it's called *Hot Socialist Licks from the Tractor Factory*. They're, like, a cross-over Russian Cajun Funk band. You don't have it, huh? Well, gee, what about *Gorby's Dead* by Boris and the Birthmarks?"

Upstairs are the t-shirts—zillions of them. Go nuts, but remember you'll be tanning in Nice (rhymes with "grease") in a few days, so be sure to pick colors that will complement that Côte d'Azur glow. We sorority gals have to think ahead.

From Virgin, it's a short walk to the **King's Road/Chelsea** section of the city. King's Road was real popular in the '60s, when it was a hangout for music's biggest names. Many a legend from the past shopped there, even people like the Beatles (you know, Paul McCartney's band before Wings). Though King's Road has fallen on hard times lately—it resembles 8th Avenue in New York and consists mainly of Indians selling genuine pleatherette jackets—it might be a good place to get a cheap jacket for the next stage of your trip, especially if you're doing a James Dean thing. Just remember the old Pakistani proverb: "One man's leather is another man's naugahyde."

If you happen to be carrying Dad's Amex Card, you may want to head over to Bond Street or Regent Street and see how the other half shops. If the prices depress you, comfort yourself with the thought that you'll be able to afford them after you get that great job on Wall Street and do a little insider trading. But on the other hand, by the time you can afford the Good Life, you'll be too old, fat, or sick to enjoy it. Ponder for a moment, if you will, the timeless dichotomy between Youth and Riches. It may be time to write in your journal again.

Another interesting area to shop/explore is **Knightsbridge**, which contains **Harrods**, the aircraft carrier of British stores. Harrods is well worth a visit, if only to inspect the food section. If you've recently come from a diet of dorm food, the sensory overload may be more than you can handle. Anything you can imagine—which, if you thought *Moby Dick* was a pretty good fishing story, is obviously not too much—is available. They sell mounds of boa constrictor steaks and scads of pickled pigs' pancreas. They sell fruits so exotic they have no name, and you order them by saying "I'll have that stinky purple one with the green fur. Yes, the one that's moving." Nobody said becoming a gourmet was going to be easy.

Day Two

After a fine English breakfast of animal by-products and eggs fried in fat—so good, and so good for you—you'll be ready for your second day in London.

First, head for the **Tower of London** (the Tower Hill stop on the Underground), an old prison where people who committed crimes (like stealing enough food to stay alive or advocating independence for the American colonies) were imprisoned and, after a fair trial in the best English tradition, had their heads chopped off in the back parking lot.

The Tower also contains instruments of torture. (Back then, they didn't have Pee-Wee Herman videos, so they had to use racks and whips and stuff.) However, the biggest draw is the **Crown Jewels**, the collection of all the loot the English plundered over a 500-year period and made into the necklaces and earrings that Princess Di now wears to Elton John concerts.

Actually, the Tower is worth the trip, if only to see more gold than around the neck of a Philadelphia crack dealer. It's also the place to watch Moms and Pops from Dearborn, Michigan not being overawed by the excess: "Herb, look at this ring! It's *almost* as big as your Elks Club signet ring," "Helen, over here. Wouldyalookatthat bracelet! It's just like the one I got for Ellie at Graceland, except mine had a picture of Elvis."

The Tower is also a good place to meet fellow travelers from back home. Determine immediately if they are serious history majors from some private school in New England: "I've always been fascinated by the socio-political implications of the dissolution of the monasteries by Henry VIII, and so when I won the Louise Cabot Harris Prize for Women Historians, I jumped at the chance to come to London to work on my senior thesis. How about you? What's your period?" If so, drop them like a hot bowling ball. Let's not forget—we are here to Party.

Next, head back to the area along Oxford Street and Tottenham Court Road and get some last-minute t-shirts, postcards, and photos of Princess Di and the Queen's horses (you can never have enough photos of the Queen's horses around, in our opinion).

By late afternoon, start thinking about catching your train to Holland. For this, you need to get to **Liverpool Street Station**.

St. Paul's Cathedral

If you have more than two days in London, **St. Paul's Cathedral** is worth a look, and you can explore the nearby financial district of London afterwards.

You'll probably need to take the Underground to reach St. Paul's, since it's quite a distance from the area around Victoria. Get off at the St. Paul's stop and, when you emerge from the bowels of the earth, you'll be facing one *muthuh* of a building. Built in the 1650's, St. Paul's contains hundreds of tombs of famous and not so famous Brits. Most of the military types appear to have met rather gruesome ends in their effort to wrest control of a godforsaken piece of desert for some old king or queen. The view from the top of the dome is amazing, and it's your Tall Thing To Climb in London.

Going To a Show

Very popular among Americans visiting London is the opportunity to take in a show. For those readers from the New York area who often attend Broadway productions, the London theater (excuse us—*theatre*) promises to be a unique experience.

Reflect for a moment on your last trip into the Rotten Apple. You and your loved ones drive into the city, accompanied by two armed escorts carrying your tickets to *Miss Saigon*, which you mortgaged your home to buy. You fight your way to the theater distric through hellacious traffic and bite your nails as you give your car to the Highly Skilled Parking Professional at the lot created last Wednesday by the fortuitous burning of a Woolworth's. The HSPP (*Nationality:* Guatemalan. *Immigration Status:* Unclear. *Previous Experience:* Driving donkeys on dirt roads outside Guatemala City) takes your car and hits 63 mph in the 40-foot-wide parking lot. You hurry for a light dinner at one of the world-famous delis in the area.

After 45 minutes in line, you get a table and eat $3 of pastrami for $15. Your meal, which will return to haunt you within the hour, becomes a delightful New York Experience thanks to the waiter's gruff wit: "More water? You want I should bring you more water? I ain't seen you piss out the last glass, pal."

You make it to the show with one second to spare, relieved that you had $20 to give the panhandlers blocking the theater doors. Another lucky break: only two picket lines to cross. The show is fine, except that you have terrible heartburn.

You go pick up your car, but the HSPP can't find your keys. A $10 bill jogs his memory. You get home at midnight after a fabulous evening in The City. Who says New York isn't the most exciting place on earth?

Going to a show in London is a bit of an anticlimax after New York. In London, you can afford to buy tickets without selling a kidney, you can take the safe, clean Tube to the theater, and you can even get tickets to *Miss Saigon* without making your sister perform in a special collector's video. For theater tickets, try the **Leicester Square Ticket Booth** or any of the ticket outlets in the city, including one in Victoria Station.

A Soccer Match

If bungee-jumping has already lost its thrill for you and you want to try something really dangerous, consider a trip to a soccer ("football") match. The season in England runs August to early May, and there are about 20 teams in the London area, including Arsenal, Chelsea, West Ham United, and Tottenham Hotspur. Funny names, huh?

If you decide to go but don't have access to a fully-armed Bradley Fighting Vehicle to drop you off and pick you up, splurge for a seat in the stands. It costs more than standing on the terraces, but you'll have a better chance of escaping with only minor contusions.

Seriously, the violence at soccer games has decreased in recent years, but you should exercise caution at the stadium.

You might even enjoy the game, but we realize soccer isn't for everyone. Who wants to see a bunch of grown men in short-shorts kicking a ball around, when you could be at Candlestick Park watching a bunch of billionaire cry-babies in tight pajamas spitting and picking at their crotches for twice the money?

Chatting With the English

London will be one of the few cities on your trip where you can chat with the natives without grunting and using your hands. A few words of advice may help you avoid awkward situations:

First, remember that the Brits are a very tight-assed lot. They have extreme difficulty discussing anything more intimate than the weather.

Second, they think it's rude to appear more than mildly interested in any topic other than the weather.

Finally, the British adorn everything they say with so many qualifying phrases that they never actually say anything.

For example, let's say a terrorist hijacked your flight to London and diverted your plane to a hot place where they speak Arabic. Then, the hijacker killed the passenger next to you because she asked to go to the bathroom. You stay on the plane for two weeks while diarrhea runs rampant, and you're finally rescued when a SWAT team storms the plane. You barely escape the bullets whizzing everywhere. You finally reach London, where it's snowing in mid-July. You are mugged at the airport and cheated by the cab driver on the ride into town. You stagger into a pub to have a beer after three weeks of Sheer Hell. After striking up a conversation with the British guy next to you, you pour out your heart to him, detailing all the terror you've endured.

In all likelihood, your drinking companion will look embarrassed and say something like, "Well, it does sound rather as if you may have had a spot of bother coming over. I say, though, it does jolly well seem as though the weather is improving to a degree. I shouldn't be too surprised if we begin to see some possibility of a slight thaw in the next few days or so. One can never predict these things, can one? I say, though, if it's not an impertinent question, was it very sunny in Beirut? Not much of a summer here, I must say, though we mustn't grumble. We did have a run of not too inclement weather during Wimbledon, and I dare say that it wouldn't be too presumptuous to expect a little more sunshine before the autumn season."

You kill him.

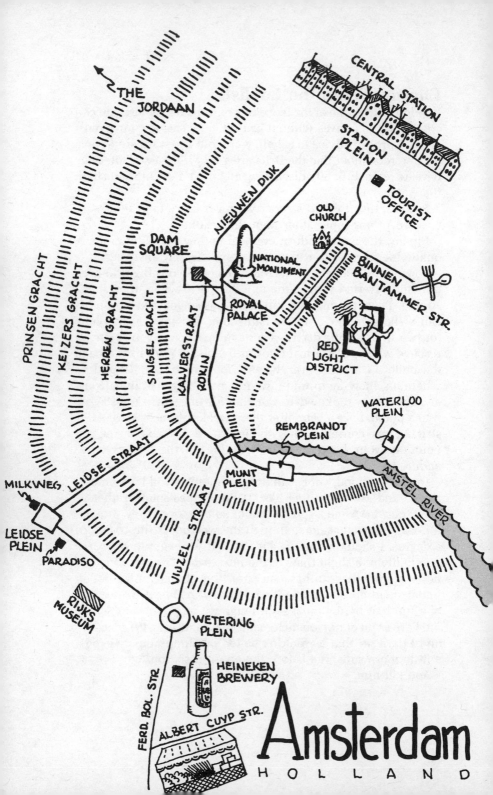

Amsterdam

Amsterdam—the city of coffee and canals, of herring and hash, where poets wander among pornography and bicycles outnumber people. It's a city filled with Japanese tourists (posing as photographers), Swedish secretaries, Canadian backpackers, and American coeds.

Upon arrival, you may be shocked by the glaring absence of high-profile office buildings or monuments like the Eiffel Tower or Seattle Space Needle. Don't despair. Holland is also called the Lowlands, and all the canals that parallel the streets are supposed to make up for this shortcoming with charm. Besides, as we will see later, the Dutch have other ways to get high.

Amsterdam will be one of the most confusing cities on your trip when it comes to nomenclature. Holland, The Netherlands, the Lowlands, Dutch—you'll find you can use these terms interchangeably when describing where you've been or where you're going. On postcards, for example, you can write "Greetings from Holland!" In conversation, you can say, "In the Netherlands we met these really rad Dutch guys." When writing your Intro Sociology paper, you can refer to "the traditional Dutch costumes of the Lowlands" you saw in Holland.

Holland is also known for artists who used to paint windmills and portraits of men with goatees. For you art buffs, there are plenty of great museums in Amsterdam, so if you must do some culture, get it out of your system here. Otherwise, just tell people you saw great "Flemish art" (yes, another somewhat interchangeable word, but use this one only in reference to painters and paintings).

Fine. Now let's orient ourselves to Amsterdam.

Getting Started

Amsterdam is the perfect city for the *Let's Blow* traveler for several reasons. First, the city is laid out nicely, like the spokes of a half-wheel, with the train station set smack in the middle. In peak tourist season, the **Centraal Station**, known as C.S., looks like a budget traveler's version of a M*A*S*H hospital. People lie around everywhere until the police move them along, and the walking wounded heft their backpacks onto trains and head out to the front lines of Europe, while raw recruits arrive on the boat-trains from London or on the subway from Schiphol Airport.

Get out of the train station as quickly as possible. Directly outside, over the tram tracks and to your left, is the **VVV**, the city tourist office. Head there and be prepared to wait while Herb Billing from Tacoma, Washington (salesman for Mutual of Omaha) tells a rambling anecdote about the last time he was over here "in YU-ROPE, during the Big One, WWII" to the young woman trying to book him into the Amsterdam Hilton. After the two nervous Turkish guys are reassured for the fourth time that their budget hotel does not serve pork products at breakfast, it's your turn.

We have found the staff at the VVV to be extremely helpful and breathtakingly efficient in at least six languages. The important thing is to know what you want. If you're traveling rock-bottom, say so. Don't turn the whole business into a kind of Dutch "Let's Make a Deal." Be prepared, though: a rock-bottom hotel usually means sharing a multi-bed room with a bunch of dope-heads, and if you have any open sores, you may not want to use the showers. However, if you're reading this and thinking we could be describing your own apartment, then you may be very happy with such a place. Rock-bottom is about $10 per night.

If you're traveling with a special someone, you should be able to find a decent room—where *you'll* be the first to mess up the sheets—for about $20-$30. Expect to pay about $60 if you want a toilet and shower in your room. Most hotels throw in some sort of breakfast—usually bread, butter, jam, coffee, and sometimes cheese and cold cuts.

Even at the peak of the tourist season, hotel space in Amsterdam is pretty easy to find. But save yourself time and trouble: for a few bucks, the VVV will get you a room, and it's money well spent. While you're at the helpful office, buy a city map for

$1.50 and a copy of *This Week in Amsterdam*. The tourist office will also call ahead to your hotel, so you can check-in at your leisure.

Now, fight your way back to the door and find the **GVB** (to the right of the VVV), where you can buy tram tickets. It's worth your while to buy a day-pass for each day you'll be staying, since they get progressively cheaper per day. Then head for your hotel and drop off your bags. Don't be in such a rush that you miss the guy **grinding his organ** and **spanking his monkey** on the bridge just outside, though.

Money

In Holland, the unit of currency is the *guilder*, which, for reasons lost in the mists of antiquity, is written as *f*. At this writing, two guilders equals about $1.00. So just divide everything by two to get prices.

Dutch paper money is the brightest in Europe. The 50-guilder note is bright yellow with sunflowers on it and looks a lot like a quality margarine wrapper.

The neat thing we noticed in Amsterdam is that most stuff costs about two guilders, or a buck. So when you go to a cafe and have a coffee, it's a buck. You wash it down with a Heineken, it's a buck. You order a delicious pastry, it's a buck. It's a lot like using Monopoly money.

Things To See

Amsterdam is definitely a city for strolling around. Starting at the train station, head up the street called Damrak (**American Express** is at #66) to **Dam Square** and mingle with the Japanese tourists. If you happen to be blond, your photo will probably be passed around as "a typical Dutch" the next time Hiro has the guys over for sushi. Dam Square itself doesn't have much in the way of entertainment, unless you enjoy standing in a crowd of burned-out youth, ankle-deep in pigeon guano, watching some sleazy characters pound on homemade drums while street vendors offer to sell you crack, coke, and various synthetic drugs.

(You've probably heard all you need to know from friends about the ready availability of drugs in Amsterdam. Most coffeehouses have a wider selection of hash, pot, and "space cakes" than artifical sweeteners. It's tough to get official information about drugs in Amsterdam. Technically, it's *all* illegal, but the police seem to have their hands full with the hard drug scene, so "soft" drugs flourish—if not with the blessing of the police, at least with their indifference.)

Heading away from Dam Square toward **Waterlooplein**, you will pass through crowded shopping streets with lots of bars and coffeehouses, and then you'll hit the canals. Congratulations, you're now in the renowned Red Light District. Close your eyes and push on through for now (we'll come back to it soon), and find your way to Waterlooplein, which sells tons of flea market merchandise as well as food. Here's where to buy the black pants, black shirts, black boots, black leather jackets, and black socks you didn't have time to buy before you left. Also, there are lots of cool jacket pins here for your daypacks to make it look like you've been on the road for months. You can even get Soviet military uniforms left over from World War II if you look hard. Pipes, rare records, movie posters, and other items—things you could never buy at the Woodvalley Village Square Mall back home—are everywhere here.

The Heineken Brewery

If it's nearly 9:00am or 1:00pm, it's time to hit the **Heineken Brewery**, recently put out to pasture, but still a fun place to tour. It's within easy walking distance of Dam Square—about 15 minutes up Rokin, turn right on Vijzelstraat. After you cross the canal at Stadhouderskade, you'll know you're there because 1) the building on your left has HEINEKEN written in 30-foot letters on its roof and looks like a brewery, and 2) there's a stream of Bobs, Debbies, Chips, and Lisas pouring in from all points of the compass. Believe us, this place can draw a crowd. What does beer have that religion doesn't?

Once you've gained entrance, you will meet the first of many polite, blond men who will joke gently with you if you're pretty and extract the princely sum of two guilders for the expense of the tour. Actually, the tour itself is non-existent. You are marched upstairs to an area with some monster copper kettles. The guide speaks English for about five nano-seconds, and then it's up to the reception lounge on the fourth floor, where busy waiters work hard to pour as many small glasses of the liquid ambrosia as you can hold. Meanwhile, the cadre of polite, blond men politely pass around plates of cheese, crackers, and salami.

The whole affair evokes Parents Day at one of the better prep schools. The flow of beer temporarily dries up while two short, slightly interesting movies are shown. Then you're invited to imbibe again, until the polite, blond men have to rush off to choir practice or something. You stagger out into the sunshine, thinking how WONDERFUL Amsterdam is and how WONDERFUL life is, and perhaps you should come back to the brewery tomorrow!

The Heineken Brewery tour is probably the best dollar you'll spend on this trip. It's certainly possible to take the tour more than once, but it does kind of put you out of action for part of the day. (Tours run at 9:00am, 9:45am, 10:30am, 1:30pm, 1:45pm, and 2:30pm.)

The Sex Museum

Where else but Amsterdam would you find a museum devoted entirely to sex? (If you're listing names of small towns in Idaho, please drop us a line.) The **Amsterdam Sex Museum**, located on Damrak, costs only $2.00.

What can we say about it? Well, it's certainly the best sex museum we've ever toured. The ground floor consists of erotic art through the ages and covers everything from the Ivory Coast to the Orient and lots of places in between. Yes, folks, these people are not bullshitting about their museum—it's sex indeed. Right way up, wrong way down, inside out—you name it and there are creatures doing it.

It is educational, though. For instance, we learned that Japanese oldtimers couldn't get it up unless there were at least two big china pots in the room with them. Must be one of those cultural things. You know, like you can never produce a urine sample for the nurse when she asks for it, but ten minutes after you leave the doctor's office you're looking for a McDonald's so you can make a pit stop.

Moving right along, you come to a room with a warning notice on the door: *Enter At Your Own Risk, You Could Be Shocked—No Complaints Please!* Inside are photographs of the biggest, longest, roundest, etc.—essentially a room full of freaks of nature. No real reason to feel shocked. Envious, yes; shocked, no. There are some photographs that may not be for the squeamish (zebras doing things they surely didn't learn on the veld, etc.).

Upstairs, there's more artwork from various periods, including a large collection of racy photos from the 1800's. Nothing very educational, really. I mean, it makes sense guys and gals were doing it back then 'cause if they weren't, we wouldn't be here, would we?

In the end, we decided the sex museum isn't worth the money. After all, sex is like softball: a great game to play with friends, but not much fun to watch. If you really need the education, save the two bucks and rent *Bimbo Bowlers from Buffalo* on video when you get home.

For you sophisticates who would never consider walking into such a sordid place but need to exercise your prurient minds nonetheless, **De 3 Gratien**, an erotic art gallery at Wetering-schans 39, offers you the chance to examine and buy sculpture, engravings, music, poetry, and books you won't find at Walden-books in the mall.

The Red Light District

Since we're on the subject of sex and presumably have your un-divided attention, let's talk a little about the famed **Red Light District**, on or near the winding street called **Zeedijk**.

As you can see from the map, Amsterdam looks like a giant amphitheater, similar to the one where they taught Intro Biolo-gy. The central railway station is where the professor would stand, and the canals spread out in concentric circles. Ironical-ly, the Red Light District is approximately where the pre-meds would sit.

Prostitution is legal in Amsterdam, and the young and not-so-young ladies sit on little stools in shop windows with a red light over the door and make goo-goo eyes at passersby. Supposedly, these women receive regular health check-ups, but some of them don't look so healthy. Hey, if you're crazy enough to risk your life, your MBA, and your future earning potential, go right ahead.

Regardless, it's a decent educational experience to wander around the Zeedijk, especially if you're with the love of your life/month. After all, it doesn't matter where you get your appe-tite, as long as you eat at home.

Many of the prostitutes are from Surinam, a former Dutch colony in South America. Just between us, if your brother ever tells you he's going to marry a Surinamese girl, don't sit up nights waiting for him to share his prize money from the Sears Baby Photo Contest. Many of these gals probably have wonderful personalities and would make fine homemakers—if you could just get them to stop hanging out in the front window and winking at the neighbors.

Oh, yeah. Be sure to get pictures of the women in their windows. They actually *like* to be photographed and may make obscene gestures to make your snapshot more erotic. If you have one of those auto-focus models, keep it concealed while you get her to come on to you. Act like you're real interested, and then pop it out and snap! They may act angry, but it's only for appearances. Say something hilarious like "Hey baby, the guys back at the frat house will go wild when I show 'em pictures of a real whore!"

There is an active hard drug scene in the Zeedijk, and it's not a good place to hang around late at night, even if you are with Todd, Scott, Toby, and Scooter. After all, if you want to get robbed at knife-point on a weeknight, it's cheaper to go to New York.

The Zeedijk also has an extensive collection of sex shops, where you can buy expensive adult toys, the uses for which you can only guess. Pornography and live sex shows surround you. It may not make a sailor blush, but it might make his loose-fitting pants less so. The store proprietors encourage you to browse, unlike at 7-Elevens. For our female readers, there's little in the way of a male sex district. But then, these Europeans are not as progressive in matters of equal opportunity as we are. There is, however, an active gay scene in Amsterdam. A good place to start inquiring is along Spuistraat.

The Jordaan

The Jordaan is fast becoming the most trendy area in the city, and it's worth a stroll through the narrow streets. Once a working-class residential area, the Jordaan has been taken over by Dutch yuppies, and it's supposed to be the equivalent of Soho in New York. It's fairly quiet, but it does have some nice small bars and restaurants.

The Jordaan is west of Amsterdam's center, beyond the main canals. We looked all over for King Hussein, but we couldn't find him.

Food

There are so many goodies to eat and drink in Amsterdam that you're never going to fit into that size 8 dress when you get back home. If you're interested in traditional Dutch food, however, you may be out of luck. One city guide lists 32 French restaurants, 16 Indian, 11 Chinese, 7 Italian, 3 Greek, and 1—count 'em, 1—Dutch restaurant.

Amsterdam has lots of Indonesian restaurants, since Holland once ran most of Indonesia the way we now run Canada. There are hundreds of the suckers around, and their specialty is a spread called a *rijstafel* (rice table). It consists of 12 to 20 or more small dishes of various curries, kebabs, salads, shredded coconut, vegetables, meats, and sauces, plus a big bowl of rice. When it's laid out in front of you, it looks just like a pot-luck supper at the V.F.W. The similarity is enhanced by the fact that, as in the pot-luck supper at the V.F.W., you can't really say what anything is, but it doesn't matter because it all slides down the hatch fine with a few Heinekens. Going for a *rijstafel* is great if you've hooked up with a few of your buddies at the hotel because, like Twister and touch football, it's more fun with a group.

We won't pretend to have tried even 1% of the Indonesian restaurants in Amsterdam, but we've tried enough to know that you'll love Indonesian food—so long as you don't think chop suey is really exotic. If so, save your money for a trip to the local Chinese take-out or Benihana Steakhouse (don't forget the ketchup!) when you get back home. Also, none of the Indonesian restaurants we tried served drinks with little paper umbrellas in them. Chop suey fans may be disappointed by this.

A good area to start looking for Indonesian restaurants is a small street called **Binnen Bantammerstraat**, right behind the Zeedijk. We really liked **Sama Sani**—about $15.00 per person for the rice table. The waitresses seemed to think that if you want something bad enough, you'll set your hair on fire to get their attention. Very understated. The **Kong Hing** on the same street is also good at about the same price. Two other safe bets are **Selecta** at Vijzelstraat 23 and, somewhat more expensive, **Djokja** at Ferdinand Bolstraat 13 (past the Heineken Brewery), about $40.00 for two.

One problem: a typical *rijstafel* tends to give you more food than a Vietnamese family that has clung to the wreckage of their fishing boat for a week could eat. The concept of doggy bags has not really hit in Europe (don't these people know *anything*?), and besides, just transporting the remains of a modest *rijstafel* would require a U-Haul and someTeamsters. Fortunately, there's a solution. Check out **Bojo** at Lange Leidsedwarstraat 51, which has pioneered the concept of a mini-*rijstafel* on a plate. It's not perfect, of course, but if you're a nervous eater and want to try a little *rijstafel* before going the whole hog, this is the place. It's also very cheap, close to the Leidseplein, and the waitresses are friendly (if overworked).

So there you are. *"Salamet mahan!"* as we say in Jakarta—which, roughly translated, means "Last one to finish the fish spleen is a water buffalo!"

Other goodies to eat in Amsterdam are french fries slathered with mayonnaise, of all things, carried in enormous paper cones. They taste pretty good, and maybe you'll get so addicted that next year you'll take the dining hall by storm: "Oh yeah, *everyone* in Europe eats mayonnaise on their french fries. You know, ketchup is just so *déjà vu.*"

If you've invested more of your money than you had planned in the Heineken Brewery, you can still get a cheap lunch by buying a couple of *krokets*, little potato cakes that look like spring rolls and are filled with a creamy meat or vegetable glop. You can buy them all over for one or two guilders, and lots of snack bars even sell them from vending machines.

Other cheap eating possibilities include many of the Italian pizzerias and restaurants clustered just off the main nightspot, the Leidseplein, an area we discuss below. In particular, check out Lange Leidsedwars, especially **Pizzeria Piccolino** at #63. It sells great pizza for about $5.00. Unfortunately, its pasta tastes like dorm food. The restaurant appears to be jammed at all times.

Sort of around the corner from Piccolino is **Seven Lanterns**, which serves much better pasta in the same price range. Eat at either of these and then head for one of the outside cafes on the Leidseplein for a cappuccino and a quiet period of reflection on why everyone in Holland, including the 6-year-olds, speaks better English than you. Promise yourself that you'll start watching foreign movies when you get home.

A final entry in the cheap Italian restaurant department is **Casa Di Marco** on Leidsestraat 54, a nondescript place with great soups and pizza and other pretty basic foods, which we found very comforting when a slight intestinal problem arose during our last stay in Amsterdam.

If you must have something truly Dutch, head down Prinsengracht to **The Pancake Bakery** at #191, where you can get huge, crêpe-like pancakes with your choice of 53 fillings, from meats and vegetables to fruits and berries. So, depending on the time of day, you can have brunch, lunch, dinner, or dessert there, all in the disguise of a pancake, for about $5.00. They serve coffee, beer, wine, and hot cider to wash it all down. Unfortunately, you'll be eating with a lot of people studiously reading a thick, orange travel book, but that's a small price to pay for pancakes filled with pork and kiwi, isn't it?

If you've misplaced Dad's Amex card, or if you're just tired of restaurants, head for the huge open-air market on **Albert Cuypstraat**. Walk past the Heineken Brewery and just keep going; it'll be on your left. Here you can find lots of fruits, vegetables, cheese stalls, and bakeries. You can pick up some lovely raw oysters and eels at 8:00am and feel them slide down your throat to your stomach, still churning from the excesses of the night before. Or how about a herring sandwich smothered with raw, chopped onions? *Ummmmm.* So good, and so good for you.

If you want to picnic by the canal for the afternoon, the Albert Cuypstraat market is a good place to load up on supplies. Everything is priced per *stuk*, which is one of those generic Germanic words that roughly means "each." The street market also sells some cheap clothing, t-shirts, and underwear. So if you're a bit tired of wearing the same undies for 18 days running, you can pick up a new pair here and save the old stuk for Sunday wear only. Look for the stand that sells *busten halters* (bras) for only $10 per stuk.

Nightlife

Moving rapidly along, we come to the issue of nightlife in Amsterdam. Essentially, there are two major areas of interest.

The first is the region around the **Leidseplein**. Before you hit the Leidseplein, mark it on your map and draw a route back to your hotel. Make sure you'll be able to see this route in the dark with minimal cerebral effort. There's also the area around **Rembrandtsplein**, to the east of Dam Square, but it's of secondary importance unless you're the sort who goes for the glitzy cabaret and topless bar scene. Both areas come to life at night with lots of bars, restaurants, outdoor cafes, and clubs.

The Leidseplein offers one-stop nightlife shopping, where you can find any bar to suit your tastes—and maybe discover some tastes you never knew you had. The bars come in two varieties: the very-crowded and the too-crowded. Look for places filled with tall, blond Scandinavians being pursued by short, dark Italians. Lots of clubs offer live music (mostly jazz and blues), and all are loud and raucous. Two clubs—the Milkweg and Paradiso—are large, rock-oriented halls that are definitely worth joining, even if you're in town for only one night.

The **Milkweg** "Multimedia Centrum" at Lijnbaansgracht 234a might be your first choice, especially if you're in town only for a night or two. For a membership investment of about $4 (good for a month) and a cover charge of another $5-$15, you'll get an evening of multimedia entertainment, so get there early. On any given night there can be a cult movie, live theater, avant-garde psycho video, and two or three bands—all at the same time.

The bands will vary depending on the night, and often there's no way of telling what to expect unless you rely on the person at the door to describe them. Sometimes it's best to look for clues on your own. If everyone is wearing dreadlocks and smoking a cigarette the size of your forearm, reggae is a reasonable guess. If the crowd has an angry, violent look and wears black leather wristbands and nose-rings, you probably won't hear polkas.

On nights we've been at the Milkweg, we've seen everything: psycho-rockabilly, soul, blues, punk, and industrial rock, plus some of the most bizarre dancing ever. You'd be hard-pressed to find such a show at such a price at home. And, if the music isn't what you were expecting or if you get bored with the movie, there's always the cafe upstairs (where more than the aroma of coffee is in the air), two bars downstairs that sell food and desserts, bookshops, and an art gallery. Be sure to try a "space cake," created to honor the brave astronauts who died in the *Challenger* explosion.

If all of this isn't enough for you, you can leave and get your hand stamped at the door to get back in. What's more, you're right at the Leidseplein. So go out and get some fresh air, and return for more multimedia fun later.

The **Paradiso**, at Weteringschans 6-8, is more of a no-frills concert hall reminiscent of the Fillmore days (a reference for those
of you who've read rock history books or have an uncle who
hasn't adjusted since Young left Crosby, Stills, & Nash). The
Paradiso generally books bigger-name bands (that is, you actually might have *heard* of them), which vary from hardcore metal to reggae to folk. Check your *Amsterdam This Week*.

To the right of the Paradiso is a bar/restaurant/theater called
de Balie, which at one time may have been a hopping nightspot
but now is as dull as golf on TV. Some outdated guidebooks might
encourage you to go there for some left-wing political discussion among the intelligentsia or something. Take it from us—
unless you speak Dutch, you may as well be at a Chinese Tup-
perware party.

For those of you inclined to the glitzy cabaret scene, the **Rembrandtsplein** is an alternative to the Leidseplein. There are a
lot of French restaurants and piano bars lining the square, and
the singers seem to compete with each other to be heard on the
street. Imagine, if you will, two Perry Como imitators duking
it out with two Tom Jones sound-alikes, all within earshot.

Probably the best entertainment of all in Amsterdam is simply to sit at a cafe, drink a cold Heineken, and watch well-fed
rich people waddle back and forth in front of you, like the Pen-
guin in *Batman*. Savor the moment as you view streams of travelers from exotic places like Hoboken and Little Rock pass by, the
women resplendent in polyester suits, their purple rinses
sheltered by wrinkled Handi-Hats. The menfolk are like pot-
bellied peacocks, each trying to outdo the other in bold colors
of Elks Club green, red, and blue. Here a rhinestone ring glit-
ters, there a turquoise bolo gleams in the evening lights.

A Diamond Factory
One fun thing to do in Amsterdam is visit a diamond cutting
factory, of which there are several in the immediate area. Almost
all have free tours, and, if you have sufficiently recovered from
your hangover after the Heineken Brewery, you may want to give
it a try.

We went to **Van Moppes Diamonds** on Albert Cuypstraat, but
it's typical of many of them. No matter what time you get there,
you'll face 60 or so Moms and Pops clutching their TWA "There

Has Never Been a Better Time to Get Away" totes. Get deep in the middle of the pack and be prepared to answer questions as diverse as "What's the name of the school in Rhode Island where Bertha's cousin's niece is flunking?" to "What's your favorite method of birth control?" The Rules of the Road for tourists in Europe allow no secrets.

Off we go then on our tour, led by a svelte blond who patiently deals with everything from comments from a nascent Shirley MacLaine about the healing powers of diamonds to sarcastic remarks about South African gems from a politically correct young activist who drives a Korean car fueled by Arabian oil.

After a walk through a series of halls where you'll observe men grinding what appear to be their fingernails, you will be escorted into a salon of jewelry. Here a bevy of blond salespeople will subject you to a sell so hard that a Bedouin trying to unload his ugly daughter on a traveling camel salesman could take lessons. Make for the door.

The Rijksmuseum

We didn't actually have time to visit the big museum in Amsterdam called the **Rijksmuseum** because, frankly, after we toured the Sex Museum we were pooped, and there's just so much culture one can absorb in a day.

But, lucky for you, we ran into Joe "The Destroyer" Kasakowski, who used to play tight end for Michigan Tech. Joe had been in Amsterdam for several days because he was missing a few credits (actually 39, but who's counting?) to graduate, and he was taking advantage of a really progressive program at Tech that awards 10 credits for every week spent in a foreign country. Joe had just completed units on Bermuda, Cancun, and Texas, and he hoped to graduate with honors by the end of his week in Amsterdam.

To cut a real long story short, Joe offered to write a little report for us on the Rijksmuseum. So, here it is:

The Rijksmuseum
by Joseph Kasakowski, Jr.

The Rijksmuseum is a big sucker. I don't know why it's called the Rijksmuseum, because I didn't see any Rijks.

I did see loads of pictures. Most of the pictures are old and kind of dark. The men all wear skirts, and I do not mind telling you that I would not like to share a locker room with them. No sir, I would not. The women in these pictures are all fat and look like they don't take very good care of themselves and work-out and stuff. None of them could ever make cheerleader.

There were lots of pictures that are drawn in pencil and have not been colored-in yet. I think for $4.00 they should only have pictures that are finished and colored-in and stuff.

Also, there were quite a few statues there. Some of those suckers are pretty heavy, I don't mind telling you. Like, I can bench-press 350, and I could barely get some of those statues off the ground! And another thing, how come there are all these statues of old guys in togas? Is it some kind of fraternity Hall of Fame or something?

All in all, the Rijksmuseum is a pretty good museum, but I think that Dinosaur World, South of the Border, and the Football Hall of Fame are more entertaining.

The End.

All right, we have to fess up. We actually *did* visit the Rijksmuseum and, though we may hate ourselves in the morning for saying this, you ought to spend some time looking around. The museum has a huge collection of Vermeers, Rembrandts, Hals, Corridors, Stairwells, and some exquisite Bathrooms. There is a really good museum shop, where you can buy copies of the paintings of all those old guys in funny hats. The Rijksmuseum, like most of Holland, is closed on Monday.

The Alkmaar Cheese Market

A really enjoyable morning excursion is a trip to the **Cheese Market** in Alkmaar, a 45-minute train ride from Amsterdam. The action only runs Friday mornings begining at 10:00am, and you must arrive before noon, when things start to shut down.

What happens, you ask? Well, all these geezers in costumes bring in thousands of wheels of cheese into a neat old cobbled square, weigh them, and then have an auction. When the cheese is sold, they have another little ceremony where they load the wheels onto cradles and four of the guys in neat old clothes take them out of the square and load them onto trucks.

Sounds like as much fun as watching bugs sleep, eh? Well it *is* fun—trust us on this one. If the weather is nice, the whole main street of Alkmaar becomes a big market, with all sorts of great things to munch on, including—surprise, surprise—lots of different cheese. You could also do worse than checking out the **Cheese Museum**, directly behind the auction area. (Boy—first the Rijksmuseum, now the Cheese Museum. Maybe we're getting soft in our old age.) Then, pick up a few kinds of cheese, some bread, and a festive beverage or two, dangle your legs over the side of a canal, and have a nice lunch before heading back to Amsterdam for another exhausting afternoon at the Heineken Brewery.

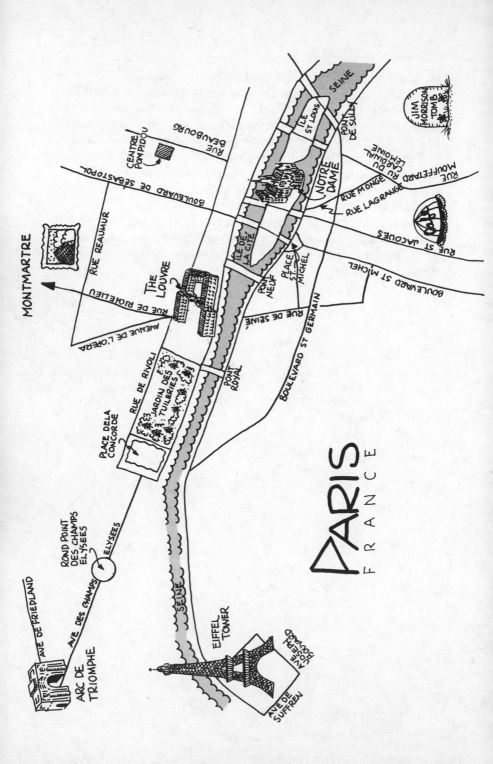

Paris

Remember in high school when you were nose guard for the Oak Hill Tigers, and you had some easy games early in the season? You guys were strutting and preening, high-fiving and butt-slapping. You thought you were *bad*.

In the back of your mind, though, you had this strange feeling—not quite worry, but, you know, a little nervous feeling. You realized that your early schedule was just a warm-up, that all these easy games were preface to the Big One, the WWIII of the season when you had to face some real opposition.

Sure, you still tackled and blocked great, and you still wolfed down steak and eggs for breakfast. And sure, you still fooled around with Julie Berkowitz in the back of your old Duster after practice. All the time, though, you had a feeling in the pit of your stomach that something heavy was coming down, something mean and nasty, something with big sharp teeth. You knew the next game was going to be against . . . **PARIS**.

Background

Paris is the capital of France, and we will be doing the city in a day or so, followed by a trip to southern France and the beaches at Nice (rhymes with "grease," not "lice").

Besides Paris and Nice, there isn't much else in France. That's not to say there aren't other cities and stuff, but nobody in the U.S. has really heard of other French places, so it's not worth spending time on them on this trip. If you really want to see places like Dijon or Strasbourg, you can always sign up for a semester abroad deal. Some of those suckers can be real blow-offs.

Before we really get into this stuff on Paris, we should clear up some misunderstandings about France and the French. There's always been this story that the French don't like Americans. Well, the truth is, the French are just jealous of us.

You see, it all boils down to the language. The French are upset because all the best movies are in English, and if you're from France and want to see *Terminator 2*, you have to learn a whole new language to do it. Think about it—it's a killer. Suppose you're a French guy and you ask this really cute French girl to the movies. You'd have to say, "Oh, by the way Giselle *ma cherie*, you must learn English by Saturday." No wonder Mickey Mouse and Clint Eastwood are so popular in France.

The other problem is the French never invent any *new* stuff. Sure they make good wine and all, and they made this superfast train, the TGV. (If they really want to travel fast, why don't they just fly?) But who invented ketchup, Twinkies, Cheerios, Cheezwhiz, and Slim-Fast? We did! Our creativity and get-up-and-go really bother the French. Plus, they can't think of any good words to describe these great new products. So they have to ask for "*le ketchup*" in restaurants, and this only reminds them that they're stuck with a language as useful these days as an eight-track tape player.

Now, a lot of French learn English so they have something to do on Saturday nights, but then they have another problem. You see, the French have a funny-shaped throat to help them to pronounce all those rolling rrrrr's. It's handy for speaking French, but try speaking English with it! You sound like an effeminate idiot.

All this gets the French pretty unsettled. As a result, they get frustrated with young American tourists who speak English much better than they do, and they act like real snobs all the time.

While it's good to understand this little problem, you've got to remember that the best defense when dealing with the French is a good offense. It's pretty useless trying to speak to a French guy in French, because he'll either pretend not to understand you or he really won't understand you. (This is going to burn all those French Lit majors out there, but that's the way things go sometimes.) The best way to communicate with French people is to say the English words slowly and loudly and use your hands a lot. This method is good for the French as well, because it helps teach them English. It's amazing how few of them understand expressions like "Eggs over easy, please" or "Gimme a short stack, and put the syrup on the side."

American Express/American Embassy

The American Express office is at 11 rue Scribe, and the American Embassy is at 2 av. Gabriel. If you're an international relations major at a good school and you're thinking of the foreign service, don't be shy about dropping by the embassy and asking for a tour. Apparently, some of the Marine Guards also offer after-hours tours which can be pretty interesting.

Money

The unit of currency in France in called the *franc*, which is, of course, a nickname. Male money is actually *francis*; female money is *frances*.

Day 1

You'll probably arrive into **Gare du Nord** about 7:00am. Since you won't be able to check into a hotel for a few hours, you might as well chill-out and get breakfast.

Pick any cafe or restaurant near the station, and grab a table near the window or, if you're really lucky, on the sidewalk. It's always fun to eat in France with a big group of people you've met on the train, so if you've brought the gang for breakfast, pull some extra chairs from nearby tables and pile your backpacks on them. If that doesn't get the waiter's attention, click your fingers in the air a few times and yell "*Gar-sun! Gar-sun!*" If you can't pronounce that, just say "Yo!"

When the waiter arrives, say slowly in English, "Hi, six *(hold up your fingers)* coffee americano, six croissants, pronto." (Note: They do not have Wheaties in France, and, believe it or not, they don't even know what french toast is.) And *voila!* as we say in French, you have just ordered your first meal.

After breakfast, start looking for a hotel. The two basic requirements are 1) it should be cheap, and 2) it should be close to the party center of town. For these reasons, we recommend the **Latin Quarter** on the Left Bank. Don't worry—you don't have to do any crazy stuff like learn yet another language here.

The Latin Quarter is the old university section of the city. To get there, hop on the subway (called the **Metro** by the French and know-it-all, artsy-fartsy types back home). Strictly speaking, you need to buy a ticket to ride on the subway, but, in fact, you can just jump the little gate (careful with your backpack!). Nobody really minds. "Crazy American kids" you can sometimes hear the old people murmur with a smile. Anyway, if you wanted to spend a fortune riding a hot, crowded subway, you'd be in New York now, right?

Take the subway to the area around rue Cardinal-Lemoine and start scouring the streets. There are lots of seedy hotels in this area, and you'll be right where the action is.

You can always get a room for two people and pile in five or six if you all have sleeping bags. The hotel owners will often do a little good-natured grumbling, but they all have hearts of gold and remember when they themselves were young and filled with *joie de vivre* (a French phrase that means "horniness"). In any event, they'll be thrilled to host a bunch of cheerful, clean youths who always floss after meals.

An interesting thing about French hotel rooms is that they often have a bidet in the room. The following tip isn't for everyone, but we've found that if you're with friends, the bidet can make a darn good punch bowl. Rinse first.

Things To See
Staying in the Latin Quarter puts you in primo partying position at night. It's best, however, to get some sightseeing out of the way early. If you really crank, you should be able to see most everything in Paris in one afternoon.

First, hop on the Metro and get to the **Eiffel Tower**, a big, old, steel structure. You can go to the top of it by elevator, but it's expensive (about $7.00). So make it your Tall Thing To Climb in Paris, and take the stairs for about $3.00. You can get some great snaps of the city from up there, and, since most cities look about the same when you're up high enough, you won't need to do any more climbing for the rest of your trip!

After your Eiffel Tower Experience, head across the river (by foot if you still have the energy) to the **Arc de Triomphe**. The French built this big, old arch before they developed the sorry habit of losing all their wars and needing the U.S. to save their butts. There's not much to see, except that the Arc is at the top of the **Champs Elysées** (pronounced "chomp a-lee-say"), a big street where the French hold bicycle races and ticker tape parades to celebrate the U.S. saving their butts again.

Both sides of the Champs are lined with airline offices, so if you want to bail out, now's the time. ("Oh, you guys, I just remembered I left my Walkman at the top of the Arc. You go on ahead and I'll catch up with you." Right.) There's also a **McDonald's** on the left side of the street where you can grab *le lunch*: *le Big Mac*, *le fries*, and *le Coke*. Hey, this French language is a breeze!

After you hike down the Champs (and it's the Mother of All Hikes), head directly for **Montmartre** (take the Metro). This region of Paris is where all the Impressionist painters used to work. These guys did the original art for the posters you find between the Budweiser calendar and the picture of the lacrosse team on sorority girls' walls.

Montmartre overlooks the city and has a lot of small, winding streets and cafes. It's also a good place to buy postcards of the blurry pictures the Impressionists used to paint. Nowadays, these guys could probably do a lot better with an airbrush or a Macintosh with MacPaint.

Unless you're an art major, you don't need to linger. However, the steps of the **Sacré-Coeur** (the big church at the top of the hill) are a good place to hang out if the weather is nice. Slip on your Raybans, ease off your Reeboks, and kick back for a while. It's the end of the first quarter, and your defense is holding.

Actually, Montmartre is a good place to score with fellow Americans, especially if you're able to draw any kind of straight line. Just whip out a piece of paper and start sketching, pausing often to stare pensively at the sky and cop a view of the t-shirt that spells University of Wisconsin in a wonderfully curved way on the brunette sitting beside you.

For men, a good opener might be something like "It's easy to see what brought these guys here, isn't it?" (Give a rueful little one-artist-to-another smile.) If she says "Who?" or "Yeah, I never thought Guns N' Roses would play a dump like Paris," forget it. But if she blushes and murmurs "Yes" in a soft voice that says "You are almost as cute as Steve Ellis, whose body I have adored in English Lit and whose children I would willingly bear," then you've struck pay dirt.

For the ladies, a good ploy is to go up to a cute guy, giggle a little nervously, drag one of your Nikes across the dirt, and open with something like "You really have great muscle tone. Could I sketch you against the background of the old church? Do you, like, work-out a lot or something?" Before you know it, you'll be walking arm-in-arm, daypacks caressing, as you blow through Europe together.

Take the steps down from the Sacré Coeur to the area around **rue de Steinkerque**. Lots of shops selling pure junk line these streets, and it's a great place to pick up some trash for an old aunt or somebody. What could be more appropriate than a plastic Eiffel Tower or a tea towel with Notre Dame in Day-Glo?

Now, swing to the right a little and walk down Boulevard de Clichy until you pass the **Moulin Rouge**, which was the hottest nightspot in Paris in, oh, 1824 or so. Today, it's a flashy, trashy club catering mainly to middle-aged American tourists, all purple rinses and white shoes—people like your parents, in fact. Definitely not worth the admission price.

Also, the area around the Moulin Rouge is a big shopping area for prostitutes. (That is, it's not an area where prostitutes buy their weekly groceries, but instead . . .)

It's probably getting late in the day by now, so head to the hotel for a quick shower and maybe a power nap. Don't forget to pick up your *Universite de Paris/Sorbonne* sweatshirt on the way home. The university is near where you're staying (if you took our advice), but there isn't much to see there. All the students are busy making money on Cape Cod for the summer.

The Evening

After your nap, it's time to strut your stuff around the Latin Quarter for the evening. Guys: wear khakis, a Lacoste shirt, and Docksiders. Ladies: it's a blue denim skirt, white (to show off your tan) t-shirt, and Candie's. Don't forget to drape your college sweatshirt casually over your shoulder.

Start the evening's entertainment along a stretch of streets that run more or less away from the **Boulevard de St-Michel**. This area has an enormous number of restaurants, all serving French specialties like shish kebab, hamburgers, and pizza.

As you stroll around this area, you may be surprised to run into people you know from back home. Well, it surprises us that people are surprised by this. Look, if you give 300,000 American kids the same travel guide to Europe (you know, the one with the bright orange cover) and send them off at the same time of year on the same itinerary, chances are some of them will meet. What's more surprising is the fact that you always meet the people you like the *least*:

Kelly: "Oh my God! I can't believe it! This is, like, really un-real! What are you guys doing here?!" *(Note: These sentences are repeated for about five minutes in various combinations.)*

Debbie: "Kelly! Oh my God! I didn't know you were in Europe!" *(Translated: Shit, why does that bitch have to show up here? If she starts flirting with Bob, I'll rip her eyes out.)* "When did you get here? You look really great! You must be starving yourself!" *(Actually, the fat cow doesn't look half bad. If Bob starts flirting with her, I'll cut his balls off.)*

Kelly: "Thanks, Debbie. You look really great yourself. It's so good to see you! I love your t-shirt! It like looks so bohemian." *(Where did she get that rag? It makes her boobs look even big-ger than usual. It's probably the only reason Bob hangs around with her. He's not bad looking, though.)*

Debbie: "Get outta here, Kelly! It's just some cheap thing I picked up in London. Oh, Kelly, have you met my friend Bob?" *(Eat your heart out, slut.)*

Bob: "Hi Kelly, how's it going?" *(You are really hot.)*

Kelly: "Just fine, Bob." *(I bet he thinks I'm really hot.)*

Debbie: "Kelly, I thought Scott was going to be traveling with you." *(I also heard Scott got smart and dumped you.)*

Kelly: "No, he couldn't make it." *(Eat shit and die, bitch.)*

Debbie: "Oh, that's too bad. Isn't Europe a blast! We are, like, having the greatest time!" *(Or we would be if Bob would keep his eyes off other women.)*

Kelly: "Yeah, I'm having *soooo* much fun! It's so cool to be traveling by myself. I think you meet more interesting people that way. So many people travel with their boyfriends or girl-friends, and I think, like, it could get really boring." *(Though I wouldn't mind traveling with Bob for a few days.)*

Bob: "Would you like to have dinner with us, Kelly?" *(You are really hot.)*

Kelly: "Hey, that's a really nice idea, Bob. I'd love to! Debbie, where have you been hiding Bob? He is just *soooo* cute. You guys are just *soooo* cute together." *(But not for much longer, if I have my way. I wonder how Bob would feel about carrying my backpack for a few days?)*

Debbie: "Great! Let's have dinner and we can catch up on some news." *(And maybe you can catch salmonella.)*

Notre Dame

After dinner, stroll over to **Notre Dame**. In all sincerity, the sight of the flood-lit cathedral on a warm, summer evening can make even a professional party animal swallow twice. The church is situated on a small island (*Ile de la Cité*). Cross over on a footbridge, spend some time around the square in front of the church (*Place du Parvis Notre Dame*), and listen to the cooing of the doves and the chorus of "Neat!" "Cool!" and "Oh my God!" from your articulate compatriots.

If you happen to be with someone cute you met earlier but still haven't—pardon the indelicacy—gone for it, this is the right time. If you can't score with props like Notre Dame in the background, maybe you should think about the priesthood. Plus, you're only minutes from your hotel, so you young lovebirds can give horizontal expression to your desires within the hour.

Day 2

Next morning, it's time to do a little more sightseeing again.

A major pain in the ass to deal with of this morning is the **Louvre**, "the most recognized symbol of art and culture in all history," according to one dorky guidebook. We say: imagine the hugest mall you've ever been in. Imagine it's as crowded as it would be on Christmas Eve, and imagine all the stores are art and frame shops. Well, that's what the Louvre is like, except they don't have any posters of Elle Macpherson.

Why do we have to go there, you ask? Well, we have to go there for a little while because, er, because, uh, you know, um . . . Hey, there isn't a reason in the world why we have to go there! Let's blow it off.

So instead of the Louvre, head down the river to the **Pompidou Centre**, a monstrosity that's an exhibition hall. Since the architect put the heating and plumbing pipes on the outside of the building, it looks like a large sugar cube being raped by serpents. If this architect ever comes to your neighborhood and offers you a deal on building a house, tell him to hit the road.

The building appears to be totally empty, except for a bunch of people in uniforms. However, you can climb onto the roof and get a great view of the city.

After you shoot a whole roll of film on your disc camera before you notice your finger is in front of the lens, climb back down to the large square in front of the Centre. The square is an interesting place, filled with weirdos, artists, drug dealers, and sorority girls. Take your pick.

By now, you'll need to start thinking about catching your train down to Nice. To do this, you'll have to get to **Gare de Lyon**. Beforehand, however, you have time for lunch.

Eating and Drinking in Paris

One of the problems you'll face in Paris is choosing from the huge range of wonderful things to eat. There are so many great restaurants that it would take a separate book to describe even a fraction of them. So, we'll just cover some good places in the center of the city that you can find easily and that we enjoyed.

Starting our search in the Latin Quarter, make your way to **Place St-Michel**, at the junction of Boulevard St-Michel and Boulevard St-Germain. Place St-Michel has a standing population of bums, drug pushers, and young folk hanging out. Stand with your back to the river, and over to your left you'll notice a little street called **rue de la Huchette**, where you'll pass countless Greek restaurants serving greasy shish kebabs to hordes of foreign tourists, most of them under 25. The food is cheap—but that's about all you can say for it.

If you aren't fussy about folks walking and sucking pig blubber off the end of a stick, you may enjoy the hustle and bustle of the street. If you were brave enough to eat the seafood there (traditionally stored in the restaurant's windows), congratulations—you've probably got some exotic French parasites camping in your small intestine right now.

At the end of rue de la Huchette, find rue de la Bûcherie, where you'll see a pleasant restaurant called **La Bûcherie** at #41. It's not cheap, but if you're celebrating a special occasion (she's finally pregnant; she's definitely not pregnant; he got his trust fund; he got a second interview with Quaker Oats; etc.), this is a lovely spot.

Down the street, there's a mandatory stop for all pseudo-intellectuals in Paris: the **Shakespeare and Company** bookstore at #37.

Maybe it's just us, you know, but look, it's not like we're morons or something. Like, once we rented a foreign movie by accident, but we watched it anyway, and *nothing* happened in it. There wasn't even a single car chase. And another thing: we'll watch public TV now and then, especially if there's a program about snakes. We really like snakes. So you see what we're saying? We're kind of intellectuals, too. But one thing we can't understand: Why would anyone come to Paris to hang out in some smelly dump of a bookstore and pay money for old paperbacks you can get for free at a yard sale back home?

Actually, nobody *reads* anything at Shakespeare and Company, because everyone is too busy looking at everyone else and trying to seem tortured and artistic. The problem is, *Let's Go* says it's "a Paris and New York institution," and now all these pimply-faced Literature majors pile ten deep inside.

Another thing we don't like about the place is they've got no books on snakes.

Near Shakespeare and Company, look for the tiny restaurant called **Specialties Antillaises** at 57 rue Galande. The lady in charge is called Madame Angele, and she serves great homemade sausage and other specialties from Martinique. Her place only has three tables, so don't plan on holding your Five Year Reunion there.

If you head further inland, you'll hit **rue Mouffetard**, which dates to the 13th century. This street and the square above it called **Place de la Contrescarpe** is full of cheap and, in most cases, decent restaurants. Certainly the quality is far better than anything you're likely to find on the more popular rue de la Huchette. Try **La Chope**, where (for our four readers who give a shit) Hemingway once hung out and wrote. ("I didn't know that **Mariel** Hemingway wrote books, too!") La Chope attracts large crowds from the local high school, so if you're into 10th graders, it's a nice place to have lunch.

One of the best things about rue Mouffetard is the outdoor market located toward the end of the street and down the hill. It's a great place to pick up the ingredients for a picnic. (It's closed Mondays.)

There's a great cafe at #116 called **Brasserie Mouffetard**, run by Papa Chartrain and the clan. You can get good lunches and snacks, and their fruit tarts will banish all thoughts of Hostess Cupcakes forever.

Finally, if you liked *Roots*, you'll love **Le Village Africain** at 2 rue de l'Arbalete (which crosses Mouffetard). It's one of the coolest stores in Paris, and, as you may have guessed, it sells stuff from Africa. We were tempted to try one of their products called "monkey bread," but we lost our nerve.

Heading in the opposite direction from Place St-Michel, you will pass **rue St. Andre-des-Arts**, which has lots of good places to eat. Don't miss the **Crêperie** at the corner of Place St-Michel and rue St. Andre-des-Arts. If you're used to eating at places in Wisconsin called Pattie's Pancake Pantry, you may die from sensory overload at the Crêperie. Cheap, too.

Keep going until you come to **rue de Buci**, which, like Mouffetard, has a pleasant street market at the corner of Buci and rue de Seine. At 25 rue de Buci, **Le Petit Zinc** stays open until 3:00am, so you and your boyfriend can have your *I-thought-you-knew-that-I-felt-that-you-would-understand* talk. You'll have lots of equally anguished company. The food is pretty good, in case you need to sustain your powers of clear, logical discourse. You can also enjoy fighting at their outside tables in the summer.

Two other good places to try in this general neighborhood are **Le Petit Vatel** (5 rue Lobineau) and **Au Savoyard** (16 rue des Quarte-Vents). Students pack the former, which serves hearty, cheap food. Au Savoyard is a lot classier and, of course, more expensive. It specializes in food from the French Alps. The St. Bernard dog steak is very good when in season. Just kidding. Try the *raclette*, a sort of pancake of Gruyère cheese with potatoes and onion.

On the right bank of the river, most of the nighttime activity centers around the Pompidou Centre and the pedestrian streets that run from there to the huge, subterranean shopping center called **Les Halles**. In particular, the main drag that connects the two places is worth cruising at night in search of food.

If you're in the mood for Tex-Mex, try **Papamaya** (94 rue Rambuteau)—great enchiladas, but be warned: it's popular, so pick your time carefully.

The other good possibility in the area is **Au Pere Tranquille**. At first, you'll think it's full of clean-cut college kids from back home, decked out in their penny loafers and college sweatshirts. Then you'll notice that the sweatshirts proclaim some non-existent school like "Harvard State University" or "Nashville Institute of Technology." Eventually, you'll figure out that all the patrons are French, and they're staring at you with the contemptuous look that trendy French youths reserve for *"les stupid Americaines"* who don't speak French. Remember, though: these are the same people who think that Jerry Lewis is our most valuable national treasure and that Nashville has an Institute of Technology. Funny folk, the French.

Another hopping place to eat in the area around Les Halles is **La Tour de Montlhery** (5 rue des Prouvaires), which serves good home-style French food in a polite, home-style way. It also keeps very late hours.

If you want to see what the French can do with something as disgusting as pig stomach, head to **Pharamond** at 24 rue de la Grande-Truanderie. It's expensive, and the waiters go out of their way to be as rude as possible. But for the chance to eat authentic French pig stomach, no price is too high, right?

For cheap and not too bad food, try the self-service cafeteria **Melodine** at 42 rue Rambuteau—a good bet if you're tired of being humiliated by waiters in real French restaurants.

Ile St-Louis (the island that Notre Dame is *not* on) has a few interesting restaurants. If you think tackiness is perfected only in the U.S., then check out **Nos Ancetres Les Gaulois** at 39 rue St-Louis-en-l'Ile. This place loosely—and we do mean loosely—evokes the Middle Ages. The decor would be a hit at a restaurant back home with a name like "Ye Olde Haunted Castle." Lots of stuffed animal heads everywhere. (Did we imagine it, or were the antelope wearing sunglasses?) The food is an all-you-can-eat-for-one-price effort, which does little to encourage the appetite, and the wine is, er, a little tart. Lots of hungry backpackers pig out there, though, so if you're in the mood for a low-quality drunken evening, this may be the place.

Finally, for the best ice cream in Paris and probably in Europe, you need to find **Berthillon** at 31 rue St-Louis-en-l'Ile. It's open from 10:00am to 8:00pm and closes all of August, when its most devoted customers, the Parisians, are all on vacation. The best flavors are the natural fruit flavors, and no, they don't do mix-ins.

Nightlife

Just because you're in Europe doesn't mean the normal night-time activities of healthy young Americans—having sex and get-ting drunk—are beyond your reach. We've got a lot of good insights on the former activity, but if we discussed them we'd have to replace our pretty cover with a plain brown wrapper. So we'll leave this delicate subject safely in your hands (no pun intended) and spend some time on the topic of good spots for drinking and music in Paris.

Probably the most pretentious cafe/bar is **Cafe Costes** at 4-6 rue Berger (near Les Halles). It's worth going in there just to take a leak, though the exotic design of the bathrooms may perplex, rather than relieve, your bladder. Cafe Costes is much loved by American college students who spent the previous semester in Paris and therefore think they're real cool. Drink prices are out-rageous, but it's worth a look.

Ditto for **Cafe Beaubourg** at 100 rue St. Martin. Though it's owned by the same family who runs Cafe Costes, the bathrooms are not as spectacular.

Among other famous bars in the center of the city, you might take a look at **La Coupole** (102 Blvd. du Montparnasse), full of trendy youths, French, Americans, and everything in between. It's closed during August.

Back on the Left Bank, the famous bar **Les Deux Magots** (6 pl. St-Germain-des-Prés) is where the intellectuals, those who wish they were intellectuals, and those who want to see people who might be intellectuals, gather. It's another Hemingway haunt. (Ernest, we think, but it could be Mariel—we always get the two confused. Ernest has more facial hair, right?) The bar lists 25 different whiskeys, not including any cheap ones. If you've come to Paris to begin your great American novel, then Les Deux Magots may be the place to lose your literary virgini-ty and write that tough opening sentence. (Good tip here: "Call me Ishmael" has been used. Sorry if that screws you up.)

For the lower end of the drinking scene—i.e., places where you and your boyfriend can actually afford a drink apiece—you need to go where French students drink. A lot of art students hang out at **La Palette** (43 rue de Seine). *Ah, what could be more roman-tic, you ask yourself, than meeting and falling in love with a real, live, penniless French artist and sharing his attic apartment, where* *you'll live on love, bread, cheese, and cheap red wine?* Nothing, except maybe a lawyer with a new Jag, a co-op overlooking the East River, a condo in Telluride, and a wealthy but seriously ill father.

You can also try the area by the **Jardin des Plantes**, especially along rue Linne, where French science students tend to gravitate (again, no pun intended). So, if you want to meet a real, live French chemistry nerd and share his attic lab . . .

You can have a lot of fun strolling around **Place St-Andre-des-Arts**, where street musicians murder the lyrics of Simon and Garfunkel songs. After you've had an earful of culture (*"I yam joust a pear bye and my starry's seldoom taud . . . "*), pop into the crowded **Le Mazet** (61 rue St-Andre-des-Arts), a nice, dirty dump where you can play pinball and drink beer until you feel strong enough to go outside again.

Near by, the **Pub St-Germain-des-Prés** (17 rue de l'Ancien Comédie) serves as a home-away-from-home for traveling American college students, where they can relax and be themselves for a change. It's a good place to meet a temporary girlfriend or boyfriend, if you've convinced yourself that a quick fling in Europe can only strengthen your relationship back home.

Music

One of the things you've probably planned to do in Paris is listen to music. It'll be great: you'll hang out in smokey clubs 'til the wee hours of the morning, drinking wine you don't really like and making yourself sick smoking stinky French cigarettes, all the while telling yourself "This is the life. I'm never going back to Kansas." Right?

Well, *malheureusement* (or "bummer," as we say on the left bank of the Atlantic). France, North Vietnam, Albania, and Equatorial Guinea have had an equal impact on the music scene. (If you're reading the Vietnamese edition of this book, please forgive our bourgeois, running-dog-of-capitalism attempt at humor.)

Suffice to say that the French are fairly clueless at producing new music. Your best bet in Paris is to look for jazz clubs, for music from France's former colonies, or for African music in general.

For jazz, start at **Le Bilboquet** (13 rue St-Benoit, in the Blvd.

St-Germain region), an up-market restaurant with local musicians. All the big names in jazz play at **New Morning** (7-9 rue des Petites-Ecuries), but it can be very pricey, so make sure you really want to see the act before you shell out the admission fee. **Le Petit Opportun** (15 rue des Lavandieres-Ste-Opportune, in the Châtelet region), a genuine club in a cramped cellar, also has big names, and there's a decent bar upstairs.

For other types of music, try **Chapelle des Lombards** (19 rue de Lappe) for salsa and African music. **Le Cloitre des Lombards** (62 rue des Lombards) offers Caribbean music, and it's not too expensive. For rock and new wave, **Gibus** (rue du Faubourg-du-Temple) gets a lot of up-and-coming British bands, interspersed with what passes for French rock. Finally, **Le Bouile Rouge** (8 rue de Lappe) is a rowdy dance spot that doesn't even have an admission charge, though drink prices are a little steep.

Other Things to Do

If you're having a slow day in Paris and can't find anything interesting or cultural to do (pretty easy to imagine, actually—after all, Paris isn't Cincinnati), the really moronic among you might consider a visit to the **Paris sewers**. These beauties, on the left bank of the Seine at Pont de l'Alma (start from the Eiffel Tower and walk along the river toward Notre Dame—Pont de l'Alma is the third bridge), are, of course, open for business 24 hours a day, but the Great Touring Public can visit them only from 2:00pm-5:00pm on Monday, Wednesday, and the last Saturday of each month (a schedule that wouldn't be too tiring even for State Liquor Store employees). A small museum with a film explains the function of the sewers (as if you couldn't figure it out for yourself), followed by a quick trip into the fascinating depths, guided by a gray-faced worker who hasn't seen the sun much. Guess what? It smells bad down there.

Fashion tip: Do not wear flip-flops or open-toe sandals on this tour because, just between us, it's tough to keep any facility clean that's used by two million people as a bathroom every day. Admission is 8 *francs*. Enjoy.

Another semi-interesting sidetrip is **Napoleon's Tomb**. Napoleon, of course, was the star quarterback for the French Army when they had a good team. He led them through a few rough but successful season before losing the Superbowl to the English at Waterloo. The French have never really been the same since. After he died, they retired his jersey and built him a tomb about the size of Shea Stadium. It's housed in a building called the **Hôtel des Invalides**, which was a hospital for pensioned soldiers and is worth a visit. The decor is Late Jim and Tammy Bakker—religious, but a bit over the top. There are loads of statues around the tomb and lots of stuff written in French. Also in the same complex, there's a cool military museum. (Sorry, but boys will be boys, so we really liked the museum.)

If you need more tomb-gawking, visit **Jim Morrison's grave** at **Père-Lachaise Cemetery**—something of a ritual pilgrimage for young visitors to Paris, especially those who immortalize Morrison as a demigod of 60's artistic vision. Other occupants of this historic cemetery—including Chopin, Oscar Wilde, Proust, and Balzac—have not rested in peace since Jimmy was planted. To get there, take the Metro to Père Lachaise, and follow the sleaze when you get out. They'll guide you right to the tomb. Be warned that the police have gotten somewhat strict about the crowds that gather, and they'll close the entire cemetery if things get out of hand.

Finally, for a glimpse of the life that only the president of a failed savings-and-loan could afford in our century, a trip to **Versailles** is a must. Versailles is a great big mother of a palace that Louis XIV (pronounced "Louie the Fourteenth" as opposed to "Louis Ex Eye Vee," just in case you're from North Dakota) built millions of years ago. It has more rooms than Indian teaching assistants in a freshman physics lab, and, the trouble is, they all look the same after a while (the rooms, not the TA's).

Versailles is not a bad little day trip from Paris, though, and you can get there using your Eurailpass from Invalides Metro Station. (Make sure you get on the right train—the one run by French National Railways, SNCF. Take it to Versailles Riv Gauche station.) You can easily walk from the station, and you can't miss the palace, because it pretty much blocks out the sun in that part of the country.

To ensure you have a perfectly miserable day, tag onto a guided tour being led by someone holding an umbrella up in the air like Lady Liberty's lamp. The sound effects go something like this: "In this room—room #135 in your book—it is thought

the Compte du Courcy may have sat at the exquisitely detailed
rosewood bureau and used the heavy gilt inkwell to write his
famous *pensees* to the Countess of Aubergine. Notice that the
satin wall coverings match rather closely those we saw in the
Petit Salon (room #102 in your book). The coverings are thought
to be the work of the master craftsman Henri de Beauchamp,
whose workshop flourished in the Marais district of Paris,
which we will be visiting tomorrow." Did we mention that people *pay* to go on these tours?

The best way to see the palace is by skateboard, but the
French, humorless as always, wouldn't let us. Our advice: Cut
right to the chase and see a few of the famous rooms like the
Hall of Mirrors, where the Treaty of Versailles was signed. Since
you are all familiar with this important event in history, we
won't embarrass you by asking you who signed it. Suffice to
say it was not Michael Jordan.

Two very important tips: Bring something to munch on, because the dining facilities are not very good. Also, don't drink
any liquids for several days before your visit, because the wait
for the bathroom will make your eyes turn yellow.

The grounds of the palace are really beautiful, and if you still
haven't been able to . . . you know . . . be with the person you
met at the bar last night, the gardens offer all sorts of interesting, secluded areas to explore. And if you still haven't met that
special someone yet, don't be afraid to . . . you know . . . *be with*
yourself.

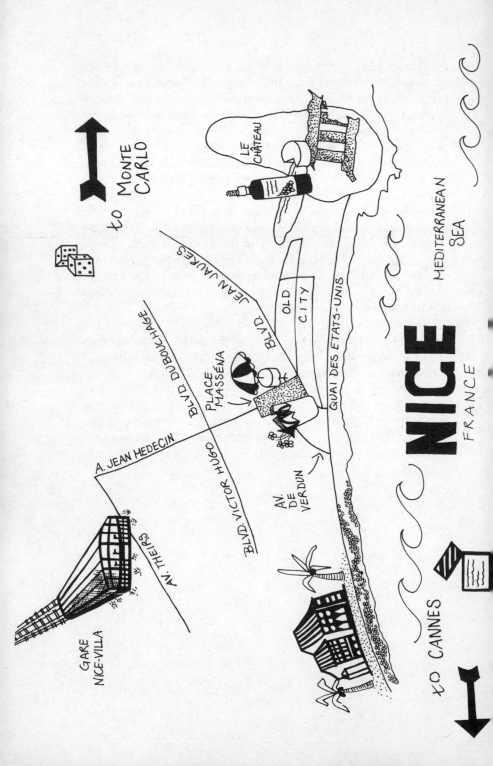

Nice

Okay, kids, it's time to hit the beach, Riviera-style. We hope you're well-rested after your overnight journey on the sleeper-train from Paris, because surf's up and it's your turn to secure a beachhead.

The reason you'll want to go to Nice rather than Monte Carlo, Cannes (you know, like the film festival), or Marseilles is that Nice is a cheaper place to stay and eat and therefore a good place to meet other travelers. Plus, those other cities are easy day-trips from Nice on the train with your Eurailpass. For example, Cannes, with its naked (bet *that* word jumped off the page at you), white, sandy beaches, is only 20 minutes away, and trains leave Nice every 20 minutes.

So, while the beach in Nice may be too rocky for building sand castles, you can scoot up to Cannes for the day to catch some rays, back to Nice for chow, over to Monte Carlo for some night-life, and back to Nice for bed. Nice, then, will be base camp for our operations on the **Côte d'Azur** (pronounced "coat da sewer").

Getting There

You can reach Nice easily from Paris by train. Simply hop on the train at Gare de Lyon, and a mere 11 hours later you'll stagger off at Nice, as fresh as a *M*A*S*H* rerun.

If 11 hours sounds a bit long, you can always take one of the famous French "bullet trains," known as the **TGV**. These trains are expensive unless you have a First Class Eurailpass, in which case you can use them by paying a small supplement. The TGV is beloved by the French as a way of showing the world that French ingenuity and commitment to excellence did not stop at inventing the guillotine, the bidet, and the french fry. The TGV *is* fast and smooth, but after the first five minutes, it becomes as interesting as a USAir flight to Buffalo.

Orientation

Nice is a small town with the diversity of a larger city—kind of like a state university town. (In fact, there is a university in Nice where you can study French history or Impressionist art next spring on your semester abroad.) It's easy to walk around in Nice and get to any hotel, restaurant, the beach, and the train station without using public transportation. After London and Paris, you'll undoubtedly find this a real blessing.

As in other cities, the Nice train station pretty much has everything you'll need to get started: a money exchange office, lockers to stow your rancid duffle bag, shady characters, and a tourist office where you can get maps, book a hotel, and ask dumb questions ("Do you, like, accept the same francs here that they do in Paris?").

Just outside the station, you'll immediately see hotels, and you should pick one so the train will be within easy reach for your excursions. Remember, you'll want to be able to find your hotel room when you come back late and drunk from Monte Carlo. Some hotel suggestions:

Hôtel Darcey (28 rue d'Angleterre, phone 93-88-6706) is a proven favorite—just use the pedestrian underpass and head to your left when you get to the other side.

Hôtel Novelty (phone 93-87-5173), next to the Darcey, is a friendly, casual place. Despite the name, the rooms do not have fake dog poop or vibrating plastic objects.

Hôtel les Orangers (10bis, av. Durante, phone 93-87-5141) will give you the feel of the apartment you rented for the last 10 years at the Jersey Shore. Most rooms have kitchenettes and up to six beds per room—for the unbelievable price of about $10 per bed.

Hôtel Little Palace (9 ave. Baquis, phone 93-88-7049) is a clean, friendly, convenient hotel, though a bit more expensive than the seedy ones near the train station.

After checking into your hotel and unloading your gear, head toward the beach. Get onto **Avenue Jean Médecin**—the "Champs" of Nice—and go south. You'll pass open-air cafes sprawling onto the sidewalks, department stores, and suntan oil shops. Don't be distracted by any of these just yet, however. We've got to keep up the pace.

The beach in Nice is like those you've seen in Maine or Oregon. It's all rocks and no sand, but at least you can swim. However, unless you're just dying to get your feet wet or your top off, stay dry until you get to Cannes.

Instead, roam through the **Old Town**, a.k.a. *vieille ville*, to your left as you face the water. Down in this quarter, you'll experience the Old World charm of the Mediterranean—butcher shops with animal carcasses hanging from hooks, cheeses as ripe as an undershirt after a hot day in Houston, and open-air markets displaying a bountiful harvest of vegetables, fruits, and audio cassettes. Load up on picnic supplies here.

The narrow streets wind through the shadows of old buildings leaning above. Old ladies peer from behind shutters, and children frolic. Photo opportunities abound ("This is the *real* Nice, dating back to around, er, ah, you know, really long ago . . . ").

From the Old Town, find the steps that lead to the cliff-top park called **Château**. The climb is worth it, for the cliff offers a magnificent view of the Riviera and Nice, and it's your Tall Thing To Climb on this leg of the trip. The park has green grass, gardens, and some old ruins. It's the perfect setting for a picnic (see end of chapter) and will inspire a journal entry:

Thursday—Here I am, finally in solitude. This is the first chance I've had to be away from people and the hustle and bustle of the city since my journey begun. I'm sitting among the ruins of something that I don't know anything about because I can't read the French on the signs. But I know they're old and therefore important. (Come to think of it, though, this place could be a construction site for condos.)

The city lies beneath me like a miniature set from Disneyland. But I know there are people down there—people who live, work, grow up, and die there. I'm wondering just how different our lives really are and if the women really do go topless on the beaches . . .

Now you're excited by the prospects ahead, so you climb down and head along the Quai des Etats-Unis, which follows the shoreline. This turns into **promenade des Anglais**, which is like Miami Beach or Highway 1 in California—lots of big hotels and palm trees.

There's nothing more of interest here, so head into the "new" town via **place Messéna**. There's a pedestrian shopping area there, and one on **rue Paradis**. (How come all tourist maps depict pedestrian areas in yellow or red, but in reality they're always white concrete?) This will be the area where you'll later congregate among fellow travelers, minstrels, artists, and fat people eating ice cream cones. Speaking of eating . . .

Food
Two things come to mind with regard to Nice: nicoise salad and seafood. Not eating seafood in Nice is like not eating lobster in Maine, pizza in Chicago, or Chinese food in bed. Be sure to try the *bouillabaisse* (fish soup), which is to Nice what barbecue is to Memphis.

The old part of Nice (*vieille ville*) has a lot of good, quaint restaurants. Try **La Socca** at 2 rue Micolleti or the **Taverne du Château** at 42 rue Droite for some of that Old World cuisine.

In the new part of town, there are a lot of places to eat on the av. Jean Médecin or rue Messéna. One we highly recommend is **Chez Diva** (11bis rue Grimaldi, near Victor Hugo Blvd.). It's a small, family place with a modest fixed-price menu that includes about five courses and wine. What's more, you'll meet mostly other travelers there, since other popular guidebooks recommend it (but tell 'em *Let's Blow* sent you).

Restaurant Aux Voyageurs Nissart (19 rue d'Alsace-Lorraine, phone 93-82-1960) offers an excellent six-course meal for about $15. Across the street, **La Saëtone** (phone 93-87-17695) has good regional fare at comparable prices. Also, there are a lot of Vietnamese restaurants in this area, in case you're hungry for some good old Hanoi favorites, just the way Mom used to make 'em.

Going Topless
Now we come to another one of those potentially difficult areas—this time for our female readers.

Your upbringing has undoubtedly taught you to keep certain parts of your anatomy under wraps, no matter how absurd it sometimes seems. What's more, these social mores are reinforced with legal consequences, unless you're in certain parts of California, Oregon, or Martha's Vineyard. Well, in France and other parts of Europe, it's quite acceptable to get that "all over" tan without going to a Tanfastic at the mall. In fact, in Nice, Cannes, and throughout the Côte d'Azur, you may feel odd if you keep your top on.

{Karen's diary entry, July 12}

Kelly kept telling me that she couldn't wait 'til Nice so she could get her "San Tropez tan." But I was as nervous about the idea as I was about Chip's intentions on our Prom Night. I mean, even in the locker rooms at school I think it's, you know, weird to let everyone see me nude, even though they are all girls of my own gender. But then, Kelly always was more bold and adventurous than me.

*She'll think I'm a real chicken if I don't go topless here. But I keep thinking about those two guys, Steve and Al, who we met on the train between Amsterdam and Paris. They said they might see us down here around this time. I'd, like, **die**, if they showed up when I was half-naked. And what about when we get back? I just know Kelly will tell everyone, and Chip will call me a slut.*

But if I don't, Kelly will be pissed and tell all our friends what a prude I am. Oh, what will I do?

{Karen's diary entry, July 13}

I can't believe what I did today! It's like I've opened a new chapter on my life! I took off my top on the beach in Cannes! I was hesitant at first, but when Kelly did it, I said, oh what the heck! And from that moment on, I felt FREE—free from all those hang-ups that male-dominated society imposes on us women and the constraints of being female. Suddenly, I was totally liberated and at one with the sea, the sand, the sky. If only all those creeps weren't taking pictures of us . . .

Taking Pictures

Now we come to one of those potentially difficult areas for male travelers in Europe. You will be confronted with beautiful scenery wherever you go, and you'll of course want to capture these sights on film so you can bore your friends when you get home.

A sure-fire way to spice up your slide show is to have shots of the topless women on the beaches in France. The techniques, however, require a bit of trickery and some patience, if you don't want to appear too crude.

(Of course, you sensitive, liberated males reading the above while watching *Donahue* are going to toss this book down and expound at length to your Significant Other ["girlfriend," "babe," or "honey" is so sexist and demeaning, isn't it?] about how disgusting and offensive we are. Meanwhile you're thinking to yourself, *Hey, I really should dig those prints out of my sock drawer and relive the old memories. I wonder if Janette and Odile remember our 'modelling studies' in Nice...*)

One technique we recommend is to spot a hot prospect and then focus your camera on an object *behind* her. Pretend you are snapping shots of the sun-crested waves or the cute cabanas by the boardwalk. Then, casually sweep your camera around and shoot without a break in the motion. Since most of you will be using auto-focus cameras, this technique should be (pardon the pun) a snap. But back home you'll find that most of your photos will be of seagulls—but *naked* seagulls, if that's any consolation.

Another plausible tactic, especially during the film festival season in Cannes, is to introduce yourself as a movie producer/director/agent, etc. Say something to your photo subjects about their "screen potential" and ask if they would mind if you took their picture. Trouble is, most producers/directors/agents wouldn't use a $29.95 disk camera, so you'll need decent photo equipment for this one to fly.

Other Things To Do In Nice

One thing a lot of travelers do in Nice is their laundry.

Another thing is rent mopeds and explore the countryside. Nice is the perfect place to satisfy this desire, because you don't have to take major freeways to get out of town. Also, there are rental places right near the train station.

You can explore some nearby quaint towns easily. One such place is **St-Paul-de-Vence**, an artists' community in a very artistic setting.

But don't follow our advice like a bunch of naked seagulls—explore on your own. The windy, hilly roads are fun, and the views can be breathtaking. Go ahead—try some stunt riding like you saw in *Terminator 2*.

Speaking of laundry, Nice may be the perfect place to take care of those ripening clothes in your dufflebag. Since you can roam the city at leisure, drop off your clothes at a laundromat. For a few bucks, the friendly proprietor will freshen your undies while you're basking on the beach in your bikini, which you can wash later in the bidet in your room. When you pick up your clothes, argue with the manager and insist that you gave him a suit jacket to clean, SO WHERE IS IT? Chances are, they'll show you their "lost and found" stuff, from which you can pick a nice jacket to wear to the casino in Monte Carlo tonight.

Cannes

Cannes is where you go to enjoy the beach experience as we Americans know it. An easy commute from Nice, Cannes has a well-groomed beach, beautiful sun worshippers, and a good boardwalk, the **Promenade de la Croisette** (just call it "The Prom"), which follows the beach and is a good spot for cruising. Walk along The Prom, scope the perfect beach spot, and try to pick out movie stars, who abound during the week of the film festival (second or third week in May). Go ahead—ask Michelle Pfieffer if she'd like to take the train to Rome with you tomorrow.

The theater where most of the movies play is on the western part of the boardwalk/beach, but it's tough to get into, especially for the hot films. There are ways to get tickets for the less popular movies, but a lot of times they involve sleeping with someone claiming to be a producer/director/agent, etc.

To get into a major film, you'll have to do worse. You must lie through your teeth and convince the guards that you're with one of the major studios (MGM, Universal, Barney's Video World, etc.) and that you've forgotten your pass or had it stolen. Frequently, though, it's like getting into a frat party if you're male and not on the guest list—even if you win by getting in, you're disappointed by what you find inside. After all, who wants to sit through four hours of subtitles of an ultra-serious epic about the leader of some backwater nation, when you could be breeching the beach in your Jams and Raybans, hitting on Michelle Pfieffer?

If you want to chow down in Cannes, keep in mind that most stores and restaurants shut down from about noon to 3:00pm for siesta. A pedestrian area along **rue Meynadier** has about all you'll need in the way of stores and restaurants.

Monaco/Monte Carlo

Monaco is another great place to go from Nice. Ride your moped or take the train there, and visit at night, when the Casino has more action.

Monaco is a "Hereditary Constitutional Monarchic Independent Principality." Loosely translated, this means it was handed down in the family.

Monaco is a small place. How small is it? Well, it's so small that if someone farts, everyone runs into France to get away from the fumes. It's so small, the main power plant is a Sears Die-Hard.

Monaco has a Prince, it used to have a Princess, and it even has its own coins—but casino chips can't be exchanged on the open market.

Don't be confused by all this. Monaco is simply a port city whose main import is money. The average container ship is about 40 feet long, sleeps 12, and has a name like *Daddy's Girl*. A lot of big tennis stars live there, which is surprising since the place is hardly big enough to play chess, let alone tennis.

There are two distinct parts of Monaco. One is the older part called **Monaco-ville**; the other is the flashy new **Monte Carlo**, home of the renowned **Casino**. When you arrive at the train station, stay right and head uphill. You'll end up in Monte Carlo.

To get into the Casino, you have to pay $9.00, show your passport, and be dressed for the part. "Right, like I really brought a tux with me from Fresno." Now wait a minute. Remember the last semi-formal you attended, when you discovered at the last minute that your only suit still has grass stains from the time you and Chrissie took that "walk" after the Alumni Appreciation Dance? You still got in, right? You've just got to make do with what you've got and try not to look too much like a slob. So, lace up that pair of Docksiders you brought along and leave the sneakers behind for tonight. No problem.

Once you get inside, the Casino's not that great. Las Vegas is a lot more fun and not nearly as stuffy. Still, any guy who can build a country that attracts rich fools willing to gamble their money away is okay by us.

You can do the whole Monaco experience in an evening, so plan to get back to Nice for a nightcap and bed.

A Picnic

One of the most pleasant things to do in Nice is have a French-style picnic, an *apres-midi pique-nique*, as they say. Here's how to go about it:

Jean-Claude (or John, as he is called around the family dinner table in Hartford) arrives, resplendent in a striped blazer, silk shirt, cravat, and white pants creased so sharp they could shave a gooseberry. His friend Michél (a.k.a. Mike) cuts an artistic figure in an artist's smock splattered with paint, his beret set at a cocky angle. *(Note: These men are paid professionals hired especially for this sketch. Do not attempt to dress like this in your hometown.)* Their lady friends, Lulu and Claudine, look enchanting in long white cotton dresses. Lulu carries a parasol.

Alors, en route! They choose a shady spot in the woods, beneath the bough of a chestnut tree. Eschewing fine furniture, they pick a simple picnic table, hewn from century-old logs, and they cover the knotty wood with a sheet ripped from their bed that morn. With a careless shrug, they toss rose petals, torn from the bud with their teeth, upon the satin surface.

Finally, they produce the feast. First, some coarse *pâté-de-terrine* and then a fine *foie gras*. Long, crusty loaves of bread come next, full of nutty grains of wheat and oat. The cheeses are ripe, oozing the fecund aroma of goats reared in the Pyrenees. Huge, turgid rods of blood sausage bring a blush to the cheeks of the fairer picnickers and a lusty grin to Michél. Dishes of plump juicy olives flank the jugs of hearty red wine.

They each quaff a glass of the *vin* and feel its heat, a certain *je ne sais quoi*, matched only by the sensation of being wrestled to the ground by a large peasant woman. Gaily, they splash the wine onto their faces and watch it stain their clothes with a Bacchanalian hue. With scant regard for social conventions, they eagerly bite into overripe peaches, relishing the feel of sticky juice flowing down their faces.

Finally, consumed by a passion too torrid to describe in a family-oriented travel guide, they throw themselves together and become a tangle of limbs, tongues, and husky moans on the verdant sward.

Later, much later, Jean-Claude plays the guitar for them.

There is also a **McDonald's** somewhere in Nice, so ask around for it.

Germany: An Introduction

The sound of your compartment door authoritatively opening jolts you awake. Towering over you are two tall, blond, Aryan men in dark uniforms, black leather pouches protruding from their belts, muttering something like "passport control." Have you entered the Twilight Zone or a bad World War II movie? You fumble through your pants for your passport—or is it your Eurailpass they want? No room for mistakes here. You've arrived in Germany!

Relax. The war is over, and Germans are more concerned about world peace than you are. So go ahead, try the German you've practiced since your sister gave you a Berlitz *German for Travelers* tape at Christmas: "Gunter TOG mine herron. Vee gates is down? Here mine passaporte donkie!"

They'll be impressed, and they'll quickly show you how well they've picked up English from their Berlitz *English for Passport Controllers* tapes.

This could go on for a while. Keep trying those well-rehearsed German lines, and they will respond in flawless English. Don't let them fool you by acting as though they don't understand your German. It's just one-upsmanship. Try the same to them. They'll probably get tired of this quickly and leave after stamping all over your passport with a device that looks like the things supermarket shelvers use to price canned goods. Bid them farewell with a fond "Alf feeterswane!"

The German Language

The single most gratifying thing about visiting Germany is that everybody speaks English. In fact, it can be downright depressing to find German nine-year-olds who can read short stories in *The New Yorker*—and actually understand them. (That puts them way ahead of most Americans who don't have an advanced degree.) It's unlikely you'll have any problem finding where you want to go and what you want to eat, but we'll offer a few pointers on the German language anyway.

Rule #1: Change all w's to v's. This is a pretty obvious tip, especially for those of you who grew up watching *Hogan's Heroes*. It should be a snap to come out with phrases like "Ve vill make you vish you vere still in Visconsin, Valter." Try a few on your own. You should get the hang of it in no time.

Rule #2: German is a language best spoken loudly, and where applicable, by slamming your fist on the table, e.g. "VILHELM, VE VOULD LIKE TWO VON-VAY TICKETS TO VIENNA, BITTE!!!" (SLAM, SLAM)

Rule #3: Germans have an unnerving habit of stringing words together to make huge, compound jawbreakers. In fact, it's a little-known fact that the evening news on German TV usually consists of a single word, which describes all the earthquakes, plane crashes, and soccer results of the day.

Some of your biggest language problems may arise when trying to figure out transportation. For example, do you know the German word for the supplement you must pay if you ride the subway after 7:00pm but are using the discounted rush hour tickets? No? Neither do we, but it probably has more syllables than antidisestablishmentarianism.

The Rhine River

Virtually all well-meaning European travel books suggest a boat trip on the Rhine River. Well, here again we're going to give you some advice that should more than return the cost of this book in the time and money you'll save.

Skip the boat trip, but see the Rhine and its splendid castles by **express train**. You can take a train between Mainz and Cologne in a fraction of the time you'd spend on an obnoxious tour boat. The trip from Cologne to Mainz takes under two hours by train, but about 10 hours by boat!

What's worse, these boats are not quaint and comfortable yachts, like Dad's back in Newport. They're huge, glass-enclosed tourist boats that seat 1,000 people. Imagine: you'll be stuck for hours—maybe a whole day—of your precious time with the Brussels Common Market Marching Band, the Richard M. Nixon High School Glee Club, and the Peckerwood (Idaho) Toastmasters, all oohing and ahhing at every castle that slowly looms out of the hazy distance, each wanting to be the first to see it.

"Lookie there kids, another big one comin' up!" band director E. F. "Buddy" Edmonson says, as the Toastmasters all plant their noses in their guidebooks, trying to figure out which castle it is, when it was built, etc. "Reminds me of those old *Abbot and Costello Meet Frankenstein* movies. Sure would like to get a photo up close!" To you, it's just another gray mass of brick and stone that's no different from the previous 18 you saw.

Let's get something straight here. Most of these castles look about the same, especially from the distances you see them from the boat. Oh sure, the first few might impress you, especially if you are a Medieval History major or a Holy Grail kook. But face it: the law of diminishing returns soon sets in, and you'll find yourself more intent on the Bluff City Girls Fife & Drum Corps wandering around the boat in their little pleated skirts and kneesocks than you will be in Castle #23.

Another thing: these boats are mostly enclosed, and we've already discussed how all Europeans smoke. If it's raining, as it often is in this river valley, you'll feel like you're inside a shower stall, trying to take pictures through the steamed-up glass.

If we haven't painted a grim enough picture yet, then imagine the children eating from the boat's snack bar and puking all over the seats. These boats are floating junk food restaurants, and you *can't leave.* The only positive thing is the cheap wine they encourage you to drink on board ($5.00 per bottle).

Now, do you want to see this lush, picturesque valley from inside a smoky shower stall plodding at the speed of an Italian postal worker, or from the comfort of your own air-conditioned train compartment at 60 miles per hour?

"Wait!" you say. "I happen to know you can take a hydrofoil on the river, and they go really fast." Fine, smartguy, but have you ever been in a high speed car wash with your seat belt fastened?

The most popular stretch of the Rhine is between Rudesheim and Koblentz—five hours by boat, less than one hour by train. The choice is yours.

Munich

When the train pulls into *München Hauptbahnhof*, Munich's Central Station, grab your bags and rush the door. You want to get to the money changer and the baggage lockers before anyone else. But take a moment to look around and see all the people eating hot dogs and drinking beer. This will be your sustenance for the next 24 hours or so.

Change a little cash before you hit the town. After you get some *marks*, buy a meat tube at one of the stands and try your first German beer. Then—out on the street.

What will amaze you most as you emerge from the train station is how clean and orderly everything seems—in sharp contrast to, say, Italy. Cars appear newer and larger. There's a noticeable absence of mopeds. Obedient drivers respect traffic lights. And although you can do most of Munich by foot, there is a clean, self-explanatory subway system. You'll see signs that say "S" or "U" all over the place. These are not convenience stores but rather the entrances to the S-Bahn and U-Bahn subway lines.

To get a place to stay, give a few bucks to the **Fremdenverkehrsamt** (Tourist Office) or **Euraide** in the station, and they'll book you a room in your price range. You could also try the **Jugendherberge Burg Schwaneck**, a youth hostel at Burgweg 4-6 (phone 793-0644) that's worth a visit if you have an extra night. It's a renovated mansion out in the woods, with lots of odd-shaped rooms and over 100 beds. It takes about half an hour from mid-Munich to get there, so you'll have to finish your beer hall drinking in time to catch the last train, or you'll be sleeping with the bums in the park. Take S-Bahn 7 to Pullach and follow the other drunks with backpacks. (Your Eurailpass is valid on the S-Bahn.)

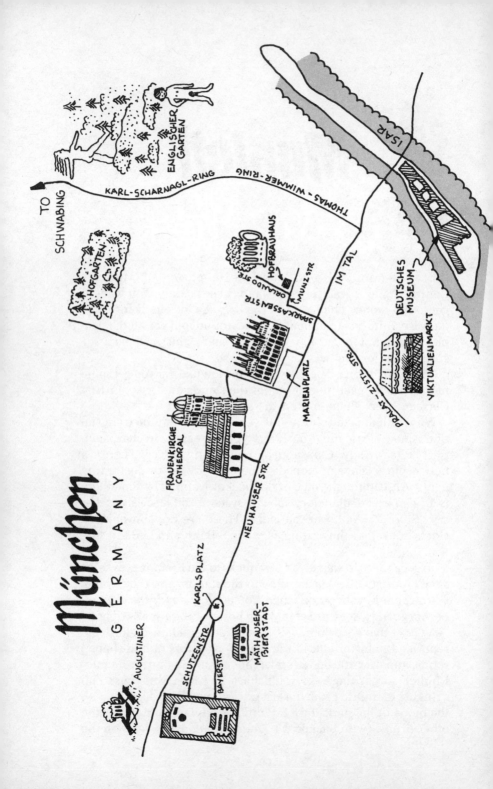

Beer Halls

The most important thing to do in Munich is **drink beer**, so get psyched for it. First, we're going to give you ground rules, and then we'll plot a game plan to visit as many breweries and beer halls as possible.

There are six breweries in Munich and quite a few others within easy reach. Many of the breweries run restaurants as a sort of public relations deal, like the way we give missiles to countries that claim to see the world the way we do. There are several of these restaurants in the center city area. At great personal cost to our livers, we have checked most of them out.

The most famous of these restaurants, of course, is the **Hofbräuhaus**, at Platzl 9 right off the Marienplatz, where you'll find long tables with benches, buxom middle-aged waitresses, a brass band playing schmaltzy music, and thousands of young travelers. Pull up a chair, set yourself down, and order yourself a big brewski. The technical name for a one-liter big boy is a *mass*, but we've found that saying something like "*Ein vant a big brewski!*" works wonders. The waitresses have seen a few young Americans in their day.

After you've bathed your tonsils with about two liters worth, take your *mass* in hand, visit with the other tables, and compare the size of your *mass* with the other fellows' (it's a guy thing). There's no need for lengthy introductions—everyone's American except for maybe a few foreigners, and they'll stay out of your way. Sit yourself at any table with a loud, "Hey, where are you guys from?" and in a few moments, you'll be swapping stories of neat cities you've visited, neat beers you've tried, and the hilarious language situations you've encountered the last few weeks:

"And the waiter kept saying, 'Do you want the *wurst*?' And I kept saying, 'No, I only want the best!'"

"Yeah, I took French I and II, so I was, like, able to order things and stuff. And, you know, it was really cool to be able to say, '*Ducks cafe, seel vou play*' and actually *see* the coffee arrive. You know what I mean?"

"I know you have a boyfriend, but we could just, like, travel together as friends."

"But I could short circuit the whole system with this keen little macro I've put together!" (Yes, even engineering majors go to Europe.)

What else is there to do at the Hofbräuhaus? You could play "Find 20 *Hard Rock Cafe/London* t-shirts in 20 Minutes." And there's always chugging contests—except these are *real* contests, with full one-liter mugs to chug. Brutal.

The best action at the Hofbräuhaus takes place after about 9:00pm. The band is warmed up, kids are dancing on the tables, and even Walter Rippendorf, that nerdy kid who normally won't even *look* at a girl, is teaching three coeds from the University of Arizona to yodel in the corner. The action continues until about midnight, at which point you can link arms with all your close personal friends who were strangers a mere three hours ago, swear to each other that this was, like, the BEST TIME EVER, agree to meet here every year on the same day in the future, promise to get together in the U.S. to relive the great moments, swap addresses with people whose faces you'll forget by morning, steal everything that isn't nailed down, and finally, your eyes brimming with tears of pride, joy, and nostalgia, you stand, your hand on your heart, and bellow the *Brady Bunch* theme song.

Important fashion note: Dress at the Hofbräuhaus is strictly casual. Jams or baggy khaki shorts are highly recommended. T-shirts should be Ocean Pacific, Hard Rock, frat shirts, or anything that speaks of other cities you've seen. It's gauche to wear a Hofbräuhaus t-shirt to the Hofbräuhaus. You may also want to ease off on the white t-shirts here. True, you've got a great tan and you look fabulous in white, but the Hofbräuhaus is a cross between an end-of-season football game and Daytona Beach during Spring Break. A lot of beer, among other things, gets thrown around. You don't want the best photo of the trip showing you, beer glass in hand, your arm around the most gorgeous guy you've ever met (Tim, or was it Tom?), with a disgusting stain on your white shirt.

The next most important stop on your tour of beer halls is the huge **Mathäser-Bierstadt** (Bayerstrasse 5, near Karlsplatz). The layout of this "beer city" is confusing. It's like registering for classes on the first day back at school, except that this is a hell of a lot more fun. Wander through a series of corridors and dining rooms filled with, for once, Germans, until you come to a staircase leading to a terrace. Up there, you'll enter a huge room with an oompah band and folks getting loaded.

Here's a tip for guys who really want some action. Buy one of those stupid Bavarian hats and a pair of suspenders. If you want to go the whole nine yards, get some leather shorts. You're bound to be a big hit with American and Japanese women. Walk around with your *mass* in hand, establish a lot of eye contact, and get the ladies to sign your shirt. You'll be surprised at what they'll write: names, suggestive comments, even phone numbers. Go for it, guys!

After two or more liters at Mathäser, next stop should probably be the **Augustinerkeller** at Neuhauserstrasse 16, on the north of the Hauptbahnhof. We really like Augustiner beer, so a visit there is much better than, say, a poke in the eye with a sharp stick. The food is also better there than at the Hofbräuhaus or Mathäser.

Finally—and by now you may be feeling the six liters of beer you have on board—carom a few doors up the street to the **Hacker-Pschorr Bierhalle**. This is probably a good *bierhalle* too, but we don't want to bullshit you: our memories of this one aren't too clear, and our notes are totally illegible. It was dark, we're pretty clear on that. And the beer was definitely cold. But beyond that ...

Okay, now you've hit four of the six big beer spots. Not a bad night's work by anyone's standards. It might be good to take a stroll to the Rathaus Square (Marienplatz), where you'll probably run into a lot of the folks you met earlier at the beer halls: "You know, I've been thinking about that do-loop feedback problem, and I think an excellent solution would be ... "

Beer Gardens

The next day, take a highly educational tour of the **beer gardens** scattered through Munich's center. Risking complete liver failure, we undertook a survey of these, too. Our results are as follows:

If it's early enough in the day and you're looking for lunch, a great place to visit is the beer garden at the **Viktualienmarkt**, a large, open-air food market south of the Marienplatz. Throughout the area are several take-out food shacks where you can buy *wurst*, bread, chicken, and large pretzels. At the center of the square, there's a shady area with lots of picnic benches beneath chestnut trees.

You can shop the food market for some goodies, pick up a *mass* of Münchner Hell beer, and relax and watch the Japanese tourist beside you eat his pretzel with a knife and fork. At **Nordsee**, a chain of German fish shops for take-out, you can get great pickled herring with dill or potato salad. After the beer hits and you don't feel like walking anymore, stop over at **Friesinger's** sauerkraut stand and watch the master himself, Ludwig, scooping more sauerkraut out of a big barrel than you've ever seen.

In the afternoon, a nice option is strolling the **Englischer Garten**. On a pretty afternoon, it's full of Munich sun-worshippers—topless, bottomless, and even some with clothes on. After a quick game of nude frisbee, head over to the **Chinesischer Turm** (Chinese Tower), where you'll find another fine beer garden. Again, sit under the trees, drink Löwenbräu, eat *wurst*, and discuss replacing all electric plants in Europe with crystal power with your new 30-year-old German friends (all members of the Green Party).

Yet another pleasant beer garden to try is in the **Botanical Gardens** near the train station—it's not bad, but nothing exceptional. Much nicer is the **Löwenbräu** beer garden at Nymphenburgerstrasse 2—a lovely place with ivy covered walls, great *wurst* platters, and, it seemed to us, no tourists.

And don't leave Munich without a trip to the **Augustinerkeller**, only a few blocks from the train station. It's huge, with lots of garden tables and stalls selling cheese, roast chicken, *wurst*, bread, and pretzels. Sit in the area for self-service so you can go to the windows and choose your own food. Otherwise, you're at the mercy of the elderly waitresses, who have all the charm of roller derby queens on a bad day.

The beer at Augustinerkeller is better than at any of the other beer gardens. On a summer evening, the garden is filled with Munich residents enjoying the weather, eating picnic suppers, chatting and gossiping. Hey, maybe you could select a table at random and introduce yourself: "Hi, I'm Chad. I'm from Bayonne, New Jersey, in the United States, you know? I'm a Virgo, and I'm, like, into anything fun. How about you folks? What are your signs?"

This beer garden is also a great place to make a dinner stop to hydrate your tissues (and your *mass*) before taking a night train to anywhere.

Food

If you're apprehensive about Germany because you don't think you can eat sausage constantly, pack plenty of tofu sandwiches. The Germans eat all kinds of sausage (*wurst*), and it varies from what we think of as a sausage (a kind of hot dog) all the way to *pâtés*, black blood sausage, and salami-looking things. *Wurst* is generally served with lots of robust mustard, sauerkraut, and heavy German bread. If you're a vegetarian, Germany is going to test your willpower. Conceivably, though, you could live on all the good soups, bread, and above all, beers.

One of the best things to order in Munich is the famous *Weisswurst* (white sausage), and one of the best places to sample it is **Brathaus Herzel** (Heiliggeiststrasse 3), a restaurant specializing in sausage dishes near the Viktualienmarkt. It's even open for breakfast.

Another great thing to eat in Munich is *Leberknodelsuppe* (liver dumpling soup). It sounds gross, we know, but have you read what goes into a Twinkie lately? Once you've tried your first bowl of *Leberknodelsuppe*, you'll never go back to boring old lobster bisque again.

Finally, you can't leave Munich without trying the famous *Leberkäse* (liver cheese). Before you throw down the book with a loud "What are they trying to do, make me *puke?!*" hear us out. *Leberkäse* contains neither liver nor cheese. It's made from ground beef and ham, and it tastes, for all the world, like really good meatloaf. Of course, "really good meatloaf" is probably an oxymoron to those of you who have survived another semester of dog food at the dorms. "I'm not going all the way to Munich to eat meatloaf when I can have it at the dining hall for free," you'll say. Well, you should try it anyway. It's quite good.

The Augustiner beer garden serves a mean *Leberkäse*, warm with lots of mustard and sauerkraut. With a plate of *Leberkäse* and a frosty *mass* (ouch!), you'll never think "dining hall" again when you hear the word meatloaf.

The Mathäser-Bierstadt also serves pretty good food, and the prices aren't bad. If you're going to be drinking a lot of beer, eat some food beforehand. But don't eat at the Hofbräuhaus, since the food there is neither good nor cheap.

Schwabing

The area of Munich that runs north of the university and west of the English Gardens is known as **Schwabing**. It's often described as "Munich's Latin Quarter" or "Munich's Greenwich Village" by outdated guidebooks. While it may have seen its hipper days, Schwabing is now filled with glitzy discos, huge restaurants, and office plazas with the charm and intimacy of a Dallas freeway.

Leopoldstrasse, the main boulevard through Schwabing, is a four-lane divided road. Quaint, eh? Then, the restaurants and discos are about a football field away from the sidewalk. You'll need binoculars to read the signs. Yet, drawn by the guidebooks and the break from beer halls, parades of tourists saunter up and down this street late into the night, and the "sidewalk" cafes seem to pack them in nonetheless.

If you are so determined to see for yourself, the best streets to check out are in the northern part of Schwabing at the end of Leopoldstrasse, which runs north from the university. Look along **Ursulastrasse** and also on **Occamstrasse** for cafes where you can debate the merits of the Strategic Defense Initiative with young German intellectuals:

Helmut: "So it is difficult for us to understand the dichotomy which exists between the socio-economic implications of trying to feed and cloth your homeless people and your government's belief of mounting offensive weapons in space, you see."

Hank: "I don't know nothin' about economics, man. All I know is that when missiles from space start flying in, our lasers are going to knock them suckers right out of the sky. Wham, bam, thank you ma'am!"

Helmut: "So, what you are telling me . . . "

Hank (*gesticulating wildly*): "Blammo! Ker-pow! Top Gun!"

The debate continues.

Haid Hausen, on the right bank of the Isar River, is the nouvelle-artistic district, but it apparently needs time to ripen before it too rots.

So take it from us and our long-suffering brain cells: the beer halls and beer gardens are your best bet in Munich if you're there for just a few days.

Things To See

Munich is another city where everything is convenient from the railway station. Leading up from the Hauptbahnhof towards the center of town is a large pedestrian area called the **Karlsplatz**. There's nothing of interest in the lower part, but as you penetrate deeper into the city along Neuhauserstrasse, you come across cafes and lots of good places to eat *wurst*.

You may be impressed with the antiquity of Munich—all the old churches and stuff—but keep in mind that the city had some rather bad times from American and British bombers in World War II. So what you see is sort of what it looked like, but even the really old buildings have been restored to some degree.

Finally, you come to the **Rathaus**, which, as we all know by now, has nothing to do with rodents. At least, not the four-legged kind. Just as Paris has its Eiffel Tower and Rome its Colosseum, Munich's eyesore is the Rathaus.

The Rathaus is the town hall, and the one in Munich is pretty, but not old. It does, however, have one of those clocks with figures that move (the **Glockenspiel**). People crowd the square below it for hours in the morning, just to see some half-broken wind-up toys go around in a circle for a few minutes. Believe us, it's not worth the effort to look up even if you happen to be passing by. But, like all obligatory Famous Things, you might as well check it out if you're in the area and between appointments at the beer halls. It's a free show, but it's not worth standing in line to see. Don't forget to snap a picture you can bore people with later.

For a real gross-out, check out the skeleton of St. Mondita at **Peterskirche** (St. Peter's Church) near the Marienplatz. It's a pretty wild sight: a jewel-encrusted skeleton of a woman with fake hair, eyes, and even jewels stuck where her teeth were. St. Mondita is the patron saint of lonely women. So, if you caught Eric cheating on you before you left home and you dumped him, maybe you should light a candle here. A more constructive approach might be to head over to the Hofbräuhaus, however, and meet some potential replacements.

Further into the square, you'll come across the **Toy Museum,** where you can trace the sociological and cultural development of children and the fascinating variety of forms of play through the ages. Or, you could head to the Hofbräuhaus.

Churches

Oh yeah, there are a couple of big churches in the middle of Munich. The biggest is the **Frauenkirche**. It's a church all right. It's big, it's empty, it has two steeples on top. Inside, it's pretty bare.

Okay, that's the churches out of the way.

Museums

In general, museums should be avoided like courses that require two semesters of calculus. "But think of all the great paintings you can experience," someone whines. Look, the only way to "experience" great paintings is to run your fingernails down them, and few museums allowed us to do that for long. Besides, all the women in those old paintings are fat, and all the men look constipated. Anyway, you can always buy a book or watch PBS if you need to know about it.

The only museum worth visiting in Munich is the **Deutsches Museum**. Located on an island in the Isar River, it's the largest scientific and technical museum in Europe. "Uh-oh, sounds like two semesters of calculus," you say. Well, not really. It's a truly neat place. It does, however, contain a lot of "guy" stuff: war planes, big diesel engines, things like that. The ladies might want to go shopping (or, you could go to the Hofbräuhaus . . .).

The Deutsches Museum is a real hands-on museum, with more levers, buttons, and knobs to push, pull, yank, squeeze, beat, bang, twist, heave, and suck (for some folks) than you can ever imagine. You can simulate flying an airplane and watch molten metal poured into molds. Don't miss the electricity show, and make sure you're near the physics halls around show time. Using wires, wood, and electricity, "Herr Science" demonstrates the consequences of playing golf in a lightning storm.

The planes in the aviation hall will evoke feelings of manliness and power within even the most peace-loving, kinder, gentler types. (In the immortal words of Foghorn Leghorn, "I say, I say, there's something, oooooh, about a boy that don't like airplanes!") Finally, the ground floors have displays of coal and mineral mines with life-size wax figures picking, drilling, hauling, and sweating to show you the days when men were men. No room for Public Relations Liasons or Software Engineers here.

The whole place is a blast and well worth the admission fee of a few bucks. It's a truly fun place, even if you think only nerds become engineers.

Sidetrips

Olympic Village

Sports freaks will find a visit to the **Olympic Village** worthwhile. You can tour the stadium and even swim in the Olympic pool from 7:00am to 10:00am ($2.00, including use of a locker). The tour of the village also costs $2.00, and you can take the subway out there. Get off at Olympic Centrum. Catchy name for the Olympic Village stop, huh?

BMW Factory

If you want to see what you won't get as a graduation present, check out the **BMW factory** near the Olympic Village, where you can drool over cars so hot they make law school a bearable option. Think how totally *bad* you'll look when you drive up in one of those beauties to evict an elderly widow with leukemia from her apartment. Go for it!

The factory gives a free tour in English.

Dachau

To put all the beer drinking and fun into some perspective, you may want to go to the **Dachau concentration camp**, about ten miles from Munich. It's hardly a fun trip for anyone, but it may help you appreciate that, for many people, Germany evokes a lot more than memories of great beer and happy people.

You can catch a train from the Hauptbahnhof to Dachau, and then take the bus marked Dachau Ost (#722) from Dachau station. The camp is the second to last stop, and admission is free.

"A mandatory pilgrimage."

"An important sidetrip."

"An obligatory visit."

"A necessary but haunting reminder."

These are some of the phrases used in various travel guides to finesse this experience. To the driver of bus #722, however, the camp is just the next-to-last stop on the run he makes several times an hour from the Dachau train station. At this peculiar stop in an otherwise normal suburb, he states "concentration camp" in somber tones, and most of his passengers alight with cameras and journals in hand. It's a grim place.

Garmisch-Partenkirchen

The Bavarian Alps, only a few hours away, make an interesting sidetrip. The hamlet of **Garmisch-Partenkirchen** has a tourist office to get you started and lots of restaurants and cafes. There's also an American military base nearby, so don't be alarmed when a low-flying F-16 rattles your molars.

Ask the tourist office to suggest a hike for however long you have to get lost. If you have time, try to get to **Partnachklamm Gorge**, where a small footbridge crosses a ravine about 800 feet deep. If you walk past the Ski School (site of the 1936 Winter Olympics) and follow the road along the stream, you'll come to a self-service cable car that helps you get closer to the trail.

You definitely get the sense of being in Heidi-land, with the tinkle of mountain goats (their bells, not their elimination of waste), alpine meadows, and crusty old Bavarian men with heavy accents. Along the road, a wagon cart pulled by giant horses may pass you. The blend of old and new is apparent in the Bavarian cart driver and his American passengers. He with his leather *Lederhosen*, felt cap, suede boots, lengthy beard, and keen eyes; they with their rayon stretch pants, polyester tops, nylon caps, manicured nails, and Kodak disk cameras.

For those of you who despise physical exertion but enjoy high places nonetheless, Germany's highest mountain, **Zugspitze**, is within your reach. Take the cog railway from the small train station (Zugspitzbahnhof, just behind the main station) toward Grainau, and get off at Hotel Schneefernerhaus. From there, take the cable car to the top. It costs a lot, but you can try telling them that you thought your Eurailpass was valid and whine and cry to the best of your abilities before handing over the cash.

At the top, sing songs from *The Sound of Music*, take some pictures, and, of course, plant the American flag. (You did bring your American flag, didn't you?)

Berlin

We used to enjoy Berlin before Good Germany and Bad Germany came together to form Big (but friendly—wouldn't hurt a fly and certainly wouldn't invade anybody) Germany. Back then, Berlin had a certain *joie de vivre*, a sort of night-before-finals-with-everybody-looking-at-F's-and-nobody-gives-a-damn-so-let's-PARTY! feel. There was a unique ambience in being in this little island of normality (or, as normal as Berlin got) surrounded by evil commies.

Half the fun, of course, was getting there by train. You felt like a character in a Le Carre novel ("Who? Did he write *Gone With the Wind*?") as the train passed through East Germany on its way to Berlin and your meeting with the mysterious Mr. Z. Nervously, you double-checked your exploding Q-Tips, your tape recorder hidden in the Maalox bottle, and your bullet-proof vest cleverly disguised as a college sweatshirt. Were the East Germans wise to you? Would you be arrested the minute you got off the train and be tortured by being forced watch hours of "Yo! MTV Raps"? You'd have to be very careful in Berlin. . .

Ooops—got a little carried away. Now, where were we?

Actually, Berlin is still an excellent spot to spend some time, even if the bad old days are over and Checkpoint Charlie is a Photomat. Berliners are a lively, cosmopolitan bunch who take their pleasures seriously, and the city has perhaps the most active nightlife in Europe. Since bars and nightclubs don't have formal closing times, many nights extend well into the day. For avant-garde (that's not a brand of antiperspirant, by the way) music and just plain weird arty stuff, few cities can match Berlin.

Note also that Berlin has the biggest university in Germany,

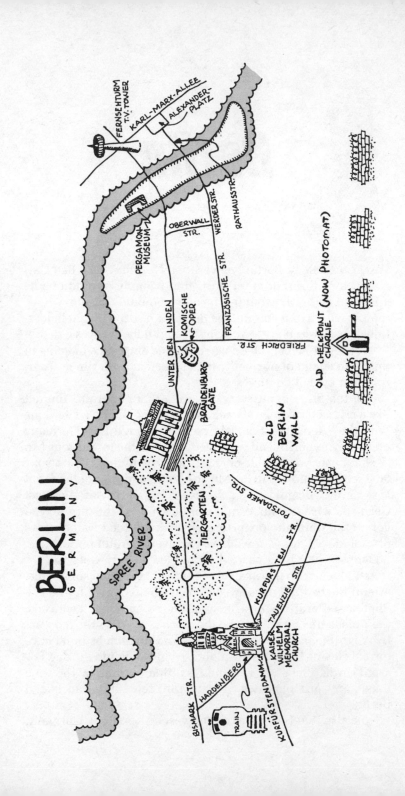

The Free University. This and other institutes of higher education (such as the Technical University and the Academy of Arts) have over 90,000 students. When you figure that the average German student spends over seven years in college, you begin to realize there could be some serious party commandos in town.

Getting There & Getting Around

If you're coming to Berlin by train—and chances are you will, since airfares are outrageous—you'll travel through what was once East Germany. This experience can be interesting in itself. Your train will arrive in **Bahnhof Zoo**, the centrally located, main train station.

First things first. Go to a tourist information office near the train station and let the efficient staff find you a hotel room. It will cost the princely sum of $2.00, and it will save you looking all over town by yourself. Note that the staff consists mainly of young people with round, rimless glasses and an excellent command of English. Good tip here: If you get lost or need something in Germany, always ask a young person wearing round, rimless glasses. They are invariably polite and speak perfect English.

Try to stay fairly close to the **Kurfürstendamm**, the main drag of Berlin. The word Kurfürstendamm is a big word, almost as big as "existentialism," and so nobody in Berlin ever says Kurfürstendamm. Instead, they call it the "Ku'damm."

The subway, known as the **U-Bahn** (Berliners also shortened this word from "Utilitarianistic-Bandolier"), dominates public transportation in Berlin and operates 4:00am-1:00am. Travel is on an honor system, but be warned that the system for catching freeloaders is fairly efficient, though that shouldn't deter the sporting types among you. A second subway line, the **S-Bahn**, takes you through what was the forbidden zone.

Things To See

Start your exploration by wandering the **Ku'damm**, which cuts through the city center. This street used to be the ritzy place to be before World War II. It's become a bit more populist now, but it still has a lot of the better stores and hotels. At night, you'll also see many beautiful ladies of the evening working the street (in case Julie ditched you in Nice for a French film director and you just want some, er, companionship).

At the corner of the Ku'damm and Tauentzienstrasse, you'll find the famous **Kaiser-Wilhelm-Gedächtniskirche**, built at the end of the 1800's. "What's so special about this dump?" you ask. "It looks like a bomb hit it." Actually, several. The ruins of this church have been basically untouched since WWII as a testament to the insanity of war.

Beside the church, a huge shopping center called the **Europa Center** contains a bunch of stores, movie theaters, restaurants, and bars. It's a good place to check out well-dressed Berliners going about their business. It's also definitely worth the time to investigate the huge water clock on the ground floor. You wouldn't want to set your watch by it during a hard frost, but it's a pretty cool sight. Also, outside the Europa Center is a weird fountain that defies description but is known locally as "The Water Dumpling."

Heading down Tauentzienstrasse, check out the stores on one of Berlin's principal shopping streets. Toward the end of the street and right before you emerge in Wittenbergplatz, you'll come to the **Kaufhaus des Westens** or, as it's known to the truncating-crazy locals, the KaDeWe. You *must* check it out.

The **KaDeWe** has the distinction of being one of the largest department stores in Europe. While that fact is not so remarkable in itself, it has the most amazing food section you'll ever see in your entire life. If you thought the only two cold cuts that really mattered were ham and bologna, you're in for a shock. You can choose from over 400 meats and *wursts* in the deli section. Although you can buy American cheese in the cheese shop, why would you when you can get pound of Peruvian llama cheese or maybe some evil-smelling sheeps cheese instead?

No food store in the world, with the possible exception of Harrods in London, comes close to the KaDeWe in sheer size and quality. A dozen snackbars and little restaurants scattered throughout the store offer everything from Chinese food to pizza. There's a huge wine and liquor section, and a fruit section that you'll remember fondly the next time you go out at midnight to buy a week's groceries at the HandiMart. Just thinking about this store has us drooling all over the word processor. (Oh, if any of you reading this happen to stop by the store, could you pick up a pound of sea slug and mail it to us in care of Mustang Publishing? Surface mail is fine.)

Passing through Wittenbergplatz, you find yourself on Kleist-strasse, which eventually leads you to **Nollendorfplatz**. An interesting sight there is the flea market located in a series of abandoned subway cars. You can get some good buys if you take the time to look. These days, you'll find all sorts of goodies from the old East German army. How about a slightly used tank? Nobody will dare cut you off in traffic when you've got a 120mm cannon mounted on the front of your wheels.

South of Tauentzienstrasse and a fairly good hike away is the **Rathaus** (City Hall), which has a special connection for all Americans. It was there that Pres. John F. Kennedy made his famous "*Ich bin ein Berliner*" address in 1963. (He was trying to say "I am a Berliner" to show solidarity with the citizens there, but his words actually translate to "I am a rump wrangler.")

If you're running for student government office in the fall, this is a good place to have your photo taken. You should stand there frowning in concentration as you consider the issues on which you'll run—legalized kegs on campus, longer gym hours, and changes in the book buy-back program at the co-op. You may have to wait in line though, since others who claim leadership roles in America—be it Rotarians, County Commissioners, or PTA Presidents—have their five seconds of glory on the steps before you. *Sheesh*. America: still the only country in the world where anybody can dream of being a rump wrangler.

Near the Rathaus is **Templehof Airfield**, where the Berlin Airlift was organized after WWII. The Airlift Memorial there commemorates the thousands of candy bars dropped by U.S. fliers so West Berlin kids wouldn't have to eat Soviet Twinkies.

Head back to the area around the railway station. You may want to visit the **Zoo**, reputed to be the world's largest. In 1943, a bombing raid made guacamole out of most of the animals. The zoo was totally rebuilt and today has 11,000 species. We didn't think there were that many species on earth, but maybe they're counting bugs or bacteria or something. They do have a neat subterranean section, where you can sit in the dark and be a Peeping Tom on the sex life of a badger family. The zoo also has Germany's only panda and a great gorilla section, where you'll see faces like those you used to date in high school.

Food

Berlin's food is typically German—heavy on beer, bread, and *wurst*. For example, a basic Berlin dish is *leber mit apfel und zwiebel* (liver with apples and onions). Sounds yummy, huh? Actually, if you swallow it fast and wash it down with a lot of beer, it tastes pretty good. Other local specialties to watch for (or avoid) are *eisbein* (pickled ham hocks), *kasseler rippenspeer* (smoked pork chops), and *hackepeter* (beef, pork, and onions ground together). Delicious, nutritious, and low, low, low in fat.

Since Berlin has no mandatory closing times, a lot of restaurants don't really get going until 9:00pm, so you should adjust yourself to eating late. For typical Berlin cuisine, try **Die Nolle** at Nollendorfplatz, or maybe **Restaurant Schultheiss-Bräuhaus** on the corner of Ku'damm and Meinekestrasse. At either place, you can load up enough cholesterol to make your arteries as clogged as the Holland Tunnel on Friday afternoon.

Finally, if you want to try something a little hokey but fun, spend an evening at **Tafelrunde**, a restaurant decorated like a medieval inn. You pay one price (about $20) and eat all you can, so make sure you're hungry when you get there. They don't provide any utensils, but that's part of the fun. Anyway, admit it: haven't you always wanted to rip a drumstick off the turkey at Thanksgiving dinner, stick the whole thing in your mouth with disgusting sucking and chomping noises, and gross out your Aunt Sophie? Well, here's your big chance to practice.

Like most big cities, Berlin has a number of ethnic eateries. Look particularly for Turkish restaurants. They've sprung up everywhere, but especially in the district called **Kreuzberg**, known as "Little Istanbul" to the natives, where many of the 100,000 Turkish inhabitants of the city live. Try **Restaurant Istanbul** at Knesebeckstrasse 77, or maybe **Kurdistan** at Kaiser-Friedrichstrasse 41. The latter restaurant is actually Kurdish, but who's counting?

Drinking

Berlin has hundreds of bars/restaurants that stay open very late, where Berliners socialize, gossip, chat, and drink. These places go by the general term *kneipe*, which loosely translates as "a hangout." *Kneipe* run the gamut from sleazy dives to high tech chrome-and-glass establishments that resemble tanning salons at a good mall.

A drink you should try at your first kneipe is the famous *Weissbier mit Schuss*. This beer, a pale malt, is served with a shot of fruit syrup dissolved in the beer. The flavor of the day is usually cherry, but sometimes you hit others. For those of you who've developed a taste for banana-blueberry-grapenut wine coolers, here's a beer you can savor.

Everybody has his own favorite kneipe. Many of us keep taking our livers to a new one every few days, hoping to find one that will stick. One of the more famous kneipe in Berlin is **Loretta im Garten** (Lietzenburgerstrasse 89), a huge outdoor garden with lots of tables, cheap beer, American college students, and live bands. You can actually get away with bringing your own food into Loretta's, so if you couldn't finish your liver mit apples und onions at lunch, whip out the squashed remains and share them with your friends.

The **Irish Pub** at the Europa Center is neither Irish nor a pub, but it is a lively place with decent (sometimes) Irish music at night and Guinness on tap.

Old East Berlin

It's still fairly obvious when you cross from what was West Berlin into what was East Berlin, mainly because the architecture is so different. Old East Berlin, though decrepit and filled with hideous, cheap buildings, is being rebuilt quickly to make Berlin fit to be the capital of the biggest country in Europe. (Not to imply that the Good Germans have any ideas about flexing their new muscles, but Germans are like that big stupid kid you knew in high school—strong as an ox, well-meaning, but easily led by the wrong crowd.)

Head for **Unter den Linden**, the main street in old East Berlin. It was the most beautiful street in Berlin until WWII, when the Allies, in a far-sighted vision of the need for inner-city parking, bombed it into dust. Note the huge old Soviet Embassy, which has enough antennae and satellite dishes to start its own Christian Broadcasting Network.

At the end of Unter den Linden is the famous **Brandenburg Gate** in Pariserplatz. This gate, the symbol of Berlin, was badly damaged during WWII. You probably caught a glimpse of it during the TV coverage of the collapse of the Berlin Wall.

By the way, there's still lots of Wall left, so don't be shy about taking the 14-pound sledgehammer you've carried in your backpack all the way from Boise and knocking off a few chunks to bring back home. Pretty soon, Martha Stewart will be coming out with a book called *Martha Stewart's Gifts You Can Make from Chunks of the Berlin Wall.*

Now turn around and walk in the other direction on Unter den Linden, away from the Brandenburg Gate. Further up the street, you'll pass **Humboldt University**, the most famous university of old East Germany. If Germany had teams in the NFL, most of its recruits would come from Humboldt. This is a definite t-shirt stop, since a t-shirt from dear ol' Humboldt U. is infinitely cooler than a Hard Rock Cafe anywhere-in-the-world t-shirt.

Keep going up the street to the **Neue Wache**, a Monument to the Victims of Fascism and Militarism. Soldiers of the old *Volksarmee* (People's Army) used to stand in front and do a little goose-step number every half hour as they changed the guard. Nostalgia—it ain't what it used to be.

We continue our stroll up Unter den Linden to where it crosses a wimpy little canal called Kupfergraben and becomes Karl-Liebknechtstrasse. You are now on the renowned **Museumsinsel** (Museum Island). There are a bunch of famous museums to the north, including the **Alte Nationalgalerie** (National Gallery), **Bodemuseum**, and the most famous of all, **Pergamonmuseum**.

Pergamonmuseum was built specifically to house Zeus' **Pergamon Altar**, dating from 180 BC (for those of you who like to get your stats straight, whether it's American League or Ancient Rocks we're talking about). According to a certain big orange guidebook, this museum is "mind-boggling." Well, you may want to take a look, but in case you're pressed for time, the altar looks like a miniature temple. To the average observer (like us), it resembles Veterans Stadium in Philadelphia, where they hold the annual Army-Navy game, though the Pergamon Altar is a lot smaller. In fact, we paced it out, and it would be tough to play even arena football in the Pergamon Altar if it were in Philadelphia, which it isn't, so that's that.

However, one of the things that will strike you at this museum is the similarity between people all over the world. Like, these Germans built a special museum just for the Pergamon Altar, while we've built museums just for Enormous Balls of String and Jumpsuits of Elvis. It's a small world, after all.

Fight your way back to the door through the throngs of *Let's Go*'ers trying to see three Astoundingly Broad Museums before lunch, and let's go get some chow. Get back onto Karl-Liebknechtstrasse and head east until you come to the area around Alexanderplatz, which your Berliner friends refer to as "The Alex."

The Alex is dominated by a huge television tower (**Fernsehturm**), which has acquired the nickname "telasparagus." This is your Tall Thing To Climb in Berlin. It's no Eiffel Tower, of course, but it's worth the trip, and there's a revolving, rather pricey restaurant on the top.

On the square itself, a bunch of food stands offer wurst, bread, mustard, and plenty of beer. This type of impromptu eating is popular with the locals, and we faced long lines before we actually got our hands on the grub. But, after an exhausting morning measuring that Pergamon Altar and having our minds boggled, the *wurst* tasted pretty good.

Some of the better places to eat in old East Berlin include **Jagdklause** (Hans-Beimler-Strasse 70), which specializes in wild game like deer, boar, etc. The **Restaurant on Top of the Television Tower** (can't remember the official name) is fun, too. The **Operncafe** (Unter den Linden 5) is a nice spot to sit in the evening and watch people stroll the street.

After dinner, take a walk and check out **Karl-Marx-Allee**, behind the Alex. This huge boulevard, one of the Communist showpieces of old East Berlin, runs for about three miles to the east. It's lined with mid-sized buildings of great ugliness.

Nightlife

There's so much happening in West Berlin at night that you may need to forgo sleep completely during your stay.

We've already dealt with the *kneipe* concept earlier, and that alone should keep you occupied and away from anything educational for quite a while. There's also a great musical nightlife in Berlin, covering jazz to punk and everything in between.

For jazz fans, excellent places to start looking are **Floz** (Nassauischestrasse 37) or **Quartier Latin** (Potsdamerstrasse 96).

One of the neatest places to go for blues and jazz is a place called **Museumkneipe** at Ku'damm-Karree 207. This place is a bizarre combination of jazz club, bar, antique shop, and museum of sorts. It's run by a homely little man who wears a t-shirt with his picture on it (which you can buy for five bucks). Museumkneipe is a great place to spend an evening, because usually they don't charge admission and the beer prices are reasonable. Plus, you get to hear good music. The tables are scattered among the goods for sale, so you can shop for antiques while enjoying the atmosphere.

Riverboat (Hohenzollerndamm 177), one of the more bizarre places to go dancing, should appeal to those of you missing the Mississippi and yearning for a mess-o-catfish. Actually, Riverboat is a fun place to spend the evening, as is the huge **Big Eden Club** (Ku'damm 202), which is big enough to host the Army-Navy game if the Pergamon Altar ever became unavailable. Both Riverboat and Big Eden cost about $3.00 to get in. A little more expensive is the **Metropol** (Nollendorfplatz 5), housed in an old theater. Some nights, it's quiet enough to study for the LSAT, and others it's an absolute madhouse.

There are several other evening entertainments available. If you want to see an old fashioned love story, Berlin-style, get yourself a ticket for the cabaret at **Chez Romy Haag** (Welserstrasse 24). It's your typical boy-meets-girl-who-turns-out-to-be-a-boy-which-is-fine-because-the-first-boy-turns-out-to-be-a-girl story. We didn't lose you there, did we? For those of you from Kansas, what we have here is a **transvestite* show.** Now, if you think transvestite is a special fabric like Gortex, you are excused from the rest of this chapter. The actors at Chez Romy Haag ain't exactly Liza Minelli and Joel Grey, but if you enjoyed dressing in mom's clothes when you were a little boy, go with it. You'll be among friends.

Of course, there are much more "exotic" clubs to visit than Chez Romy Haag, if you're in the mood for interesting nightlife. Since this is a family book, we'll leave you to find them on your own. But if you want a hint, begin your search around **Liet-**

---

* Note: **Transvestites** grow *down* from the cave's ceiling; **transvesmites** grow *up* from the cave's floor.

zenburgerstrasse, where you can check out such exotica as a "bathtub act," which has little to do with getting clean but may help you relax.

For a good sense of what's going on in town, two biweekly magazines carry listings, *Zitty* (which is thinking of changing its name to *Clearasil*) and *Tip*. Much of their text is in English.

Alternative Berlin

Finally, a few words on "alternative" Berlin. The city has a reputation for tolerating some pretty bizarre stuff. As a result, Berlin has attracted a lot of people who pursue what's known as an "alternative lifestyle."

The **Kreuzberg district** is especially interesting in this context, as is the area around the **Free University** in Dahlem, where you'll find enough vegetarian food to turn your entire digestive tract into a botanical garden. You'll also find folks wearing weird clothes and, of course, round, rimless glasses, the true mark of a young German intellectual. It's an interesting area to wander, though you may stand out like an English major in Chem Lab if you show up in your Joe College outfits. (For assistance, see "What To Wear" in the Introduction.)

The New Eastern Europe

Those of you familiar with the first edition of this book may recall how we encouraged you to travel into the bowels of the socialist paradises of Hungary, Czechoslovakia, and East Germany. Since we last wrote, the Eastern Europe of communism, bad food, crummy hotels, and relentless bureaucracy has gone the way of Eastern Airlines.

Frankly, we miss the old Eastern Europe (and the old Eastern Airlines, too, for that matter), where getting a bite to eat was an adventure and smuggling the *International Herald Tribune* in your shorts was a capital crime. Visiting Eastern Europe used to be like dating someone in high school who had really strict parents. You remember: the clumsy kisses on the doorstep, the furtive groping in the car outside her house, always with one eye on the porch, scared shitless that the light would come on or that her father would rap on the steamed-up car window. Every time you picked her up, you were grilled by her parents, who just knew your pockets were filled with drugs, condoms, vibrators, and flasks of gin. Her dad made it quite clear that if there was even the hint you had, er, damaged the goods, he would be only too happy to emasculate you with his power drill.

Years later, you meet again. Now, she has an MBA/CPA, a large apartment with lots throw pillows, and a cellular phone that rings at the worst times. Her first words after you make love are, "I wonder how Tokyo opened."

It's like that with the New Eastern Europe. Things aren't quite that grim, of course. There's still plenty of lousy food and rude, petty bureaucrats, but in the rush for every Czech and Hungarian to have their a Gameboy, these countries have gone a bit limp and just aren't as interesting anymore. Real, live Communists have become as rare as eight-track tape players.

So, to summarize for those who may have lost us above and are now reading this with a woody for sweet ol' Mindy (or was it Mandy?) from Jefferson High, the countries once owned by the old USSR (collectively referred to as "Eastern Europe") have gone the way of many 1960's rock bands: split-up, gone solo, reunited, and sold out. They've declared their independence and invited MBA's over to engineer supply-side, service-oriented, consumer-driven economies. You can now get MTV and CNN in places like Budapest and Prague. Big hairstyles, Blockbuster Video, and 1-900-PHONE-SEX lines are on the way. Sadly, the black market has dried up, and you can no longer get your thrills trading a pair of ratty Levi's for a 15th-century religious relic or a worker's monthly wages.

The Evil Empire is gone, the Berlin Wall is small chunks suitable for framing, and Checkpoint Charlie is a Photomat. There's a Big Germany in place of Two Germanies. One Berlin instead of Good Berlin and Bad Berlin. Damn! If the commies hadn't all kicked the bucket, we never would have had to go back to Europe to research this Revised! Expanded! edition.

While all this may dampen your expectations, there is a positive side. Things have gotten simpler for the *Let's Blower*. While you once needed a visa to get into Hungary, Czechoslovakia, and Poland—a real pain in the butt—this requirement has been removed for Americans. And all we had to do was promise billions in foreign aid to be relieved of this chore. (You still need a visa for Russia at this writing, but a few billion ought to do the trick. . .)

The currency situation has also improved. You can now convert dollars into *forints*, *koruny*, and *zloty* easily, and even get back dollars again. A hundred bucks will make you a millionaire in Polish *zloty*. What's more, there's now real food in restaurants and decent stuff to buy in stores. The God-awful National Tourist Organizations of Hungary and Czechoslovakia are still around, but they're losing their control of hotel rooms to free-market forces. So, although the situation is still changing rapidly, it's not as tough as it once was to get simple things like a bed and a meal in Eastern Europe.

There is however, still one great big place that you thrill-seeking, culture-shockster, intrepid types can experience without getting special shots or joining the Navy. Mathias Rust broke the ice by flying his Cessna into Red Square, and now you can do it by more conventional means. Comrades, on to Moscow!

Moscow

The old USSR was a very big country that has become many little countries. At this writing, most of the old Soviet Republics are now countries in their own right and have joined the new Commonwealth of Independent States—but we're not betting our royalty checks on that concept lasting. We thought about including a few key cities, but we decided to wait until they finish renaming them all. By the time this book hits your local bookstore, St. Petersburg may be called Sleepy Valley Estates, and you may have to drive a Range Rover and be a successful proctologist to live there. It's bad enough trying to keep up with the street names. Glorious Workers' Collective Road is now Free Enterprise Highway, and if you ask Russians about Lenin, they look puzzled and ask if he and McCartney are still writing songs.

So, we decided to confine ourselves to a trip to Moscow. If you decide to venture further afield, you're on your own as far as we're concerned! The important town is Moscow, and we'll hedge our bets and guess it's the one that'll be around for a while.

The old Gorby-coup thing is past, and those coup people either committed suicide or got jobs as night watchmen at the Warehouse for Fallen Statues. Of course, we can't predict what has happened since this book went to press. For all we know, the only visa you'll need for Moscow will be the kind that competes with American Express and Mastercard. But whatever happens, Moscow will still be there. Moscow remains a solid reminder of power run amok, and there's still plenty to see of the old order.

MOSCOW

- Rossiya Hotel
- RAZINA
- St. Basils
- CHERKASKY B
- KUYBYSHEVA
- MOSKVORETSKAYA
- GUM →
- MARKSA
- PROSPEKT
- Red Square
- Pl. Revolutsii
- Kremlin
- MOSKVA
- Inturist Hotel
- KALININA PROSPEKT
- Arbat Pedestrian Mall
- BOROVITSKAYA PL.
- Pushkin Museum

First thing, though: Forget all this nonsense about how "Westernized" Moscow has become. O.K., you know there's a McDonald's, a Pizza Hut, and Baskin-Robbins there, but they aren't making any money. Mostly, they were installed as tourist gimmicks to supplement the usual stuff like Red Square and Lenin's Tomb. The Ministry of Internal Tourism thought the Kremlin was losing its appeal (and Lenin's body its skin), so they struck a deal with McDonald's to build an enormous Golden Arches outlet. Shrewdly, they figured this would comfort most Americans, who refuse to travel to a country where they can't get an Egg McMuffin to go.

The Russian Language

We need to say a little something about the Russian language:
    You won't understand it.
    There—so much for that important cultural item.
    Since the Russian language uses a lot of funny characters that don't bear much resemblance to normal letters, finding your way around is tough, since there's little English on street signs or Metro stops. There's not even any helpful scheme to guide you through the Metro, like the #7 train or the Blue Line. One small comfort: there's little chance you'll be killed on the Moscow subway.
    Incidentally, don't expect much help when you ask Yuri the best way to get to the Kosmos Hotel. English is not as common in Moscow as it is in, say, England.

Toilet Paper

Do not forget to bring **toilet paper** with you. Chances are, you won't find any in the public restrooms, and what you do find resembles Astroturf. We'd hate to think what you'll do if the cabbage you've been eating for breakfast, lunch, and dinner decides to stage a coup in your colon and you are caught, as it were, with your pants down.
    If you do find yourself bereft, consider using your big guidebook with the bright orange cover. Travelers around the world have discovered that its paper has marvelous absorbency. The chapter on Albania should hold you for a day.

Arriving in Moscow

You'll likely arrive either by air at **Sheremetyevo-2 Airport** (which might be called "Donald Trump Airport" by now, but just go with it. . .) or by train at **Byelorusskiy station** or **Kievskiy station**. The airport is a lot like Kennedy Airport in New York—crowded, disorganized, and full of foreigners. If you've brought any valuables like a camera, Walkman, toilet paper, etc., stuff them down your shorts or, failing that, do not let them out of your sight for one second. Be sure to carry all of your important things with you, and never check any item you'd like to see again. The baggage handlers, socialists to the core, believe fervently in the distribution of wealth, starting with themselves, and tend to "distribute" bourgeois items like cameras.

Having successfully registered for classes several times at your own personal diploma mills, the intricacies of getting through immigration and customs should present little problem.

Getting from the airport to the city will be one of your first tests of survival. Taxis are generally not considered legitimate means of transportation by experienced travelers to Moscow because, although cabbies are State employees and receive salaries of about $40 a month, they are also agents of the Moscow Mob, a crime ring that preys on people with hard currency, like you. At press time, the rate for a cab ride to Moscow was $40.

An alternative to the taxi gouge is a bus which stops at the airport (behind the parking area). It runs to the nearest Metro stop, Rechnoy Vokzal, from 6:00am-11:40pm, about every 20 minutes. You'll have to pay in rubles, so change some money at the airport.

All guidebooks will describe Moscow as a "ringed city," and we suppose it looks that way on a map. However, these rings are not readily apparent to the visitor navigating on foot or by Metro.

The subway (**Metro**), efficient and reliable (hmmm, must be run by the Japanese), is by far the best way to get from one major area to another. Some of the stations are like museums ("Ugh— not in Moscow, too!"). Check out the Metro commemorating the People of the Revolution (pl. Revolyutsii), adjacent to Red Square, with statues of the working-class heroes of the Bolshevik uprising (not the 1991 coup attempt).

Where To Stay

Chances are you'll be staying at one of the fine Intourist hotels, each as quaint and intimate as your freshman dorm. The most infamous are the Mezh, the Rossiya, the Intourist, and the Kosmos. Unless you have reservations or booked through Intourist, you may not have much luck getting into any of these hotels.

The Intourist hotels have a fascinating labor-intensive mechanism for controlling security known as the *dezhurnaya*, or, in technical terms, "Key Lady." Key Lady is big, brash, and a trained killer. On each floor of most hotels, Key Lady controls the use of your room key with an iron fist. You want to leave? Key Lady takes your key, jots down some notes, and locks it into a drawer in her desk. Key Lady is a vigilant guard who never leaves her post, except for a two-hour bathroom break whenever you need your key. But don't worry, she'll be back—she's KEY LADY! (Key Lady will also sell you a bottle of just about anything for hard currency.)

A quick jaunt from Red Square is the infamous **Intourist** (ul. Tverskaya 3/5, phone 203-4008). Even if you don't have the displeasure of sleeping there, the bar is worth a late night pop or two, if only to see the internationally acclaimed prostitution capital of Russia.

The **Rossiya** (ul. Razina 6, phone 298-5531), a monstrosity that almost dwarfs the Kremlin, is adjacent to Red Square. The largest hotel in the world (over 3,000 rooms), it's the setting for many spy novels. You'll see why when you roam its cavernous lobbies and corridors. The area just outside is an interesting hang-out for Russians and tourists alike.

The newly refurbished, art deco **Metropole** (phone 927-6039) is almost adjacent to Red Square. At $300 a night, though, you'll probably just want to visit the lobby and check out the impressive main dining room.

If you head straight down pr. Kalinina from Red Square and turn right when you hit the river, you'll find the **Mezhdunarodnaya** (a.k.a. the "Mezh") at Krasnopresenskaya nab. 12, a huge complex that will remind you of an early mall. It's where journalists and business people drink, swap war stories, and wait for their plane home. A very sleazy Irish pub inside (sleazy even by Irish standards) sells Guinness on tap for hard currency.

The grand lady of them all is the **Kosmos**, about 45 minutes from Red Square by Metro (pr. Mira 150, phone 217-0785), built to accommodate the crowds of the 1980 Olympics. The Kosmos has over 2,000 rooms and restaurants large enough to comfortably seat the allied troops from Operation Desert Storm. The rooms, which smell like a smoke-out clinic and are heated to a comfy 98° year-round, are carpeted (floor to ceiling!) with attractive patterns of burn marks and stains. The furniture is worse. Most rooms offer a view of the Kosmos Metro station, with its funny Sputnik thrusting skyward. On a positive note, the Kosmos has a large indoor pool, sauna, and notorious late-night bars, including the famous **Heineken Cash Bar.** If you want to evoke those memories of your freshman dorm, the Kosmos is the place.

Across from the Kosmos is the **Exhibition of Economic Achievements**, which is about the biggest oxymoron we can think of.

If you're really desperate and willing to part with some hard currency, there are several hotels that will take you on short notice. One is on a boat in the Moskva River across from the Mezh, called the **Alexander Block**. There are rumors that it's also a brothel, but what do you care as long as they wash the sheets? Another possibility is the **Hotel Visit** (phone 202-2848). There are also numerous agencies springing up that will find you room in private apartments. We recommend this alternative if the room isn't far from the city center.

What To See

Your first impressions upon looking around town will be of drab contrasts, shades of grey and dirty yellow. The skies are dotted with red stars, and there are no glass skyscrapers—only a few old monsters Stalin built with slave labor.

First, head down to Red Square, the center of Moscow. This is the place you always see in the background on the news, where every film crew in town feels obliged to broadcast from. If you're lucky, they might be shooting *Arsenio Hall—Live From Moscow*, and you can creep up behind the set and jump up and down yelling "Whooo! Whooo! Whooo!" In the crowd, you'll spot Sally Jessy Raphaël looking pissed, wondering how long

Arsenio will tie up this prime real estate. She's got a whole show to shoot, and at this rate, she'll have to cut the segment on Transvestite Russian Love Slaves and go straight to Richard Simmons' Cabbage Diet.

There's not much to do in Red Square except look around and take pictures of the **Kremlin** and **St. Basil's Cathedral**, but the area does become a nice hanging spot when there's good weather. It's a popular place for Eastern Europe tourists too, and you can see some characters who'll make the folks displaying their pigs at the State Fair back home seem pretty normal. Take note of the bizarre cameras people use. Moscow is virgin territory as far as Japanese imports are concerned.

GUM department store, across from the Kremlin, is worth a look inside, if not for the quirky stores, then at least for the architecture. Built in the 1930's (and presumably high-tech for its time), GUM calls itself the biggest department store in the world, but there's little to buy. A well-known joke about GUM goes something like this: A man walks into one of the shops and, looking at the empty shelves, asks, "No shirts?" The clerk replies, "Sorry, sir. You're in the No Shoes department. The No Shirts department is upstairs."

From Red Square, you can walk to a number of interesting places or hop the Metro to get you anywhere else.

Where To Eat

Forget all the bad things we said about English and German food. Nothing can compare with Russian cuisine. If rotten, dried, salted, rancid, smelly fish—the kind fishermen leave behind on docks, the kind even the gulls won't eat—is your thing, you'll savor the prospects. If you like pickles as a main-course vegetable and are enticed by the thought of boiled, tri-colored meats, then come prepared to chow down. What's worse, there's this quaint Russian tradition of washing down each delectable mouthful with industrial-grade vodka or brandy. Trying to force the liquid down while keeping the food from coming up is one of the great challenges of the Russian meal—and something you'll long remember. Remember, don't forget the toilet paper.

Many of the so-called fancy restaurants in Moscow are still state-owned, and you can't eat there without a reservation. A dining experience at a state-owned restaurant goes something like this:

You arrive at the restaurant with a reservation, but you're kept at the door for several hours. After a lot of discussion with three stern bouncers who appear to have little to do except keep you at the door, you get into the dining room. Peering through thick clouds of cigarette smoke, you notice many empty tables and no shortage of waiters or waitresses, either. You are seated next to a table of 12 loud, drunk men with facial scars—the Executive Committee of Moscow Taxi Mob. They make sure the smoke near your table is up to the required concentration.

In front of you are plates of assorted cabbages and pickles (zakuski), no more than four days old—a week at most. Then comes the bottle brigade. The waiter will bring several dozen bottles of green, yellow, and clear liquids and open them all around you. Go for the clear ones. If you want beer or wine with your meal, forget it; you'll have to settle for brandy or vodka. You may get some cabbage soup, and they are pretty liberal with caviar (ikra), if you like that sort of thing. The main course is usually salted fish or boiled meat, with a potato and cabbage.

By now the drunks next to you have linked arms and are singing loudly. Two have fallen face first in their cabbage soup. Across the floor of empty tables, a band comes on the stage and starts to play a Russian version of We've Only Just Begun. Time to get out of here. Someone might want to dance.

The good news is, there are number of alternative restaurants springing up that offer fare which more closely resembles food. Yep, there's the world's largest **McDonald's** at Pushkin Square and the nearby **Pizza Hut** at pr. Kutuzovsky 17 and one on ul. Tverskaya that delivers for a 10% commission (phone 229-2013). Pizza Hut has a special entrance allowing those with hard currency and little social conscience to breeze past the rubles-only line.

Many restaurants have hard currency sections and rubles-only sections. The former are filled with foreigners, while the latter have long lines. If you have the patience to wait in a rubles-only line, you'll meet real Russians and pay a fraction of the amount you'd pay in dollars, usually for the same food. If you want to meet other Americans or Brits or perhaps that cute Scandinavian of your dreams, try the hard currency section.

Below are a few restaurants to try, but we advise you to get *Moscow Magazine* (printed in English, available at most major hotels), which describes the best and newest possibilities.

Tren-Mos (pr. Komsomolskiy 21, phone 245-1216), an American (TRENton) and Soviet (MOScow) joint venture, is about as close to a Friday's as you'll find in Moscow. It features a French waiter and an optimistic proprietor, who sometimes has theme nights with things like a Cajun buffet with a jazz band and Dixie Beer. On those nights, Tren-Mos can have a fun atmosphere, and you'll forget where you are, until you step back outside.

Cafe Viru (Ostozhneka 50, near the Kropotkinskaya Metro) offers salads and sandwiches and is a popular hang-out for youth at night.

Tanganka Cafe (ul. Chkalova 76) has a pleasant dining area upstairs. It serves *pelmeni* (a kind of ravioli), plus beer.

Farkhad (Bolshaya Marfinsdaya 4, phone 218-4136), a lively Azerbaijani cooperative restaurant, offers wonderful, exotic dishes and fresh fruits and vegetables.

Two areas to scope out for rubles-only fast-food are along **pr. Kalinina** and **Arbat**. You can try to make reservations in advance by calling (good luck!) the restaurant and telling them you're from an American delegation promoting free-enterprise and you have lots of dollars. That should get you in the door, and once you're in, you're in.

For a tasty snack on the run, try **Bread Store #102** (formerly Dante & Puccini's Trattoria, but the Soviet Government didn't think that was catchy enough) at pr. Kalinina 42, which has all kinds of fresh breads and pastries. You can have a coffee upstairs in the cafe to wash down your selection. There's no place to sit, but the standard chest-high tables will do. Across the street at #29, check out the **Biryusa Cafe and Kulinariya**, a Russian version of a deli.

If you're lucky enough to get invited to a Russian home, you'll discover that Russian food can be quite wonderful. Delightful dishes such as *pirozhki* (warm breads filled with wild mushrooms or meats) or *pelmeni* (a meat-filled ravioli) are hard to find outside of the home. Remember, a typical Russian wife (usually responsible for all household activities, plus a full-time job) doesn't have the option of stopping off at the A&P on her way home from the tennis club, loading up the Volvo with goodies from the deli counter, and deciding whether to serve her special duck in raspberry sauce or her famous raspberries in duck sauce. Whatever you're served in a Russian home has often been fought for (literally) in long lines that people spend their lives in. As in many cultures where the people have very little, they give more than they can afford to guests. So, if you're invited to a Russian home, load up with as much booze, flowers, fruit, or candy as you can and be a good guest.

Bars

The **Red Lion Pub** (Hotel Mezhdunarodnaya, 2nd level, phone 253-2283) combines the world's worst cuisines (Soviet and British) in a dreary pub. But who cares when there's Guinness on tap?

The **Hard Rock Cafe Moscow** (basement of Victoria Restaurant, near Zelyeni Theater in Gorky Park) is a popular hang-out for heavy metal types, especially late at night. They even have food here, and accept cash or rubles. Go late for some real memories. (Any day now, Moscow will get a few Banana Republics, a Body Shop, and a Spencer Gifts to go with the Hard Rock.)

Outside of the Mezh and Intourist hotel bars (see *Places To Stay*), the most popular bar is the **Spanish Bar** at the Hotel Moskva (Manezhnaya pl.), a very happening place late at night for locals and foreigners.

Things To Do

If you're in total despair (and, if you've followed our advice, you should be), then go to the circus, a Russian entertainment institution, and it isn't just for kids. In contrast to the circus experience in the U.S., which usually involves going to some vacant lot on the edge of town and paying money to park, only to watch a bunch of abused animals perform unnatural acts with sleazy carnies, the **Moscow Circus** is an upbeat, fun time.

Two permanent arenas house the circuses. One is near Moscow State University (Metro: Universitet); the other at Tsvetnoy Bulvar 13 (Metro of the same name). While they utilize high-tech stage props and polished performers, the quirky music from a live orchestra gives an Old World (though surreal) atmosphere. You'll be amazed and amused by beautiful acrobatics, old-fashion magic tricks, clowns, and animal shows. If you time it right, you'll see Arabian horsemen trying daring feats and bears dancing with elephants (the bear usually leads). At intermission, check out the refreshment stand in the lobby—a marvel in itself.

Circus performances run every evening and twice a day on weekends. Buy tickets before going out there.

A nice spot to visit on a warm summer eve or a cold winter night is the wooded park called **Kolomenskoye Summer Residence** (of the Czar in the 16th century), accessible by a short hike from the Kolomenskaya Metro stop. It's situated along the banks of the Moskva River, and you Film Studies majors may recognize it from *The Russia House*. They dragged an 18th-century wooden prison here from Siberia (in which, as *Let's Go* dutifully informs us, "Archpriest Avvakum wrote his celebrated autobiography." *Celebrated*?! Get a life, you guys.), plus Peter the Great's log cabin, so you'll really get a sense of life in the good old days.

Shopping

Shopping in Moscow is an experience you may only want to observe from a distance—say, Chicago. The rules of purchasing items are byzantine, and often shopkeepers won't even let you in their store. It's becoming more popular for shops to require an invitation to enter, supposedly to prevent hoarding.

If you do get in and decide you want to buy something, it's very complicated. Let's say you want to buy a bottle of water at a food store. First, pick out what you want, go to a cashier, and pay for it. The cashier may ask for your Moscow proof of residency, a means of distribution control. Sometimes a passport will get you by. You may also be required to present an empty "return" bottle. You'll be taxed 5% on the item—but at local prices, this shouldn't break you. Then it's back to the original place you saw the bottle to pick it up. You may need help with this process and a lot of patience (17 years of Zen training should suffice). We hate to think what buying a week's worth of groceries or, God forbid, last-minute Christmas shopping must be like.

The main shopping streets in Moscow are **pr. Kalinina**, **Arbat**, and **ul. Petrovka**. A lot of people sell antiques and craft items along these streets, but be careful about offering dollars. It might get both you and the seller in trouble.

Several open-air markets are definitely worth the trip by Metro. The most notorious, at **Rizhsky Park** (Metro: Rizhsky), offers free enterprise at its best, and some of the stuff you'll see there looks like it was made on a different planet. Pack your pockets full of rubles and head there on a warm afternoon.

If you're shopping for arts and crafts, try the market at **Izmailovskiy Park** (Metro: Izmailovskiy). There's also an outdoor pet market near the Taganskaya Metro that's an interesting diversion, but, of course, you can't actually *buy* a kitten because you could never pronounce "Here kitty, kitty" in Russian and the poor little thing would just get totally confused and run away.

Prague

Prague, the capital of Czechoslovakia, ranks as one of the most beautiful cities in Europe. Because the Germans swallowed up Czechoslovakia before the start of the World War II, Prague was never subjected to the bombing and street fighting that ruined so many European cities. The old part of Prague is still a maze of winding streets and faded yellow houses with red-tiled roofs. On a hill overlooking the city, a collection of huge buildings constitute the former royal palaces and the museums.

A Communist government was installed there after WWII, and Czechoslovakia was moving toward a fairly liberal form of socialism when the Soviets sent in tanks in 1968 to reinforce a hard line. Most Czechs recall this event with great bitterness (sort of like our Vietnam or Watergate).

In 1989, the "Velvet Revolution" —which has nothing to do with paintings of Elvis imported from Mexico—finished the job begun 21 years prior and banished Communism once and for all. Vaclav Havel, a playwright who had been imprisoned for his democratic views, was elected President, and the country started the difficult transition toward an open, democratic, free-market society.

Arrival and Accommodations
Your train will most likely arrive in **Hlavani** station, the biggest and most modern of the several depots in Prague. A number of accommodation service bureaus have opened in Prague recently, and the station has a ton of them. For a small fee, they'll book you into the hotel or private residence of your budgetary preference, starting at about $5/night. Arrive early though,

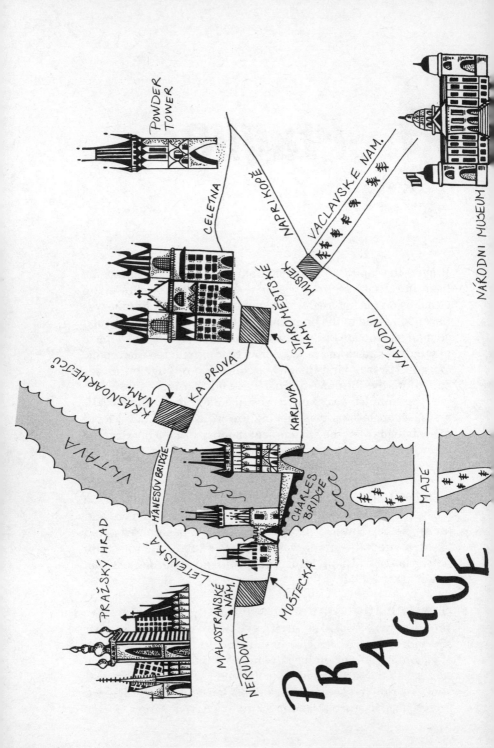

since most bureaus close by 7:30pm (4:30pm on Sundays). **VES-TA**, **ACE Travel Agency**, and **Natura** are among the more relia-ble agencies.

If you want to experience the pleasures of staying with a Czech family in a private home, you'll have an advantage over those who want a hotel room, because there's a severe short-age of hotel space in Prague. Plus, staying in a home will make your visit more interesting. When booking a room in a private home, make it clear you don't want to stay so far out from the city that you have to set your watch back one hour when you take the train to Prague each morning.

Though there are exceptions, it's best to have low expecta-tions when staying in private homes. Most of them are not so great by American standards. Although we've assumed throughout this book that you have the cultural sensitivity of Muslim fundamentalists, try to tone down the "Rah, rah, U.S.A. #1!" exuberance in Prague. The average Czech has a pretty good idea how his home compares to what you take for granted back in Ohio, so don't rub it in too much. Unless, of course, your host starts dumping on CNN or Burger King or Barbara Bush or our other cultural treasures, then feel free to give the little slob a piece of your mind.

If you arrive too late for help at the station, get on the subway in the direction of HAJE. It costs the grand total of four *koruny* (about 13 cents), and it's done on the honor system—with fre-quent checks by plain clothes inspectors. Despite our usual cavalier attitude about paying for public transportation, pay the fare and be a good citizen. There's no sense getting in trouble to save a few dimes.

The subway is quite impressive. Spotless, well-lit, and effi-cient, it was built for the Czechs by their friendly neighbors, the Soviets. If you thought the Soviets could produce only bad vodka and athletes addicted to steroids, you're in for quite a surprise. "Oh yeah, what about graffiti?" you ask. "I'll bet they don't have any cool graffiti on the walls." Well, you're right, they don't.

Get off the subway at the first stop on the line going towards HAJE. The stop you want is called **Muzeum**, the site of the Na-tional Museum. Climb the steps, and you'll find yourself at the top of the hill looking down the wide main drag of Prague,

known as **Vaclavske nam**. This was the venue of the mass pro-
tests that freed the Czechs from their Communist captors in
1989. Just below the Museum, there's a memorial to the defeat
of Communism, commemorating those who died in the 45-year
struggle. This may come as quite a shock to you Young Repub-
licans who fervently believe it was Ronald Reagan and George
Bush who crushed the Commies with their strong rhetoric.

Head down the street, past many of Prague's fancy hotels and
restaurants. There are lots of places here to change money, and
dozens of tourist and lodging services have appeared in the last
few years. But don't attempt to change money on the street with
anyone offering a better exchange rate. The *koruny* ("krown")
has been floating freely on the world market and is quite sta-
ble. The sleazes offering a better rate probably will give you
worthless Polish *zlotys*, which look a lot like *koruny* to a
newcomer.

What To See

Once you've dropped your stuff and slapped a new disk in your
camera, it's time to hit the town.

There are a number of spectacular sights in Prague, and it's
best to start at **Staromestske namesti**, the huge old town square
near the river, where you'll find the **Old Town Hall**, which has
a clock from the 15th century. Don't you wish your Swatch
would last as long? Actually, the clock is a bit of a dud. It's neat
to look at, but it doesn't do a whole helluva lot (sort of like Van-
na White).

However, it's nice to wander around the square. To attract
tourists, the Czechs have been spending a lot of money on
renovating Prague, so things are clean and polished. Also of
interest in the square, but probably still closed for repairs, is
the **Bethlehem Church**, built way back in 1391. To give you some
perspective, Christopher Columbus' father wasn't even a twin-
kle in his father's eye back then.

Several cafes in the square offer a chance for you to sit and
reflect on the significance of your Czech adventure so far.
Perhaps you could take the opportunity to write a postcard
home: "Dear Mom—Here I am in Prague, capital of Czechoslovakia. I am probably one of the first Americans to see the
city since it became free. Don't worry though, Mom—everything

is cool. There is even food here now, and beer, and t-shirts, and everything. . ."

The square sees a lot of action in the summer, and lots of new fashionable shops are claiming space around its perimeter. Near Staromestske nam., but closer to the river, is the remains of the old **Jewish Quarter** in Prague, including the oldest synagogue in Europe, between Parizska and Hrvitova. This area also holds the Nazi-built **State Museum of Judaism**, created by Hitler to show the "decadence" of Jewish culture. There's also an eerie Jewish graveyard, which contains thousands of gravestones, all piled atop each other. This whole area has a creepy, surreal feeling to it. From Staromestske nam., walk up the pedestrian street called Celetna to the **Powder Tower**, another pile of old rocks from the 15th century. Take a right under the archway, and you're on **Na Prikope**, a favorite pedestrian shopping street. Continue along Na Prikope to Mustek, at the intersection of the lower end of Vaclavske nam.

Shopping

You'll find the main shopping areas of Prague along the **Mustek** area and also down a street called **Narodni**. There are lots of cafes, shops, and bookstores in this area. It's well worth the time to look inside the decrepit **Maj**, one of the city's big department stores, located on Narodni. Basically, Maj is a pitiful version of K-Mart. Now, we've got nothing against K-Mart, and probably a lot of you have made some fine Blue Light Special purchases there. Well, Maj is to K-Mart what K-Mart is to Saks or Tiffany.

You may want to browse some of the bookstores. The Czechs are voracious readers and, although your level of Czech may not allow you to peruse the scintillating *Czech Dairy Industry Bill, Amended 1989*, there's often a good selection of art and souvenir books about the city. Several of these are in English, and you can pick them up for a few bucks.

Some of the older bookstores still stock titles published as part of cultural treaties between former socialist countries. But these books don't seem to be flying off the shelves. We bought a few copies off a big pile of dandy little *Czechoslovakian-Mongolian Phrase Books* one year, and darned if the pile hadn't gone down very much when we returned a year later. It's a shame, really. Imagine how impressed the babes would be if you had the contents of that little jewel mastered.

Speaking of language, Czech is rather peculiar and tough to master, because it minimizes vowels. To give you an idea, the Czech word for ice cream is zmrzlina. This probably has something to do with *Wheel of Fortune*, where you have to pay for vowels, but we're not sure.

More Things to See

Walk through the winding streets until you hit Karlova St., which takes you to the river and the lovely **Charles Bridge**. This pedestrians-only bridge spanning the Vltava is lined with statues dating from the 15th century. (Prague is so old you'll find yourself longing for something modern and tacky—a Goofy Golf or a wax museum, for example.) A favorite gathering place for tourists and Czechs alike, the Charles Bridge is especially lively at night, when you can find lots of young people gathered to play music and people-watch. You'll hear strains of Bob Dylan, Simon and Garfunkel, Neil Young, and other great Czech composers from small circles of the New Youth. It's worth lingering on the bridge for a while to view both sides of the river.

Across the river, the castle complex with the spires of the Cathedral of St. Vitus dominate the skyline. To the left, you'll see the strange sight of the American stars-and-stripes fluttering in the breeze. No, don't get your hopes up—it's not a VFW hall or a Ford dealership. The building is actually the summer residence of the American ambassador. Stop by later and ask if you can take a dip in his pool and maybe make a few phone calls.

Cross the bridge and pass under the tower on the castle-side of the bridge. This tower, the **Little Quarter Tower**, dates from— you guessed it—the 15th century, and for the princely sum of 20 cents, you can climb the steep wooden stairs and get a great view. This is your Tall Thing To Climb in Prague.

Go downstairs, and you'll emerge on a street called **Mostecka**, lined with interesting stores, including a "Columbian Cafe," which serves the only cup of coffee in the city that doesn't taste like it was brewed from kidney beans. Savor it.

After you pass the square called Malostranske nam, the street winds steeply, and, after much huffing and puffing, you'll come to the large complex of buildings that contains the **former roy-**

al palace. Part of the complex now houses the Czech President, and another part is an art gallery which we, of course, skipped. However, there's a decent **military museum** with lots of cool guy-stuff like machine guns, axes, and chunks of things that were the business ends of torture tools in less enlightened days. A portion of the museum is devoted to the "liberation" of Czechoslovakia by their good pals the Ruskies after WWII.

In the same area, the huge **Cathedral of St. Vitus** is worth a look. Don't be as impressed as the other ooohing and ahhing Japanese and Albanian tourists—it's actually a fake, built in the 19th century. You can even go inside and gawk at the tombs of ancient Czech kings if you want. We, however, thought we'd done our quota of tomb-gawking for one lifetime, so we blew it off.

While you're still up on the hill, you might want to check out a large **jewel collection** there, too. But you know, jewels aren't really interesting to look at unless you knew the people who owned them, like Elvis or Liberace or your great aunt who died a month ago and named you in her will. However, if you have the urge, it only costs a few cents to see the loot. One note of caution: In general, Europeans don't shower with the same ferocity and frequency as Americans, and the small jewel halls get lots of visitors. Suffice to say that the air can become a little, er, ripe—probably like your socks are right now.

Stumble back outside and spend a few moments gazing at the expanse of the city. It truly is one of the most beautiful sights in Europe. You can count a hundred church spires in every direction. (Well, maybe not *exactly* a hundred, but we didn't want to spoil the mood by writing "a whole shitload of church spires . . .")

Where To Eat

By now, you've no doubt discovered that all this *gittin' culchure* sure can work up a powerful appetite. So, let's try to find a Czech restaurant.

No sweat, you think. We'll just cruise down the block and choose one. Not so fast, bub—remember, all restaurants and shops were run by the iron fist of the state only a few years ago. Many restaurants are still accustomed to seating only groups of 100 or more at a time and serving them a fixed menu. Slogans like "The customer always comes first" and "Quality is Job 1" haven't yet caught on in many of the traditional Czech restaurants.

Assuming you've found a restaurant that's open, just walk in and seat yourself at any empty seat. It's rare to get a table to yourself, and even if you do, the next folks who walk in will join you. Actually, it's a good way to meet people. In most cases, people will make an effort to talk to you, even if the conversation involves only griping about the bad service.

The **Automat Koruna**, a snack bar/take-out on the corner of Na Prikope and Vaclavske nam, is a lifesaver in Prague, with outrageously low prices. It serves many kinds of food, including open-faced sandwiches, sausages, etc., and it even has pastries of some sort. And let's not forget the beer. The Automat is always packed at lunchtime, but if you get there early, you can at least find a place to stand. It's also open early enough for breakfast, when the Czechs go for a kind of doughnut that's not exactly Dunkin' quality and doesn't come in Frosted Chocolate Kiwi Creme-Filled flavors, but it's still pretty tasty. They also serve weak, milky, hot chocolate with powerful laxative properties.

The best places to look for meals are **vinarny**, which serve cheap food, decent wine, and often excellent beer. The prices are astonishingly low. On a recent trip, we never spent more than $12 for five-course meals—including drinks—for two people. And we certainly did not skimp on the drinks. Our favorite place to eat is **U. Kalicha** at Na bojisti 12. Their goulash is the best in Prague, and they serve Pilsner Urquell on tap. To get there, get off at metro stop Pavlova (line C) and walk a short way down Vitezneho unora. Na bojisti is a side street on the right. You can also walk there from the National Museum, but you must get there before 8:00pm or you'll get shut out. A good *vinarna* in the lesser town (over the Charles Bridge) is **Mararska Vinarna** at Malostranske nam 2. Nearby, **U. Patrona** at Drazickeho namesti 4 is a bit more quaint. **Klasterni Vinarna** (Narodni 8) offers wine from Moravia and Nitra, plus an extensive menu. The restaurant at **Hotel Pariz** at u. Obecniho Domu 1 was also okay, but neither we, nor our publisher, nor our children, nor our children's children accept any liability. . .

Drinking

Czechoslovakia produces great beer, and we enthusiastically explored this aspect of Czech life. Most of you need no introduction to **Pilsner Urquell**, which, together with **Budvar**, is available in the U.S. Budvar, of course, is the precursor to a famous American beer. Can you guess which one? The only difference between Budvar and Budweiser is that Budvar actually has a taste.

Nearly 120 breweries operate in Czechoslovakia, and thanks to a strange distribution system, only certain pubs sell each variety of beer. As a result, finding a particular beer can be tough. Some of the best beers to hunt for include *Zoloty Bazant* (Golden Pheasant), *Flekouske Pivo* (Fleks Beer), and *Staropramen* (The Old Well).

Only three bars in Prague serve *Velkopopovicky Kozl* (Old Billy Goat), arguably the best beer in the country. The only convenient place to get it is a bar called **U Betlemske Kaple** at Betlemske nam 1 in Prague. It's a famous landmark, so you should be able to find it easily. Their food tastes a lot like old billy goats, but the beer compensates.

Another pleasant drinking spot is near the **Wallenstein Gardens** (the palace north of Wenceslaus Square). The gardens themselves are pretty, but you can't do a little necking on the grass because stern-faced guards are everywhere. Just outside the walls (actually, set in the walls) is the famous **St. Thomas Restaurant**, which serves St. Thomas beer (*Svaty Tomas*)— excellent stuff, and the food is nearly edible, too. The restaurant, set deep inside a vaulted cellar, even has decent service and a beer hall atmosphere at times. The street address is Letenska 12.

A final drinking spot is **U Bonaparta** on Nerudova 29, about half way up the winding street you climbed to get to the castle. Though their food would not win any awards at a Denny's Taste-Alike Cook-off, it's a convenient rest stop and has an interesting stream of customers. Don't even *think* about using the bathrooms.

Nightlife

For the most part, nightlife in Prague consists of walking around the city hoping your dinner stays down, then maybe a visit to a jazz club later in the evening. Most of the city's attractions are lit at night, and while crime is becoming more of a problem than it was in the police-state days, you can feel fairly safe if you take the usual precautions.

A visit to the **Charles Bridge** at night is a must. As it grows late, the bridge fills with young people clustered in groups and, as a Czech friend put it, "singing songs of peace and protest." It's all pretty cute, though it's strange to hear a young Czech belting out old chestnuts like *Blowin' in the Wind* while surrounded by his peers, who wonder what the hell this business of "antlers glowing in the wind" is all about. You can also find jewelers and artists selling their wares on the bridge, and you can pick up some nice little mementos for a few bucks.

Many restaurants become nightclubs after a certain hour, and several offer jazz. It's merely a matter of trying to spot the entrances, since the doorways are usually dark and have only the shadowy figure of the doorman to tell you there's something of interest inside. Expect to pay a few bucks to get in, and drinks will be quite expensive by Czech standards. However, if you're accustomed to big city prices from the States, you'll think you've died and gone to heaven.

Czechs, like all Europeans, love jazz and have produced their share of great musicians, none of whom come to mind right now. It's easy to meet local artists at these clubs during their breaks, especially if you remember to be a little sensitive and don't start talking about the 39 incredible concerts you heard at Ronnie Scott's during your junior year in London. Since Czechs don't get to travel much, this would be like telling a starving Ethiopian your mom's recipe for fudge brownies.

The best places to find good jazz in Prague vary from year to year, but start by checking the restaurants along Vaclavske nam. **Foyer Supraclub** at Opletalova 5 (a block from Vaclavske nam) offers live jazz Friday through Sunday beginning at 9:00pm. **Press Jazz Club** (Parizska 9, upstairs) is open Monday through Saturday from 9:00pm-2:00am.

Budapest

Hungary, a former Communist nation, is a fascinating country to visit for a day or so. Budapest, its beautiful, lively capital, spans both sides of the famous Danube River. Except for their relentless bureaucracy, Hungarians were always less than enthusiastic Communists. Indeed, Hungarians are now proving to be passionate capitalists, with a willingness to hustle tourists that would awe any used Buick salesman back home.

Arrival and Lodging

Americans and Europeans no longer need a visa to enter Hungary, and the Eurailpass is now valid there. The most convenient route to Hungary is by direct train from Vienna. In fact, if you make it to Vienna, you really should take at least a day trip to Budapest. It's only about three hours by train.

The arrival in Budapest is a spectacular sight: the train swoops around a bend, and, in the distance, you can see the Danube bisecting the city. Your train from Vienna will arrive in either **Déli Station** or **Keleti Station**, both of which have an Old World, *Murder on the Orient Express* look about them. Get off the train and go straight to the **IBUSZ** office in the station or to **Budapest Tourist** outside. The latter lists fewer private rooms, but it's staffed with friendly people who'll do anything to help. Budapest Tourist is an especially welcome alternative if the IBUSZ line stretches all the way back to the border.

By far the most interesting lodging option in Budapest is a private house. You may have some odd experiences, but it's the best way to get a feeling for the way ordinary people live in this part of the Communist legacy. Hold out for a place near the city. That is, don't listen to the instructions for getting off bus

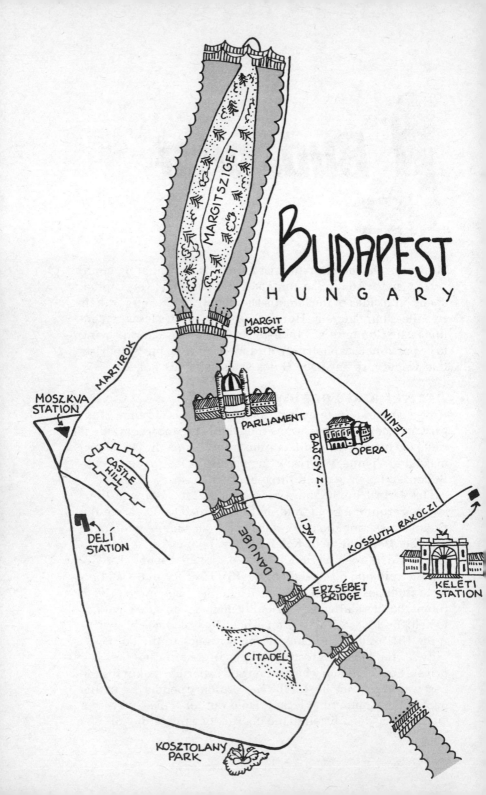

#478, taking the #965 for 15 stops, then transferring at the Revolutionary Bulldozer Factory #31. There are private rooms near the center of the city, and you can get one if you're a little stubborn. But don't expect a split-level, landscaped home with a three-car garage and a cute guest room with a private bath. Chances are, the family will sleep in the living room, while you get to sleep in *their* room. The one bathroom may also serve as a laundry room, closet, pantry, art studio, and tool room—sort of like a New York co-op. Check your expectations at the door, please.

If you can't take the risk and absolutely need a bathroom of your own, the **Hotel Ifjusag** at 1024 Zivatar u. (phone 135-3331) is a no-frills motel (with a real Ho-Jo look about it), conveniently located and clean, for about $30, including breakfast. It even has a disco in the basement, where you can dance the night away with some Albanian tourists (world-renowned party animals, those Albanians). Take a taxi from the Moskwa metro station. At the rock-bottom end but with an interesting location, the **Hotel Citadella** on Gellért Hill (phone 166-5794) has rooms for under $10.

Orientation

Basically, Budapest consists of two districts on opposite sides of the Danube. **Buda** (and also a district known as **Obuda**) is on the left bank, and **Pest**, the old district, is on the right. Most of the natives live in neither, but rather way out in the boonies in huge, ugly apartment buildings. We stayed with a family out there on one of our visits, and we had to leave a trail of bread crumbs from the apartment to the bus stop so we could find our way back at night.

Though you don't want to stay out there, a bus trip to the 'burbs is educational—you'll get a glimpse of how the Communists felt people should live in a workers' paradise. Our impression: the middle class lived at the same level as the poor people in our housing projects. There is one big difference, though. Our housing projects get cable TV.

Public transportation is dirt cheap in Budapest. A bus ride costs about a dime, and the subway and tram cost even less. As we advise in the chapter on Prague, you may as well pay for your transportation in Budapest, since the fare is so cheap and the consequences of being caught may be unpleasant.

You can buy a 24-hour pass for about 50 cents, so go ahead and splurge. But you can't buy the passes on the buses or the trams. You have to get them at newspaper stands, tobacco shops, or subway stops. Once you board a bus or train, validate your pass by sticking it into the machine provided for the purpose.

Be warned: almost everyone uses the buses and trams to go to and from work. Therefore, in the interest of keeping your various body parts from being squashed, avoid riding public transportation during anything approaching rush hour.

Traffic jams are a universal problem. Cars, as in all countries, are becoming the most visible expression of status in Budapest, but you'll recognize few models. The most common is an old East German beauty called a Trout (in translation). It's the only auto whose engine is built from old sewing machines, and its exhaust system can produce more fumes in ten minutes than a commune of vegetarians after a bean supper. Most taxis are Trouts, so be sure to enjoy the stylish handling as your cabby pushes on the gearshift with both feet to coax it into third. And—*whoa!*—is that rich Corinthian leather? Nah, it's cheap Yugoslavian vinyl.

Money

The unit of currency in Hungary is the *forint*. There are about 75 *forints* to the dollar, so think of a *forint* as a big penny.

As in Czechoslovakia, there is no advantage to changing money with people who approach you on the street.

Drugs

Former Soviet bloc countries take a hard line on drugs of any kind, including pot. If you're stupid enough to bring dope into either Czechoslovakia or Hungary, you deserve to make license plates for Trouts for a long, long time. So chew gum or something for a few days and enjoy the rare sensation of having your pupils at their natural size for the first time in five years.

Things To See

Once you've found a room in a private house, it's off on your sightseeing trip around the city. First, check out the map we've provided.

Buda, on the left bank of the river, is very hilly and offers some great views of the city. The first landmark to make for is the **Fisherman's Bastion**, an old castle (come to think of it, it would be more surprising if it were a supermarket) that's one of the principal landmarks of Budapest. You can get there by subway: Get off at the Moskwa or Déli Station stop, and it's an easy walk from there, up about 400 steep steps. A more interesting way up is the **cog railway**, which you catch from the front of the Hotel Budapest, along Szilagyi Erzébet fasor.

If churches are your thing (and they are *not* ours), then you should check out the **Mátyás templom**, behind the castle. Watch out for earnest *Let's Go*'ers searching for the spot where Queen Maria Theresa stubbed her toe in 1740. They'll also be practicing the three lines of Hungarian they memorized at the youth hostel last night.

In the same area, the **National Gallery** may be worth a look if you're not already burned out by all the eager scholarship you witnessed at the Mátyás. Don't expect to see any Andy Warhol's there, but if busty Holy Virgins and fat babies make your wheels squeal, then it's the museum for you.

After all this excitement, head down the hill and back across the river to **Roosevelt Square**, located in one of the busier parts of town, just across the Széchényi lánc híd (Chain Bridge) in Pest. There are a number of pretty cafes and coffee shops in this area, where you can savor bad Hungarian coffee and some of the little cream cakes the natives wolf down in great numbers. It's funny: all the little cakes, while different in appearance, taste just about the same. This fact led us to speculate that all baked goods in the city are produced at the Cream Cake, Doughnut, and Cannoli Factory #4, somewhere on the outskirts of town.

Roosevelt Square has a pedestrian mall that parallels the river on Váci utca. Note the anxious youth cruising at a brisk pace with their boom boxes perched on their shoulders. Many cafes, tourist stores, and shops line the way, and the proprietors are happy to help you part with your *forints*.

Turn left when you reach Kossuth Rakoczi (a major shopping street), stroll north along the banks of the Danube (known to the natives as the *Duna*), and you'll come to the impressive **Houses of Parliament** on Kossuth Square overlooking the river.

We tried to amble in to see if Hungarian congressmen spend their time on the same weighty matters that occupy our legislators. (E.g., Should the first week in August be National Wig Week or National Be Kind to Your Appliances Week?) Unfortunately, the soldier with the rifle at the door didn't feel we would benefit from the experience, so we never did learn if July 17th was declared National Blind Beekeepers' Day.

Walk in the opposite direction from the Houses of Parliament, stay by the river, cut inland a bit, and you'll find the **National Museum** at 14-16 Museum Square. It boasts a little of everything, and its jewel collection is particularly mediocre. It's usually crowded, mostly with Hungarians and an occasional busload of American tourists. If you want to take the metro to this museum, get off at the Kalvin stop.

From the river near the museum, you can gaze across at the huge Soviet **Liberation Memorial** on the other side. This is your Tall Thing To Climb in Budapest, so take a tram over the Szabadság híd (híd means "bridge") and get off at the first stop. Transfer to the #27 bus, which will take you all the way up to the Citadella, where you can pay a few *forints* to climb a few more yards and experience the view. You can see for miles and miles, but it isn't the most impressive skyline you'll ever see. The city sprawls aimlessly, and there are no high rises to provide perspective. The best views of Budapest are from below, along the bridges and the banks of the Danube.

Eating

Hungary, of course, is famous for *goulash*, and you can get it just about anywhere. Paprika, a favorite spice, is used liberally in just about any meat dish you order. You can get wild boar in some restaurants, but it sounds more exotic than it tastes, unless the idea of globs of fat clinging to pieces of stringy dark meat activates your salivary glands.

Our favorite restaurant in Budapest is the **Park Étterem** in Kosztolányi Park. Go over the Petöfi híd into Buda, turn right down Karinthy Fr. St., and the park will be on your left. Bus #7 from Rakoczi St. will take you there, too. The restaurant has lots of outdoor seats on a terrace overlooking a pond framed in weeping willows, with the city skyline as a backdrop. The food is superb and cheap. You can get a full meal—goulash, entrée, vegetables, dessert, and a few beers—for about $7.00. And you can discuss the plight of the proletariat while eating like a king or queen.

Shopping

Some of the best sights in Eastern European countries are the downtown department stores. The big ones—**Corvin**, **Csillag**, **Florian**, **Lotto**, and **Verseny**—are concentrated along Kozzuth, Rakoczi, and Lenin Avenues. They're open until 6:00pm on weekdays and 5:00pm on Saturdays. Explore one of these stores and you've explored 'em all. Be sure to check out the bogus sports teams on the sweatshirts—Boston National Football League, Michigan State Lions—and the nonsense English slogans on sportswear. We wrote some down to preserve the precise wording: "Sport Fishing Deep See Fishing Senior," "Miami I am BIG BOSS USA," "Member Leader Club," and the ever-fashionable "Mild Airport Miss VP Club." Awesome gifts.

The selections at the cosmetics counter might explain why Eastern European women have a better record in weightlifting contests than beauty pageants. The toothpaste, toilet paper, perfume, and condoms all share the same shelf. The good news is, condoms are a steal at a dime each.

St. Margit's Island

Margitsziget (St. Margit's Island), located north of the Parliament buildings in the middle of the Danube, is a pleasant place to spend the evening after dinner. It's sort of a city park, where citizens spend their afternoons and evenings strolling, roller-skating, listening to music, or eating and drinking at the restaurants and outdoor cafes spread among the trees.

It's also popular with Tour Bus Brigades from countries so obscure that even the Communists never bothered them much. While you're downing another Pilsner Urquell, look for roaming herds of huge peasant women in black dresses and babushkas, hunched over their canes, moving slowly across the park. Those thin, frail men behind them are their husbands, talking about the winter wheat harvest of '49.

Since most young Hungarians live at home and have no privacy for, er, amorous activities, they use the island for their rendezvous. In fact, like walking through a cow pasture, you'll need to be careful where you step on St. Margit's. You're likely to turn a corner and find Endré and Mädgy engaged in gymnastics that may convince you Hungary has indeed become a liberal country.

Concerts are a common feature on the island during the summer, and most of them are free. It's also very pleasant to sit at an outdoor cafe and sip good Hungarian wine. If this is the wreckage of Marxism, you'll say to yourself, it ain't all that bad.

In the afternoon, you can rent "bicycles" on the island. They resemble three-wheeled rickshaws with pedals, and they're expensive (by Hungarian standards): $2.00 per half-hour. The rental shop is across from the **Thermal Hotel** on the northern part of the island, where you can get a Turkish bath and massage for about $4.00.

Alongside and associated with the hotel, a variety of outdoor cafes offer live jazz on Sundays. The food isn't bad either, but let's leave it at that. For about $10 for a full meal (including drinks), you can sit at outdoor tables with real tablecloths. We tried a place called **The Grill Terrace**, which advertised food "grilled alongside your table." The truth is, they wheel out a gas grill and fry your turkey breast in the same fat used for the previous customer's pork fillets. So much for the *haute cuisine* of Hungary.

At night, discos on the island roar their insipid beat and play the latest video hits imported from—Guess where? Yes, you guessed.—MTV.

Lake Balaton

If you happen to have a few free days and are tired of Budapest, consider a side-trip to **Lake Balaton**, the largest lake in Hungary and a favorite vacation spot for Central Europeans. You can reach the lake by train from Budapest, but note that the trains to the lake leave from **Déli pu.**, in Buda on Krisztina St. It costs only a few bucks to ride to the lake, but the trains are painfully slow, so be sure to bring something interesting and long—*The Collected Works of Thomas Jefferson* springs to mind—to read.

The best town on the lake is called **Siófok**. Get off the train there and head for your favorite IBUSZ office at Fö u. 174. Actually, this branch of IBUSZ is the only one we found to be

genuinely pleasant and helpful. Lots of ugly concrete hotels line
the lakeside, and they're not worth the money. Instead, go for
the private room option, which, in many cases, will get you a
small apartment built onto someone's house, specifically to rent
to tourists.

Once you've established base camp, wander down to the lake.
If you enjoy water sports, you'll have a great time. They have
power boats, row boats, and windsurfers for rent, and prices
are ridiculously cheap. Passenger boats tour the lake and run
to the small, pretty peninsula called **Tihany**.

Siófok comes alive at night, particularly on the main drag
where all the restaurants are. Most serve the specialty of the
region: fresh pike from the lake. It tastes as good as a pin cushion
soaked in the juice from a can of tuna fish.

**The most interesting thing about Siófok is the fact that the
main language is German, and Lake Balaton is a popular
meeting place for Germans. They come here to vacation mainly because it's so cheap and the beer is as good as back home.**

The discos themselves are a real blast. Most have hostesses
dressed like Barbie dolls, serving drinks at outrageous (by Hungarian standards) prices, as Western hits from 1985 blare over
a speaker system that's barely adequate for a VW Rabbit.

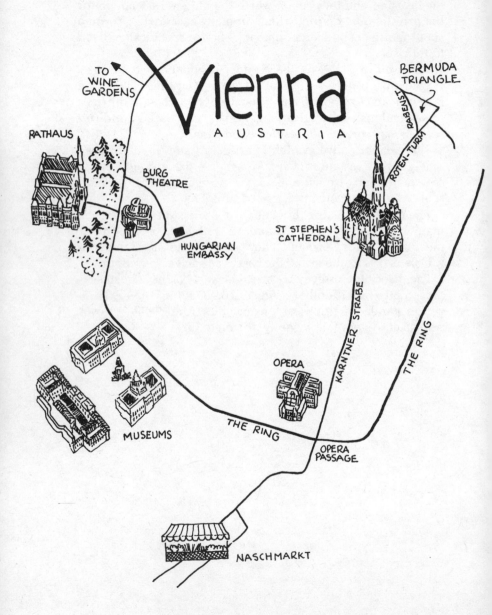

Vienna

Mozart called Vienna home. So did Brahms, Beethoven, Chopin, Dvorak, Haydn, Liszt, Strauss, Wagner, The Vienna Choir Boys, the Vienna Sausage Boys, the Pet Shop Boys, Lennon, McCartney, and Wings. You Psych majors will be psyched to learn that Sigmund Freud went through his anal fixation stage in Vienna. And how many of you History majors knew that young Adolph Hitler failed miserably painting postcards in Vienna before starting a career in public speaking and genocide?

You see, Vienna is much more than sausages and pastries. In fact, Vienna could serve as the introduction to art and culture that will inspire your talents—or expose your lack of them. But first, a little geography:

Orientation

Vienna is in Austria, a country that is, admittedly, not one of your headline-grabbing, economic powerhouses. It's probably best known today for skiing and *The Sound of Music*. The Austrians don't even have their own language, so don't waste time looking for an *Austrian Living Language Cassette Course*. Speak English, speak German, or use body language.

Austria is bordered to the east by Hungary, to the north by Czechoslovakia, and to the south by Yugoslavia—all former communist countries in varying degrees of turmoil. You will therefore be in a peninsula of sanity and stability. This should give you a great feeling of risk and danger.

If you make it as far as Vienna, definitely consider a visit to Budapest, Hungary. It's only a few hours away by train, and it's easy to get there and back (see Budapest chapter for more details).

The train ride across Austria to Vienna is quite beautiful, so take a day train if possible. You'll see spectacular mountains, quaint chalets, and alpine villages modeled after Vail, Colorado. Be sure to get a compartment with clean windows, and put high-speed film in your camera.

You'll likely arrive in the **Westbahnhof** if you're coming from Germany, or the **Sudbahnhof** if you're coming from Italy. Both of these stations are large and efficiently arranged. Get some *Austrian shillings* (AS), which go for about 13 to the dollar. If you're arriving from Italy, the currency transition is easy, because a *shilling* is like *lire* with the zeros lopped-off.

Tourist offices in both train stations (open until 10:00pm in Sudbahnhof, 'til 11:00pm in Westbahnhof) offer room-finding services, maps, and excellent pamphlets. Ask for a brochure called *Vienna Live*, which lists accommodations, restaurants, bars, discos, coffeehouses, and other essential stuff, all in English. Also, *Falter*, a weekly culture magazine, discusses current concerts, movies, etc.

If the tourist office in the train station is too crowded because trains from Rome, Munich, and a town you've never heard of all arrived at the same time, you can visit the offices at Opernpassage or the Rathaus. These are both conveniently off the **Ring**, the boulevard that defines the central area of Vienna.

For lodging, try to stay close to the Ring. There are numerous *pensions* that are somewhat evenly dispersed, but the area behind the **Rathaus**, close to the University, is a great place to start. The Rathaus, the "new" city hall, is a landmark that's hard to miss. If you choose not to use the tourist office room-finding service, at least ask them for their listing of hotels. They've got an excellent guide that provides a map, a table of services, prices, phone numbers, etc. Here are a few of our suggestions:

Pension Wild, at 8 Lange Gasse 10 (phone 43-51-74), is friendly and inexpensive, but call ahead because it's popular. **Pension Auer** at Lazarettgasse 3 (phone 43-21-21), next to the hospital, has rooms for $20-$30. **Pension Adria** on Wickenburggasse 23 (phone 42-02-38) is behind the Rathaus and has large rooms with elaborate, tacky furnishings. Some of the rooms even have a TV and an "Orgasmitron"-like shower, right next to the couch, for $29 single, $45 double. **Pension Edelweiss**, Lange Gasse 61, also behind the Rathaus, has 20 rooms with private baths from $36-$55.

Next, find your way to a tram going toward the Ring. You can buy tram tickets from a machine in the station lobby, but these are expensive on a per-trip basis ($1.50 each, or $5.00 for a book of five). You can buy a three-day pass for $7.00, good on all trams, buses, and the subway. From the Sudbahnhof, take the D tram; from the Westbahnhof, take the #52 or #58 tram and transfer to the D tram on the Ring.

If you plan to go to Budapest from Vienna, check with the **Hungarian Embassy** at 1 Bankgasse 4-6 (phone 533-2631), behind the Burg Theater. Go to the Burg Theater stop on The Ring where Dr. Karl Renner-Ring turns into Dr. Karl Lueger-Ring. The Embassy is open only on weekdays and closes early in the day.

History

As you travel through the streets of Vienna, you'll see a lot of enormous buildings and statues, particularly as you wind along the Ring. These monstrosities are from the time when Vienna was the capital of a great empire that encompassed Austria, some of modern Hungary, and bits and pieces of its other neighbors. The **Habsburgs** ruled this empire, and their ideas for urban renewal projects are the palaces you now see.

That concludes the historical background portion of our chapter. If you need to know more, get a copy of *Vienna from A to Z: A Guide to Sightseeing on Your Own* at the tourist office. It lists over 250 buildings, museums, monuments, and other mildly interesting stuff. With this booklet in hand, you'll be able to uncover such treasures as the **Undertaker's Museum** at Goldeggasse 19, or the 2.4 million places Beethoven inhabited. (Like George Washington, Ludwig was a ramblin' kind of guy.)

The Danube River

Many guidebooks describe Vienna as being "nestled" on the **Danube River**. This may be true, in the same sense that New York City is nestled next to New Jersey.

You'll never really see the Danube if you're in Vienna for a short visit, because its banks are pretty far from the central area. We don't know why anyone would want to see it anyway. The "blue Danube" is brown, and it looks like any other river in an industrial plain. So forget the Danube.

Cultural Activities

Other things guidebooks will insist you do, besides the usual museum and church thing, is to visit an opera, the Vienna Choir Boys, and the Spanish Riding School. Our advice—well, you guessed it, didn't you?—don't waste your time.

As for the **opera**, do you have a suit and dress shoes in your dufflebag? You'd be lucky to have clean socks, probably. You can't go to an opera in a Hofbräuhaus t-shirt.

Second, the **Vienna Choir Boys**. Who wants to hear a bunch of boys, stripped of their masculinity, sing in voices that make Tiny Tim seem macho? Plus, they don't take requests from the audience—not even for *Stairway to Heaven*.

Third, the **Spanish Riding School**. Look, if you want to see horses, go to a circus. You don't have to spend the airfare to Europe to see a bunch of over-groomed animals cared for by prissy short guys.

Food

Remember the awful comments we made about the German passion for processed meats? They're true for Austrian food, too.

If you're a vegetarian, pack a picnic, and the best place to go is the **Naschmarkt**, the biggest produce market in Vienna. You'll find it between Linke Wienzeile and Rechte Wienzeile (get off the tram or U-Bahn at Karlsplatz). Also, a great vegetarian restaurant in a quiet garden setting is **Gasthaus Wrenkh** at Hollergasse 9. They have limited days and hours, so call ahead (phone 83-41-28).

For those of you studly enough to handle the traditional Viennese meal of bread, meat, and beer, go to a *beisl*, which is to Vienna what pubs are to London and Dublin. They're best visited at midday, when the crust has not yet formed on the fat covering the meat dishes.

You have to be tough to eat in a *beisl*, and you can't eat there without a draft or two from the bar. All you sushi and white-winers, stick close to the Hilton. Vegetarians who wish to experience a *beisl* should proceed with caution and a menu translation book in hand. Don't try to impress your friends with your limited knowledge of German, like Robin:

Robin: "Sherri, I'll order something from the menu."

Sherri: "How will you know what you're ordering? It's all in Austrian."

Robin: "C'mon, Sher, I took German I back at Oregon State, remember? I'm more of an international person than you think. And don't worry, I'll make sure it's all vegetarian." *(She calls a waiter over.)* "Waiter, I'd like to eatten *(points to menu)* some *hirn,* two orders of *gemischter aufschnitt*— that's salad, right? *(the waiter nods indifferently as he stares down Robin's t-shirt)*—and some *eisbein* for dessert."

Waiter: "*Alles?*"

Robin: "No, thank you. We'll have some burgundy."

Sherri: "I'm impressed. What did you order for dessert?"

Robin: "*Eisbein*—it's ice cream!"

(Twenty minutes later the waiter brings a plate of brains served on a bed of lettuce, an assortment of cold cuts, including head cheese and liverwurst, and some pig's kidneys for dessert.)

Robin: "Well, uh, there's lettuce and parsley we can share. How about some bread?" *(Sherri ralphs into her silk scarf.)*

One *beisl* that has a menu in three languages and is near the university is **Zur Weinperle** at Alserbachstrasse 2 (phone 34-32-52). It's open weekdays until 9:30pm and 'til 2:30pm on Saturday. A hearty, satisfying lunch costs about $5.00. **Zur Stadt Paris**, at Josefstadter Strasse 4 (phone 42-14-67), is open Saturday through Wednesday until midnight, and it's a hip place. **Gasthaus Reinthaler**, an inexpensive alternative at Gluckgasse 5 (phone 52-33-66), is open weekdays until 10:00pm, Fridays until 4:00pm. Behind St. Stephan's Church is **Dombeisl** at Schulerstrasse 4, on the corner of Domgasse. It's a favorite place of the horse-taxi drivers, who wear bowler caps on their heads, horse dung on their boots, and goulash on their chins.

If you think Vienna is as far east as you'll ever go and therefore the Chinese food *must* be fresher there because it's closer to China, then try **Guo Ji** at Getreidemarkt 11 or **Mondial** at Berggasse 20.

There's also decent food at the **Tunnel**, Florianigasse 39 (see Nightlife, below), a few blocks from the Rathaus. And you'll pass several Italian restaurants on Florianigasse, most with reasonable prices and atmosphere. It may be noteworthy to some that there are no fewer than seven McDonald's in Vienna—America's contribution to international cuisine.

You can also eat at *Heurigen* ("wine taverns" — see below), where there is pork, cheese, and bread aplenty.

Shopping

Shopping is out of the question in Vienna because of the ridiculously high value added tax (VAT)—up to 30% on most stuff. A **flea market** operates at the southern end of the Naschmarkt every Saturday from 8:00am to 6:00pm. There, free enterprise, laissez faire, and supply-side economics occur unmolested from the stifling iron fist of government. Otherwise, save your credit line for places where you can get more bang for the buck.

For window shopping (but how are you going to carry windows with you the rest of your trip?), **Karntner** is the strasse. Start at Opernpassage and work your way to Stephansplatz, sort of the center of things. There's a big old church there, so you'll know when you've arrived.

Karntnerstrasse is a pedestrians-only shopping street with the usual flurry of activity. Vienna, being a city of great musical heritage, has better street performers than most cities. You may see chamber orchestras playing concertos with their instrument cases open for cash. You'll probably even hear some street opera, so don't be alarmed if you walk around a corner and it sounds like there's a rape in progress. The minstrels from Ecuador, playing their unique form of music, are popular throughout European cities, but the ones in Vienna are the best. It's only a matter of time before they hit America and take the streets by storm—the next big musical invasion, and *you* saw them first!

Things To Do

Vienna has miles of bike paths, and you can rent a bike for about $3.00 an hour from several shops. **Franz Josefs-Kai der Salztorbrucke**, on the right bank of the Danube Canal, is one such place.

For you mansion maniacs, there's **Schloss Schonbrunn** (Schonbrunn Palace), an extravagant estate once home to Maria Theresa. Among its guests were Mozart, who played a concerto for a luncheon, and John Kennedy and Nikita Kruschev, who didn't. The tour takes you through room after room after room, usually with some cute gimmick for each. We bailed out after about ten. There's a zoo on the grounds, too, but it's one of those old, depressing kind where you just want to shoot the animals to put them out of their misery.

Donauinsel (Danube Island), between the real Danube and the fake Danube, is a recreational area with bikes and boats for rent. And if you miss the Riviera, there are nude beaches there, too. Take U-Bahn #1 to get to the island.

The **Prater**, a large park with an old-world amusement park, is a nice place to stroll or picnic. Some outdoor *beisls* there will keep your thirst quenched.

Coffeehouses

Coffeehouses, a cultural institution in Vienna, serve as the haunts of writers, literati, artists, journalists, philosophers, political activists, political inactivists, business people, losers, winners, middle-class, upper-class, upper-middle-class, and tourists hoping to meet writers, literati, artists, journalists, etc. . . . The coffeehouses vary from dives to class establishments where waiters serve coffee in silver carafes on silver trays. Typically, they serve a glass of water alongside the coffee to create the image of a service-oriented atmosphere.

For those of you whose only container for coffee is a dashboard-mounted cup from Dunkin' Donuts, this may seem a little excessive. The coffee resembles cappuccino, with your choice of steamed (*melange*) or condensed (*brauner*) milk. This may be more of a challenge than the "reg'lar or decaf, hon?" choice at the 76 Auto/Truck Family Restaurant just off I-80.

The coffeehouses usually provide newspapers, but unless you read German, you'll have to stare at the walls. Similarly, don't get all caught up in the idea of meeting some intellectual or getting involved in a lively discussion about South Africa or nuclear missiles or something. Unless you speak fluent German, you'll never know if the group at the next table is comparing George Bush to Hitler or *Rocky III* to *Rocky IV*. So, sorry to let you down, but you're better off writing in your journal or filling out those damn postcards.

Two coffeehouses we enjoyed are **Cafe Hawelka** at Dorotheergasse 6 (open until 2:00am Wednesday through Sunday) and **Cafe Museum** at Friedrichstrasse 6, which has chess tables, serves breakfast, and stays open until 11:00pm every day.

When the coffee really starts coursing through your blood and there's absolutely no chance of sleep, try the few coffeehouses that pride themselves on keeping late hours. And we needn't tell you what sort of crowd *that* draws. Remember those nights after the best frat party ever, when you just couldn't go back to your dorm, so you headed for the local diner for coffee and grilled food? **Beatrixstuberl**, at Ungargasse 8, could revive those memories. They keep very standard hours: 6:00pm-2:00am and 4:00am-8:00am.

So what do you do between 2:00am and 4:00am? Simple. Go to **Cafe Kammerspiele** at Rotenturmstrasse 25. It's open 'round the clock.

Nightlife

Begin at least one night of your stay in Vienna with a visit to a *Heurigen* (wine tavern), usually in the suburbs but accessible nonetheless. Apparently, some law stipulates that only a wine tavern that grows its grapes entirely on its own land within the surrounding rural districts may call itself a *Heurigen*. A *Heurigen* can be identified by a sprig of pine hung above the door, akin to a neon Budweiser sign but a lot more rustic.

However, you won't need a sprig of pine to find your way. Simply follow the hordes of tourists lurching from their buses. The **Grinzing** area, with over 20 *Heurigen*, is the most popular with the bus brigades, so it's usually the most lively. Take the #38 from the Ring to the last stop, and you won't miss a thing.

If you desire a more peaceful setting, take the D tram from the Ring to the end (**Nussdorf**) or to the next-to-last stop at **Heiligenstadt**. There are about 18 *Heurigen* in this area. Some offer "live music," but unless you think an old man playing an accordion about three inches from your face or yet another decrepit oompah band playing the same tired tunes you heard at the Hofbräuhaus qualify as "live," don't get your hopes up.

The wine, usually served in mugs (we suppose this is a tradition or something) is not the world's best, and we're told it's often a mixture of several varieties. Let's face it: a *Heurigen* is a place to drink and get drunk. It must be quite a thrill to ride a tour bus after a night at a *Heurigen*, winding along the narrow roads with a bunch of geezers who hadn't had that much booze since they wuz SAE's at Ole Miss in the '40s. Yee hah.

After the *Heurigen*, head back into town for some honest live music and city life. The best places to head, in order, are the **Bermuda Dreieck** (Bermuda Triangle) area at Seitenstettengasse and Rabensteig, the area around **Schonlaterngasse** and **Backerstrasse**, and behind the Rathaus along **Florianigasse**.

The Bermuda Triangle is full of bars, restaurants, and shops. **Alt Wien** (Backerstrasse 9) is worth checking out, as is **Krah Krah** at Rabensteig 8. Just a few doors away is **Roter Engel**, which usually features two live bands a night, with anything from folk to jazz. Listen to the music seeping out the door before you decide to go in. **Kitsch and Bitter Biergartl** is a crowded place with a good old singles-bar, pick-up feel about it. There are lots of art photographs of nudes on the walls to get you in the proper frame of mind.

A few blocks away, Schonlaterngasse, the old University area, has quieter restaurants and folksy bars. **Wunderbar**, at Schonlaterngasse 8 is a cool place, and **Die Bar** at Sonnenfelsgasse 9 is open to 4:00am daily. For eating, **Pizzeria La Lantern** is a good place to starch down and drink up, and you'll be surrounded by movie posters and really "now" people.

Behind the Rathaus along Florianigasse is another area with late night bars, restaurants, and cafes. The **Tunnel**, at #39, is an interesting place with roots in the '60s and three floors. The basement is a cafe where the bands and folkies play. Upstairs there's a great bar and kitchen with friendly staff and clientele. From the balcony, you can sip coffee and people-watch.

For you disco junkies, try **U4** (you know, like U2, only twice as good), which just about everyone thinks is the hottest spot in Vienna. It's at Schonbrunnerstrasse 222. You can shake your booty until 5:00am, and they even have live bands. Franz Schubert used to dance at U4, and historians believe he developed his rhythmic sense there.

Italy:
An Introduction

We wera gonna writa da whola chapter lika dis, but we couldn't keep up the pace. For the thousands of you out there with big noses, lots of facial hair, and family names that sound like a pizza sauce made in Cleveland, relax: you're going to a country where there will be lots of people who look justa lika you.

Now, many of you may already be pissed from reading the above. You are sick of these negative Italian stereotypes, and you're tired of hearing about Italy being incredibly disorganized, where nothing works properly, everything takes forever to get done, and the cash is worth a little less than Monopoly money. Well, you are absolutely right. These are false stereotypes. Italy is actually a lot worse.

Just kidding. Italy is a really fun place to visit, with enough old paintings, ruins, and rubble to satisfy everyone. Plus, there's all that great pasta and ice cream to eat. If you already had a little cellulite problem before your trip, you'll need to have your thighs shipped home as excess baggage when you return.

There's a lot to see in Italy, from the villages in the north all the way down to Sicily. In between, there are these famous cities like Rome, Naples, Florence, and Venice. The main problem is deciding what you should see in the very limited time available.

Perhaps the biggest disappointment will be faced by those of you with big noses, lots of facial hair, and pizza-sauce names, because you actually have relatives in the Old Country. You see, you'll discover that none of your kinfolk lives in a civilized place like Rome or Florence. ("Civilized" in this context means a city with an AmEx Office, good nightlife, and lots of other young Americans around). In fact, you will quickly learn that all your relatives live in nasty little towns on some mountain, where the only nightlife is in-breeding. Why do you think your ancestors left Italy in the first place?

And another thing: what the hell are you—raised in the suburbs of Philadelphia where the only Italian you had to know was "cheesesteak" —going to say to your great great aunt once removed, who thinks you're your own grandfather coming back to the village after 60 years. Well, you could add the letter "a" to every word and maybe fake her out for 10 minutes, but what will you do when she starts asking complicated stuff, like whether Aunt Rosa still suffers from gout?

Are we getting through to you here? What we're trying to do is help you to maximize your time and enjoyment in Italy. The only must-see places are Rome, Florence, and Venice, and even hitting one or two of these is pretty darn good. If you've got "family obligations," blow them off. Just buy postcards with bucolic scenes featuring lots of scrawny animals and smiling peasants, and who's to say it's not a picture of the ancestral home in Santa Maria Riunite, or wherever your grandparents were from, right?

Now, on to the cities.

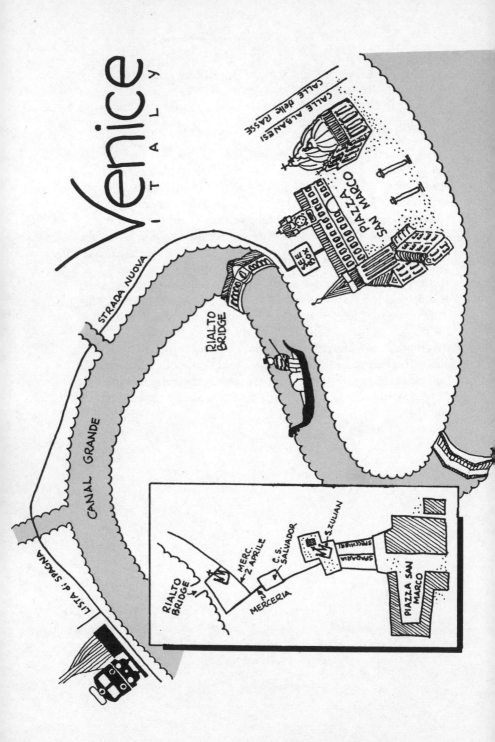

Venice

Unless you can swim ashore from Dad's yacht, chances are you'll arrive in Venice at the train station, **Stazione di Santa Lucia**. The train ride from Rome is about five hours, from Florence about four hours, and from Munich about nine hours, depending on who's at the wheel. There's also an airport about nine miles out of town called **Marco Polo**, named after the guy who invented a swimming pool game.

If you've arrived at the train station, collect your bag and head across the street. *Whoa!* The street is flooded!

Now you remember! *Gondolas!* Man, you need to rent a gondola! Head back into the train station and go to Budget Rent-a-Car. "*Bonjourno*, sir. I'd like to rent a mid-sized gondola for three days with collision waiver, air conditioning, and, uh, make it a hatchback, because we brought our water skis." "Sir, this is a *car* rental agency." "No gondolas?" "No sir." "Okay, then, rent me a car. But don't blame me if I flood the engine."

So, how *do* you get around in Venice? Well, gondolas are out of the question, because they cost about $60 for the first hour and another $30 or so for each successive hour. We'll talk more about gondolas later, but first let's get a few things about Venice straight.

It's easy to get around Venice by boat, and there are several ways to do this. The most useful to you are the *vaporetti*, which operate like buses in the main canals. They cost about $2.00-$3.00, and a one-day ticket for all the boats costs about $8.00. If you prefer to save your money for pasta, buy one ticket and reuse it. No one ever looks at the ticket, and if by chance they do, you can always play the dumb American, a skill you should have honed in Munich, Paris, and Amsterdam.

You'll find that a room in the center of Venice is very expensive. An alternative is to stay out in **Venice Mestre**, the more regular part of the city, or out on the **Lido**, the beach area. If you want to stay in the city proper, check the hotels on **Lista di Spagna** directly on your left as you leave the train station. Expect to spend $30 on a single. Doubles are quite a bit cheaper per person, so if there was ever an economic inducement to immorality, this is probably it. After you've dumped your bags at the hotel, it's time to explore.

Orientation

Venice, or at least the older part (which most concerns us), is shaped like an S (see map). The train station is more or less at one end, near the open-sea side of the city.

To orient yourself, take a *vaporetto* (see how well your Italian is coming along!) from the train station to **Piazza San Marco** (St. Mark's Square). The boat meanders up the **Grand Canal**, and you can gawk at lots of neato buildings. Try to avoid looking at the water, though. It's dark, wet, smelly, and, in case you decide to fall in, be warned—it's not pleasant.

Piazza San Marco

Piazza San Marco, the center of activity in Venice, consists of two wide squares set at right angles. You'll find many old buildings, including a cathedral, a palace, and several museums. It's also the place in Venice to hang out and meet people.

In addition, St. Mark's Square is the sight of the main industry in Venice: pigeon guano. You can watch thousands of pigeons, in a manner somewhat reminiscent of worker bees, digesting packets of grain that tourists feed them (at 75 cents a pop) and then shitting their brains out all over the Square. It's swept up late at night and sold to Japan, where it is considered a delicacy.

To escape the nasty birds' target practice, duck into the **Basilica**. This is a very old church. It's so old that almost nothing inside is made of vinyl. You can buy a guidebook to figure out the who, what, why, and where of the building, and you'll have to pay a little extra to climb the stairs and look down on the mosaic floors. There is also a jewel and gold collection to peruse, if you are so inclined. But, you know, you get kind of burned-out with stuff like that after a while.

After the Basilica, the next sight on the agenda is the palace of the former ruler of Venice. This guy was known as the "Doge," and he later started the Brooklyn Dogers.

The Doge lived pretty high on the hog. You can tour his palace (**Palazzo Ducale**), see his party room, basement, utility rooms, etc. If you can ignore the fact that the Doge didn't have electricity, a VCR, Jacuzzi, Soloflex, or any of the other necessities, you can say he had a pretty decent lifestyle.

At one time, the Venetians ruled half of eastern Europe—and that's before eastern Europe went commie and got all poor and run-down. So, presumably, the Doge could motor around in his gondola on weekends, checking up on the countries his men had conquered that week. Nice life.

Next door to the palace is the **prison**, where anyone who pissed-off the Doge spent his days picking lice out of his hair and wishing that it was all a bad Italian movie. You reach the prison from the palace by passing through an enclosed stone bridge, the famous **Ponte dei Sospiri** (Bridge of Sighs). Pause in the middle of the bridge and wave at Hiro and his wife Yuki from Osaka, who are busy videotaping anything that moves.

Back outside in the piazza again, you'll notice the **Campanile** tower directly opposite. This structure is your Tall Thing To Climb in Venice. From the top of the tower, you have a fine view and can get some pictures.

After your attack of vertigo has passed, wander back down into the square. Maybe it's time to sit in one of the many outdoor cafes scattered around and have an iced coffee. Listen to the cacophony of chatter around you. Sometimes, if you listen very carefully, you can even hear a few words of Italian.

The Rialto Bridge

From Piazza San Marco, venture inland to the second most famous landmark in Venice, **Ponte Rialto** (Rialto Bridge). The bridge spans the Grand Canal—a good thing, because it would look pretty dumb if it didn't span something—and it's covered with shops, mostly selling leather goods and jewelry made of the pink coral found in stores all over Venice. If you're interested in buying leather, you may want to wait until you reach Athens, where prices are about half as much.

On one side of the Rialto Bridge is a large, covered food market open only in the morning. It's a good place to buy the ingredients for a picnic lunch, which you can later eat by the side of a canal and play "Guess the Garbage." As you get better at the game, close your eyes and play the advanced version, "Smell & Tell."

To reach the Rialto Bridge from St. Mark's Square, just follow signs saying *Per Rialto*, which will lead you on a meandering stroll through a maze of narrow streets on what appears to be the least direct route. The experience is reminiscent of the experiments you did in Psychology class, when you fed Ronald the Rat amphetamines and let him loose to find the cheddar. If you were the suspicious type, you would swear that certain shopkeepers had paid the city to position the *Per Rialto* signs to lead tourists past their stores.

No sense fighting it, though. Just join the line and make your way through the streets, always keeping the 300-pound lady with the "Venice Is For Lovers" t-shirt in sight.

One aspect of Venice we should note is the little problem of overcrowding. During the summer, the streets become so packed that there's no room to change you mind, let alone swing your cat, sling a hammock, or play Twister. You can get a good feeling for the summertime ambiance of Venice by wearing a parka while eating a slice of pizza in any New Jersey mall at 3:00pm on Christmas Eve.

The peculiar combination of tourist hordes, Italian food, and hot, cross shoppers makes Venice a unique experience for any visitor. And if you get your jollies by having strangers rub against your body, you won't even have time for lunch in this town.

Gondolas

Now for gondolas: Everyone who comes to Venice wants to ride in a gondola. The gondola owners know this, of course, and that's why it costs a whole lot of money, even for a short ride. (Yes, good ol' American supply-and-demand works in foreign countries, too!) You should negotiate with the *gondolier* before getting in the boat, but expect to pay at least $60.00 an hour.

If you want to invest this year's income from your trust fund in a gondola ride with Carl, go ahead. You can sit side by side, your blond tresses resting on his chest, your hand in his, your hearts beating as one. You close your eyes and sigh, and all is romantic and peaceful—except for the slap of the foul water against the hull and the click and whir of 35mm cameras, as tourists photograph you from every bridge.

Occasionally, your *gondolier* will call a friendly greeting to a fellow *gondolier*: "Yo Luigi! Thatsa a couple-a fat mommas you gotta in your boat! Snort, snort." Periodically, a motor boat will go by and spray your hair with water so polluted that it isn't even wet anymore. Meanwhile, the sun smiles down at a balmy 98 degrees, you can feel a migraine coming on, and Carl keeps belching garlic. Now, that's *amore!*

The Lido

The Lido is Venice's answer to the Jersey Shore. It's easily reached from St. Mark's Square by taking *vaporetto* #6 (board near the Bridge of Sighs). Once you get to the island called the Lido, walk up the main drag **(Viale S. M. Elisabetta)**, and you've reached the beach.

One of the funky things about the beach here is that if you opt for one of the private beaches (which are a lot cleaner than the public ones), you have to pay admission. The only good thing about the admission charge is that it includes the rental of a *camerini*, a little beach hut for changing into your swimsuit. If you've been sharing a hotel room with four other people, renting a *camerini* offers you and your special someone a cramped measure of privacy in which to unfetter your thoughts and anything else that may need unfettering. But remember, you didn't hear it from us.

After a swim to bring your racing hearts back to their resting pulse, sit at one of the outdoor restaurants, light up cigarettes, and ask the questions that have concerned young lovers for hundreds of years, like "Is it true you can't get pregnant if you do it standing up?"

The closest beach to the end of the Viale S. M. Elisabetta is called **Bucintoro** (on your left as you reach the end of the street and face the ocean). A good place to eat there is the **Onda Azurra**.

Eating and Drinking

You'll find the cost of eating and drinking to be pretty high in Venice. You may want to consider getting a picnic lunch from the main food markets on **campo Santa Margherita** and the **Rialto**, and then be prepared to spend a bit more on dinner. Keep an eye out for places that offer a set menu for one price. These meals will be called *pranzo a prezzo fisso*. Even better, if you can find it, is a *menu turistico*. The only difference is the *menu turistico* by law must include the cost of the beverage and the cover charge (or *coperto*, which itself can be a buck or two before you even eat anything).

Beware of restaurants that offer *menu turistico* and then try to add a service charge at the end. Remember, a *menu turistico* includes everything. The other option, the *pranzo a prezzo fisso* may or may not include beverage and service charge in the price, so look carefully before you sit down.

A good place to start looking for food is along the **Lista di Spagna**, the street that runs to the left of the railway station. There are a bunch of restaurants along this street, and the best advice is to just cruise up and down until you find one that looks right for you. If you're interested in a good pizza and a couple of brews, try **Beau Brummel** at Lista di Spagna 160a, where you can devour your pizza while sitting outside, watching the crowds wandering up and down looking for food. The only other restaurant we tried on the street and liked is the **Trattoria Spaccanapoli** at #1518. Go for their roast chicken, if they happen to have it on the menu that evening.

As you reach the end of Lista di Spagna, the street continues as **Strada Nouva**, and you can also find many restaurants there.

If you have set your heart on eating near piazza San Marco, your best bet is to move a little inland. Right next to the ritzy Hotel Royal Danelli is an alleyway called **Calle delle Rasse**, which contains a bunch of restaurants. Other guidebooks recommend several of them. We didn't find anything very remarkable, and we recommend staying *away* from **La Gondola**, which added an extra $6.00 to our *menu turistico* for service and tax.

Nightlife
You don't visit Venice to hit the music clubs, any more than you would visit Iowa to hit the canals. So what are you going to do at night?

Well, one pleasant thing to do is hop a *vaporetto* and get a tour of the city at dusk. It's one of the most romantic things you could ever imagine. Stand on the bow of the boat, pleasantly buzzed from the wine at dinner, and with your arm around your honey, watch the lights of the historic city slip past. From deep within you comes the urge to sing *O Sole Mio*, which is the Italian version of Elvis' *It's Now or Never*. At first you're a little tentative, but then your voice swells to the starlit skies: "*O sole mio! O sole mio! O sole mio, hmmmmmmm, hmm, hmm, hmmmmm! O sole mio, hmmmmm, hmmmmmmm . . .*" until the driver comes over and tells you to either learn the words or get off his damn boat.

What else can you do at night? The city government sponsors concerts in Piazza San Marco three times a week, where you can hear people sing *O Sole Mio* properly. Don't even think about sitting in one of the outdoor cafes that line the square to listen, however. The prices rise to astronomical levels while the music is playing, and unless you're willing to go home with one of the waiters in exchange for an espresso, it's not worth it. You can just as easily sit out in the piazza and listen to the music. Then, you'll have that special Venetian touch of pigeons crapping all over your head during the performance.

There's not much in the way of a good music scene in Venice. It's probably true to say the Italians have done for rock music what the Minnesota Vikings have done for Thai cuisine. The few concerts we saw in Italy consisted of young men wearing incredibly tight pants and singing *O Sole Mio* in an arrangement Barry Manilow would find wimpy.

Probably the best thing to do at night is just wander, stopping here and there to have an espresso (cappuccino is strictly a breakfast drink in Italy) or maybe a glass of wine. Piazza San Marco is usually hopping until late at night, and you can hang out there and, with any luck, meet some kindred spirits.

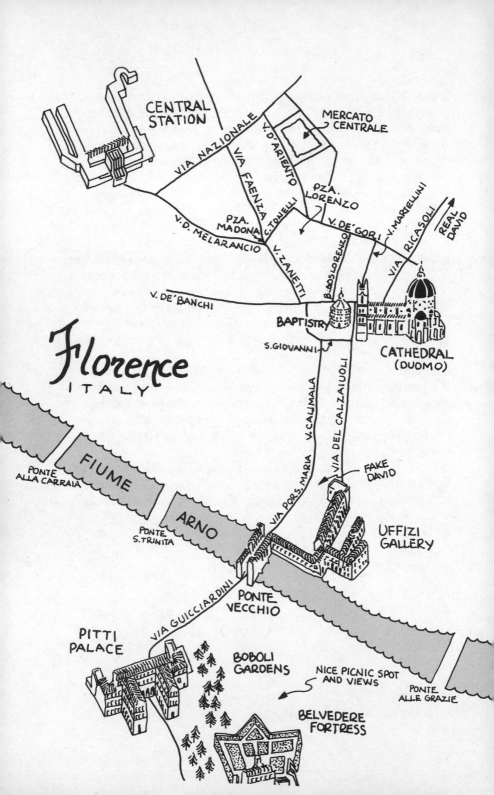

Florence

Florence, like Nice, offers the perfect respite from the hustle and bustle of larger European cities. It's a city small enough to explore without the need of buses, trams, or subways, yet it has enough of the charm, art, and life of a big city to keep you entertained. Florence is between Rome and Venice, so stop by if you're traveling between these cities. It's just a few hours from each.

Florence also has the distinction of being one of the most visited cities in Italy. Be prepared to be elbowed off the sidewalks by tourist armies determined to see the Great Cities of Italy, even if you have to die beneath the wheels of a passing Fiat so they can get to the next Big Cultural Thing.

Don't be led astray by guidebooks that say you'll need at least a week in a city as cultured and diverse as Florence. To paraphrase Hanns Johst, when we hear the word "culture," we reach for a beer. We did Florence in a day, so take it from us: you can see everything in one afternoon. We'll outline a quick tour that will give you all the background you need to describe the place to your grandparents when you get home.

History

Though Florence was founded by the Romans two million years ago, it didn't really take off until the 15th and 16th centuries. That's when a developer named **Duke Cosimo Medici**, sort of like Donald Trump, spent lots of money on impressive mansions and supported all the struggling artists who had been unable to get government grants since the Roman Empire crumbled. Maybe you've even heard of some of those artists: Botticelli, Leonardo da Vinci, Michelangelo. Ring any bells?

Unfortunately, all those good artists died about 400 years ago. Today, the art scene in Florence has fallen into the hands of bad street musicians, amateur caricaturists, and people who make "art" on the street with chalk. Luckily for the *Let's Go*'ers, somebody was able to squirrel away enough of the good, old art to fill a few museums.

If you must, check out a museum called the **Uffizi**, which houses a lot of this old art. You can also use the Uffizi to pick up some souvenirs, like art books and postcards of just the, er, johnson (a.k.a. "trouser snake," "wingwang," "Little Elvis," etc.) on the statue *David*.

Orientation

Arriving at the Central Station (**Santa Maria Novella**) should be a breeze for you by now. If you're staying overnight and not taking the midnight train elsewhere, first thing to do is book a room.

The **Informazioni Turistiche Alberghiere** (ITA) office, to the left as you come off the trains, offers an excellent room-finding service for about $2.00. It's well worth the price, since there is often a shortage of rooms during the summer, and you could get shut-out without ITA's help. This is also good practice for the time when you'll be talking to your first real estate agent. Ask for a *pensione* near the *duomo* (cathedral), Florence's geographical and cultural epicenter.

If you're desperate, try the hotel row on **via della Scala,** just across from the station and to the right. However, many of these places are of the flea-bag variety. And unless you cross the Arno River, you'll find that most *pensioni* are on the top floor of an old building on a noisy street. In fact, we believe that Italians hide amplifiers inside window frames to make the charming sounds of buses, mopeds, and street cleaners clearer.

Things To See

After settling in your room or stowing your bags, head right for the *duomo*. From there, you can walk all of Florence in about an hour. If you've been punctual up to this point and have more time, we'll also suggest some diversions.

From the **Piazza del Duomo**, you get a fabulous view (day or night) of this colorful marble church started 700 years ago. It's more impressive outside than inside, so don't get bummed if it's closed. If it's open, you can climb the long staircase to the dome for a good panorama of the city. It costs $4.00, and it's your Tall Thing To Climb in Florence.

Outside on the piazza, you'll see many of the unemployed pigeons from *Mary Poppins* trying to be rediscovered by an Italian movie director.

From the *duomo*, head past the little round building (the **Battistero**) in front of the church and turn left onto via Roma. Well, heck. Stop a second. Since you're in the vicinity, you might as well spend 30 seconds looking at the doors of the Battistero, which attract more rubber-neckers than the Oscar Mayer Weinermobile.

Push yourself through the mob and take a peek. Supposedly, Michelangelo himself proclaimed them good enough to stand at the gates of Paradise. The guy who made them, Ghiberti, spent 27 years on the job. Let's hope he was paid by the hour.

Now, follow via Roma down through the Piazza della Repubblica until you come to the **Piazza del Mercato Nuovo** on your right, an outdoor market selling mostly junk from carts. The street now changes names to Via Por Santa Maria, and it leads to the famed **Ponte Vecchio**, a bridge you've seen on many dorm posters, usually photographed using a red filter and a setting sun. It will probably remind many of you of lying on Karen's bed, wondering when her roommate was going to return and if you should both start getting some clothes on.

During the day, the shops along the Ponte Vecchio sell mostly gold jewelry and leather. If you arrive early enough, you may see the city workers hosing the puke off the street from the night before.

Crossing to the other side of the river, you'll be in an area known as the **Oltrarno**. Continue walking away from the bridge on via de Guicciardini—where you'll pass the American Express office at #49r—and you'll come upon a huge **Medici mansion** at the Piazza del Pitti. Turn left through the main entrance and go straight through to the other side. On the way, however, notice the semi-indoor fish pond with the swimming nymphs. Go ahead—toss in one of those 50-lire coins for good luck. When you get home, tell your friends that you felt so good you threw not one, but **50**, lire in!

Now, climb through the **Boboli Gardens** in the back. Mr. Medici must have thrown some serious barbecues in those days. And here's an interesting fact for you Medici trivia buffs: Talk about the Smiths keeping up with the Joneses—the palace was first built by Luca Pitti in the 15th century to one-up the Medicis, by then well-established as the social elite. But that brazen social-climber Pitti died before the palace was finished, and it was eventually sold to one of Cosimo's wives, who invited the entire Medici entourage to move in and raid the 'fridge. Ironic, huh?

Walk through the entrance, climb to your left, and there's a coffee house where you can slug down a beer in the great out-of-doors with a fine panoramic view of Florence. (Note: This is the second Tall Thing To Climb in Florence.) It's a great spot for a picnic, too. Also on top, there's an outdoor movie theater—like a drive-in without the cars—which even has outdoor Dolby sound on first-run films, so you may want to check the schedule posted near the **Forte Belvedere** housing the Modern Sculpture Museum.

Walk back down, recross the Ponte Vecchio, and turn right along the river. Turn left onto the **Piazza de Uffizi**, where there's another pseudo-market selling the same jewelry, leather, and stuff that the other ones have. The good thing about this market, though, is the "art guidebooks" of the museums. With these books, you can skip the museums but still make out like you've been there! Who knows—maybe in ten years you'll have an interest in old paintings and be glad you bought the books. And by then you'll have forgotten whether you actually visited the museums anyway.

Next, you'll emerge upon the **Piazza della Signoria**, where, among lots of scaffolding and archaeological debris, the fake statue *David* stands. Take some pictures and tell your friends it's the real one. (Incidentally, they're hiding the real one in the **Accademia** on via Ricasoli to protect it from the pigeons. No need to see it though, unless you're the type who would fly to California to see the *real* Disneyland because the one in Florida is just a cheap knock-off.)

There are lots of interesting statues on the steps of **Loggia dei Lanzi**, but, naturally, all were behind scaffolding when we were there. You'll just have to point your camera through the iron mesh and hope for the best. Be sure to check out the big fountain with a man holding three imps (identified by their Mr. Spock ears) between his legs. The imps are blowing water from hoses. You may want a guidebook to explain this one. Then again, you might as well concoct your own interpretation.

In this piazza, you'll probably find a sight common throughout Europe's *platzes* and *pleins*: bad musicians who can't make a dime in the subways, so they're trying a new venue to showcase their lack of talent. After you've had enough of them—and this should take a few femto-seconds—start walking up via dei Calzaioli toward the *duomo*.

One thing you'll be sure to see while walking through Florence are the street "chalk artists." These guys take their art very seriously, and some of their work is quite impressive. It's so good, in fact, that many won't draw directly on the sidewalk anymore. Instead, they tape a large sheet of poster paper to the pavement so they can take it up at night and sell it. Let's follow Edith and George, from the American Express Silver Wheels Bus Tour, as they stumble upon one of these guys:

Edith: "Looky here, hon—it says in this guidebook there's some old bridge around here we oughta see called the Pointy Veecheeo."

George: "Maybe it's one of those covered jobs, like we have back in Pennsylvania."

(Paying too much attention to their guidebook and not enough to where they are walking, they step right onto a chalk painting depicting the plight of the Kurdish sorghum farmer.)

Artist *(in Italian)*: "Hey you stupid American pigs! Get the hell off my painting and watch where you're walking!"

Edith: "What's that man saying to us, George?"

George: "Prob'ly trying to help us, dear. You know how friendly these foreigners can be. He prob'ly just wants to help us find that old bridge. Uh, Prego, fettucini! Avanti Pointy Veckio?" *(George, pivoting to ask the artist how to get to the bridge, tears a huge hole in the poster paper.)* "Ooops! Mucho scuzzi there, son. Say, can you help us find this Pontie Veecheese bridge?"

Artist: "Idiot! Look what you've done to my masterpiece!"

(Now the artist and his friends stand up and point angrily at

the painting. Edith gets frightened and thinks they are gyp-
sies like the ones in Rome who swiped George's wallet. She
drops her bottle of Fresca, and it shatters and fizzes all over
the torn painting.)

Edith: "Good heavens! Oh, I'm so sorry. *(In a loud voice:)*
  Mia very-a apologia, señor. Here, let me wipe it up." *(She*
  tries to wipe up the mess and smears the drawing
  horribly.)

George: "Careful, hon. Watch out for the glass." *(He kicks a*
  jagged piece of Fresca bottle out of her way, tearing an
  even larger hole across the rustic Kurdish scene which now
  looks like it was bombed by a squadron of F-15's.)

From the *duomo*, head out Borgo S. Lorenzo and turn left into
the piazza of the same name, where there's yet another market
selling the same jewelry, leather, and junk as the others. You can
either follow the path of this market or take a short cut through
Borgo la Noce to emerge in the **Mercato Centrale**, where there's
a huge indoor fruit, vegetable, and meat market—just like the
Ye Olde Food Court at the mall back home. Hours are limited,
so get there early for your picnic needs. There are some nice
outdoor cafes along this piazza, too, and it's a pleasant place to
relax with a beer at the end of the day and watch the vendors
push home for the evening.

Congratulations! You've just blown through Florence!

Renting a Moped

When you get bored of the shopping, tour buses, and fake art,
consider this: the Tuscany countryside is within walking distance—or better yet, *moped distance*—of the city.

One of the things you may find most annoying about Florence—and most of Italy, for that matter—are the obnoxious
mopeds screaming around corners, spewing their disgusting
blue smoke. Our advice: don't fight this pestilence—join it. Don't
try driving a "ped" through a big city like Rome, but Florence
is a piece of cake.

Once you cross the Ponte Vecchio or any of the other bridges,
you'll soon be safely on the back roads of picturesque countryside, where things are peaceful and tranquil. Peaceful and tranquil, that is, until you come speeding down the lanes of the

ancient hamlets, belching your two-cycle soot. Hey, it's their problem now!

Be sure to demonstrate the good moped form you've learned from in-town observation: rev your engine up to oh, 180 decibels or so whenever you can, and really crank it on the straights. If you see pedestrians, especially elderly tourists, speed up and beep them out of your way. You may even need to swerve at them to make your point.

Look for an enthusiastic Argentinean entrepreneur who left a successful business in Buenos Aires and risked it all to rent mopeds in Florence. He is very helpful and will gladly rent you a moped for about $10 per half-day, which includes insurance, his personal maintenance anywhere you might break down, and gas. What's more, he requires no money for a deposit, and he even pro-rates his hourly charges for fractions of an hour. And for you wimps, he also rents bicycles. You'll likely find him at **Mercato del Porcellino**, near the market with the bronze boar, just down from the Piazza della Repubblica ("For Rent," **Mr. Coto**, phone 234-3594).

Nightlife

As in Rome, you'll find most of the evening entertainment in Florence on the streets. If you have any nostalgia for the '60s, don't miss the **Ponte Vecchio** at night. It becomes a major hangout for the underlife—bongo players, guitar folkies who know the usual three chords and the "night merchants" selling fake Louis Vuitton bags and Lacoste shirts. If you enjoy hanging out with a bunch of low-lifes and singing maudlin old protest songs, you'll fit right in. You can get, like, really close to each other and share the togetherness and, like, drink wine straight from the bottle and stuff. But beware of ChiChi of Medici, the Night Stalker of Florence. He could be anyone.

There are lots of tarot card readers on the bridge as well. Look especially for the Truman Capote look-alike. But don't be tempted into getting your caricature done. We saw artists who displayed good examples of Mick Jagger and Jim Morrison, but their drawings of tourists were about as good as the ones your mom used to put on the refrigerator.

The **Piazza Signoria** is also a good place to hang and roam. First, get yourselves some *gelato* (a fancy name for ice cream) at **L'Granduca** at via de Calzaioli 57, at the corner of via della Speziali. They help you overcome language barriers by putting fresh fruit on the top of each flavor so you know what you've ordered. Or try **Festival del Gelato** with its neon cones and music videos, just around the corner at via del Corso 75. Both are near the Piazza della Repubblica and have thousands of flavors.

The biggest, hottest disco in town is **Space Electronic** on via Palazzuolo 37 (phone 29-30-82). This place has the familiar beat that will drive you into a dancing fool after a few beers. In addition to a fish tank filled with piranhas, there are more lights, mirrors, motors, and speakers in this club than in your average pimp-mobile. Female visitors probably will have to deal with the advances of pushy Italian stallions in tight-fitting pants, who are anxious to show that David's isn't the only penis you can inspect closely in Florence.

If you feel you're a bit more cultured than all this (after all, you are in *Florence*) and want to hear some jazz, try **Bebop** on via dei Servi (phone 26-30-04) or **Salt Peanuts** at Piazza S. Maria Novella (phone 29-33-76).

Rome

Rome, as the old saying goes, was not built in a day. That's not to say it can't be *seen* in a day. Well, let's give it a day and a night.

Rome is an obligatory stop on any European trip, and it will consistently inspire you with its ruins, relics, antiquity, and other neat old things. The whole city is like the set of the play you did in senior year of *Julius Caesar*. Even if you've never had any interest in history or histrionics, you'll be hard pressed not to be impressed.

The best places to see in Rome are all outdoors, on the streets and piazzas. Stay outside, because that's where you'll find the good action—and all the old buildings, statues, and fountains will equal anything you'd find inside a museum, anyway. (Since we agreed to blow off most museums on this trip, Rome is a perfect place to acquaint yourself with the art you are otherwise foregoing.) Rome, as the name implies, is for roamin'. (Our apologies to readers living in Intercourse, PA.)

Art History

For those of you who slept through Art History 101, here is a short primer to make you sound more sophisticated than you really are:

Whenever you stop to look at anything in Rome, like a statue or a fountain, utter something about the "romantic influences" and "ideals" of Bernini or Michelangelo. You're bound to impress anyone within earshot, and you'll be correct about 90% of the time (plus or minus three percentage points, according to the latest *CNN/USA Today* poll). These two artists/architects are to Roman art what Frank Perdue is to chicken.

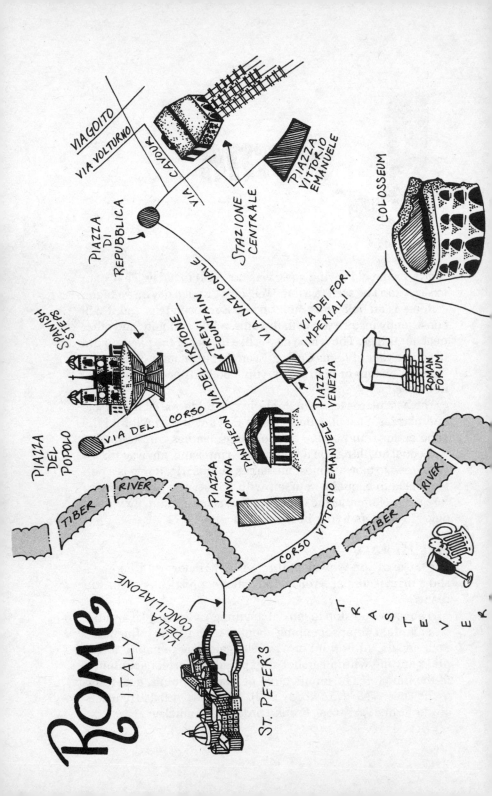

When To Go
Not in August. It is hot then and everything is closed and what isn't closed smells funny.

Orientation
If you arrive by air, you'll land at **Leonardo da Vinci Airport**. (Imagine, da Vinci built an airport hundreds of years ago! Was that guy ahead of his time, or what?!) Take a bus to the **Central Station** (*Stazione Termini*). If you arrive by train, get out at the Central Station. If you arrive by chariot, chances are those hash brownies in Amsterdam were more potent than you thought.

Leave your packs at the baggage check in the station (near track 22), especially in summer, because the streets are long and hot, and the sidewalks are narrow and littered with dog-dootie.

The station is a city in itself and has a tourist office (**EPT**) that can help you find a hotel. This will be your first test in patience. It's a beloved Italian tradition to create long lines and be utterly inefficient. If the people behind the counter see the line getting short, it is their civic responsibility, under the Charter of Roman Law, to slow things down or close for siesta. When you finally do get to the window, be crystal clear as to how much you're willing to pay, buy a street map, and ask for *Roma Giovane* (*Young Rome*), a listing of current goings-on.

If you wish to strike out on your own to find a hotel or *pension*, try the area to the right as you leave the front of the station. Head out along via Voltumo, turn right onto via Montebello, and look around on via Goito and via Castelfidardo. Avoid the area to the left of the station, especially after dark, unless you're the sort who welcomes danger.

The *pensioni* are typically on the top floors of buildings with very high ceilings. If there is an elevator, it probably doesn't work, or it requires coins that you won't have. The rooms are a bit cramped, too—about two feet by two feet—and have a series of doors that open inward. So until you get the room you want, leave your packs at the tracks.

At first the city may seem huge and overbearing, with pedestrians elbowing for sidewalk space, lots of traffic, pollution, noise, and bustle. This is apparently what people find charming about Rome. There are a few "escape hatches," however, where you can dismantle your defenses and have a look around. These include Trastevere, Piazza Navona, Piazza di Spagna (where the Spanish Steps are), Piazza d. Rotonda, and Piazza Trevi. More on these later.

If you need instant gratification just for making it to Rome, head toward **Piazza della Repubblica**, near the train station. There's nothing really interesting there unless you'd like to sit at a *trattoria* or visit some old Roman bath ruins (**Baths of Diocletian**) or a **wax museum** with characters that, for the most part, have no meaning to you. In fact, the only useful thing about Piazza della Repubblica is you can catch a bus or the subway there to a more interesting place. But you can do that from the train station, so just skip Pz. d. Repubblica. Oh, except for one thing—at night there's a low-key prostitution scene along via Cernaia, next to the ruins. Some things never change.

Public Transportation

The subway system (Metro) in Rome has two lines, and you may want to highlight this section of the book or jot down some notes in the margin. Ready? Here goes: One of the lines is called the "A" line. It goes to the Vatican. The other line, called the "B" line, goes to the Colosseum.

Now that we've mastered the Metro, let's take a little time to understand the buses, which use a complicated, meaningless numbering scheme, so don't bother trying to figure it out. Instead, just hop on any bus you see and ask the driver if it goes where you want. Stand in the doorway so no one else can get on and the driver can't pull away unless he helps you.

Buy a booklet of tickets at *tabacchi* (convenience stores) and validate them as you go. The #64 bus takes you to the Vatican from the Termini, and the #71 is useful for the heart of the city, along via del Corso. If you choose to park yourself several miles out of the city because of an obscure lead in a pretentious travel guide claiming "quaint charm at a budget price," you're on your own.

SPQR

One thing you'll notice a lot in Rome are the letters SPQR. They're on buildings, paintings, historical markers, public notices, and even manhole covers.

SPQR is not advertising for a nightclub or the Italian spelling of Benetton. It's an acronym for The Government. Translated from Latin (*senatus populusque Romanus*), it stands for "the senate and the people of Rome," and it signifies the development of the Roman Republic way back in the old days, when senators wore togas and argued over the big threat from Gaul. Since no one hears much from Gaul these days, you can assume SPQR took care of the threat.

Shopping

Shopping is one of the more complicated things you'll have to do in Rome—and all of Italy, for that matter. The problem is, you have to deal with currency so badly devalued that you need a golf cart to carry pocket change. While we touched on this earlier, reinforcement may be necessary.

First thing: ignore the three digits at the end of all prices. You'd have to take Italian VII to understand the price of a Happy Meal, major in trig to count your change, and use a calculator with 16 digits to figure the equivalent in dollars. (Besides, most calculators don't use Roman numerals.) Why haven't the Italians realized that they could lop off a bunch of zeros without disrupting their economy? We suppose they probably want to feel like they're a wealthier nation than the ones the tourists come from. Or maybe they just like displaying big bulges in their pockets.

Rome is perhaps the best place to try using the U.S. greenback, as we advised in the Introduction. Slap down a few dollars on a 7,000-lire item and don't mess around.

Leather, gold, and plastic religious icons seem to be the big things to buy in Rome. Italian shoes are too narrow for American men's feet and, like the money, clothing sizes have too many numbers. We all know Benetton clothes are available in any city in the world (but you may want to brag of having *real* Benetton clothes). So when buying gifts for others back home, stick to the plastic items at St. Peter's. One thing that is quite popular and hard to get elsewhere are the 3-D pictures of Jesus that blink.

There are a number of outdoor markets in Rome that are good for picking up vegetables, cheeses, and fresh fruit—which your body may be severely missing by this point. (Limes consumed while shooting tequila don't count as "fresh fruit.") Usually, the markets are open in the morning only and closed on Sunday.

The largest is to the left and behind the train station at **Piazza Vittorio Emanuele II**. The more elegant and flowery one, complete with cabanas, is at **Piazza Campo dei Fiori**, near Piazza Navona. Smaller markets offering books and art are found at **Piazza Borghese** and at **Piazza Santa Maria** in Trastevere. On Sunday morning, there's a good flea market at **Porta di Portese** (take bus #57 from the train station).

Food

One of the big misconceptions about Italy is that you can get great pizza there. Ditto for spaghetti. Sorry, but these both are, for the most part, American inventions (pizza was invented in New Haven, Conn.), and nothing in Italy compares to what you can buy at your basic strip-mall pizza/sub shop. In fact, pizzas in Italy resemble the cardboard "heat-n-serve" tray that comes under a frozen pizza back home. And if you want something as exotic as tomato sauce or cheese, you've got to ask for it. Tomato sauce is applied with a perfume mister. Then, the pizza sits in a glass case for several days to acquire the unique texture found most often in frisbees.

While the "pasta" dishes are sometimes tolerable, heed this word of caution when ordering: don't go asking for the gourmet, spinach-type pasta sold in mega-supermarkets back home. If you request the "green" noodles, you'll probably get something that has reached the sporophyte stage of mold development.

With that in mind, **Monte Arei**, a restaurant at 33 via Castelfidardo, is a good bet for pasta, and it's close to the Termini and *pensioni*. Nearby is **Il Passatore** at 31 via Cernaia, also a good choice.

Ice cream is another oddity that Americans can't wait to eat when they get to Italy. In response to that demand, the Italians have constructed many *gelatia* stands on the sidewalks. A single serving of the stuff, while small in quantity, typically contains enough sugar to form rock candy in your mouth. Nonetheless, there are many coneheads in Rome, and even the Italians have copied the American habit of walking around while eating ice cream. A flashy place to sample this confection is **Gelateria della Palma** at 23 via della Maddalena.

Wine

The main thing to remember about eating in Italy is to drink a lot of wine with your meals. The wine is as cheap as water (and safer) and more plentiful than acne at a New Kids' concert.

First, some wine-ordering etiquette. Don't ask right off for a glass of the house wine or a blush wine from Gallo. Instead, use a little local sophistication and ask for "the kind the Pope drinks," or "something that goes well with pizza." If you want to make a big hit with the waiter, ask for a good local Bordeaux or Rhine wine.

But seriously, you can get a fine vintage wine (in a bottle covered with real dust, no less) at almost any restaurant for the price you'd pay for a single wine cooler back home. Don't simply ask for a bottle of red wine or white wine, or you'll get a carafe of the house wine diluted 4:1 with dirty water.

The beer of Italy is Peroni. It tastes like what you'd expect from a beer brewed in a country famous for wine.

Things To See

Since time is of the essence and you've probably got tons of things to buy, we'll suggest a walking tour you should be able to knock off in a day, with plenty of time to spare.

As in every other city, we'll begin at the train station. We'll walk past great buildings and famous fountains, and we'll pause on the Spanish Steps, a place to recount in your diary what you've seen, felt, and been felt by. (Or, you can sketch the American Express office on your artist's pad.) We'll stop at a vantage point where you can see most of the historic sights, like the Forum and Colosseum, without ever having to climb aboard a tour bus. More importantly, we'll sample the local flavor by eating and drinking in quaint *trattorie* (Italy's answer to Subway Sandwich Shops) along the way.

Rome is easy to see on foot in one day. We suggest arriving early in the morning so you can get cracking right as the old town awakes. Because of the ridiculous afternoon closing hours the Italians get away with, it's best to divide our tour of Rome into day and night.

Rome By Day

Though there are certain places you can see only by day because of their hours, it is true that the Rome is best seen at night. The things you should see in the day are the Vatican, the Colosseum, and the ruins between the Colosseum and P. Venezia. And, if you need a Tall Thing To Climb for your snapshots, the view from **Piazza Garibaldi** (via bus #41) is quite nice.

First, the **Vatican**. Rome is the Pope's town, and the Vatican is his city. You can't possibly say you've been to Rome but not to the Vatican, so by all means, find your way there. From the Ottaviano stop on the Metro, follow the crowd down via Ottaviano until you hit the guy selling plastic religious things at the corner of the wall that surrounds the Pope's digs. Turn right and follow the signs along a sidewalk mobbed with tourists and about two angstroms wide to the **Vatican Museum**.

Vatican City is a sovereign state created in a pact between the Fascist leader Mussolini and the Pope about 60 years ago. The Popes have done all right here, with a private railroad station, a college, a radio station (playing those rockin' hymnal faves), and beautifully landscaped yards. Sort of like Heritage USA before Jim Bakker got busted.

Go in through the museum entrance. "*Museum?!*" you shriek. "I thought there were no museums on this trip!" Well, you're right again. We were just testing. Unless you're into a lot of boring religious art and stained glass, you can skip the whole idea.

The only thing people really come to "experience" at the Vatican is the **Sistine Chapel**, and only so they can brag about it later. When we were there, they were doing a lot of touch-up work on the frescoes (the paintings on the walls and ceilings), but they may be finished by now, and the renovation is supposed to be quite stunning, if you're stunned by that sort of thing.

Spread out on the floor of the chapel, have a picnic, and lie back to see the ceiling. Apparently, that's what you're supposed to look at. Occasionally the Vatican Police (an interesting concept, fraught with comic potential, eh? But, we don't have time . . .) will impose silence on everyone, and the shouting dies to a murmur for a few nano-seconds before resuming the normal roar. Imagine—you *pay* to get in there, and then you're supposed to act like you're in church or something.

On the way out of the museum, there are a lot of statues

without heads and limbs. These make great photo props, like the plywood cut-outs you stand behind at amusement parks. But with the statues you can be more creative. Simply stand behind these ancient pieces of art and pose your arms, legs, and face in wacky, obscene ways. As far as we can tell, it's the reason the museum curators put them there.

If you're not inclined to see the Vatican Museum, and we certainly hope you're not, then head for **St. Peter's Square**. If you can make it on Wednesday mornings, the Pope gives Mass here, unless he's off skiing in the Alps or kissing an airport tarmac somewhere. But hey, you didn't come all the way to Europe to go to church, and odds are you're not even Catholic, so skip St. Peter's on Wednesdays.

It is worth going into the **Basilica di San Pietro** and climbing to the top of the 550-foot dome for your Tall Thing To Climb in Rome. It costs about $1.50 to climb up. This dome is the biggest in all of Europe—the Pope doesn't like to be upstaged. There's a coffee shop up there, as well as a post office to get your official Vatican City postmark on the cards of St. Paul's you bought back in London. The famous Michelangelo statue *Pieta* is to the right as you enter the Basilica. You can oooh and ahhhh if you want—we don't care.

Walk away from the Vatican down via della Conciliazione if you want to shop, or along Borgo Pio if you want to eat. **Trattoria Il Pozzetto** at 168 Borgo Pio (at the corner of Degli Ombrellari) is a good place for food and a beer. They have a tourist menu for about $9.00 that is quite satisfying.

Grab the #64 bus back toward the train station. It travels along Vittorio Emanuele. Get off at **Piazza Venezia**, distinguished by its huge, white wedding cake building, the monument to Victor Emanuele. Have a beer at the very popular **Bar Brasile** (295 via del Corso), conveniently across from a Benetton store. Bar Brasile serves Kronenborg and other Roman delights to a crowd of locals and tourists, mingling, pinching, laughing, pinching, scoping, and pinching.

Walk to the back of the monument along via dei Fori Imperiali, and find your way into the ruins of the **Roman Forum**, to the right. In this museum-park, you'll pass Caesar's old house and various important old temples, many of which are under scaffolding, so be prepared for more steel and green plastic in your photos. This area is open from 9:00am until one hour before sunset (closed Tuesdays).

While wandering among the ruins, don't get all caught up in romanticizing about life in ancient times. As Thomas Hobbes said, life back then was "solitary, poor, nasty, brutish, and short." Plus, there was no such thing as Domino's Pizza or 24-hour video stores. However, they did have weekly chariot races and drunken orgies, so it was kind of cool.

Now, work your way down to the sight that best defines Rome—the **Colosseum**.

While it is a great photo opportunity, the Colosseum is a lot like Giants Stadium in New Jersey during a home game. There are busloads of tourists pouring in from all sides, people selling food and souvenirs, and lots of very uncomfortable seats. Inside, it's a real disappointment—mostly just rubble and weeds. At least at Giants Stadium they're organized enough to have artificial turf. The Colosseum, along with its reputation as the venue of various human- and animal-rights violations, was built by Jewish slaves who did not enjoy union privileges. What's more, the Colosseum used to have a dome, but it just wouldn't hold up over the years.

Besides the pickpockets outside, you have to watch out for the notorious **gypsy children**, an organized ring of kids trained by professional thieves. They live, well, like gypsies, outside the city. Their *modus operandi* (whoops, there we go with those $10 words again. But hey, we're in Rome, so we can indulge in a little Latin if we want.) is to surround you as though they are playing or begging, and then make off with anything their little hands can seize. They hand-off to one another even better than the Chicago Bears, so it's impossible to chase your wallet once it leaves your pocket. Let's follow Larry and Irv as they walk in wonderment among the monuments of history and meet a band of gypsy children:

Larry: "Wow Irv, these kids are pretty friendly, huh?"

Irv: "Yeah, I think they want to play ring-around-the-rosie or something." *(The kids close in on Larry, who reaches out and offers his hand to participate in the frolic.)* "Hey, whaddya suppose these cardboard things are they're pushing against us?"

Larry: "I dunno, maybe they want us to, like, autograph it or something." (*As Irv reaches for one of the pens in his pocket protector, his wallet is delicately hoisted from his bulging back pocket.*)

Irv: "Hey, these kids are really cute—more friendly than the kids back home, ya know?" (*Larry's camera is lifted from his belt pouch and disappears in a matter of seconds, while he dances around a circle holding a young girl's hand.*)

Larry: "Yeah, they're not afraid of us at all, and I think they want to talk to us. *Buenos dias ninos und ninnies!*"

(*As Irv bends over to pick up the pen he dropped, the inside of his day pack is quickly and professionally explored by four pairs of eager hands.*)

Irv (*whose passport is now being auctioned a few blocks away by the older children*): "I'm really gonna try to learn to speak Italian so's I can at least communicate with little kids. Hey, ya know, I wish we had something to give 'em." (*He reaches into his empty pockets for a few coins while, one block away, a 10-year-old takes a picture of his fellow thieves with Irv's new auto-focus camera.*)

From the Colosseum, get on the Metro, ride two stops to the Termini (train station), and change there to the A line in the direction of Ottaviano. Get off at via Spagna. This is the famous **Spanish Steps**, and it's where your Roman night begins.

Rome By Night

Try to arrive at the Spanish Steps around dusk, when you can experience the transition to night. This is the best place to hang out in Rome and see how the locals get their kicks. In good weather, guitar players, bongo beaters, straight and gay vagrant youth from all over find their way here to see and be seen.

The area in front of the Spanish Steps (**via Borghese Condotti**) is Rome's swank shopping area, where you can stock up on Cartier watches, Gucci bags, and elegant clothing at very unreasonable prices. Don't hold back! You're only in Rome once, and your Amex card is getting lonely. So what's a few hundred thousand lire anyway? (Oh, did we mention American Express? Yes, it's right nearby, in front of the column of the Immaculate Conception.)

When you've seen enough, bought enough, and met enough, stroll toward the **Fountain of Trevi**, another great place to hang at night. From the Spanish Steps, walk down via Condotti, turn left onto via del Corso and left again just past Piazza Colonna onto via de Sabini, which becomes via de Crociferi. Eventually you'll find a crowded, intimate square with an impressively lit fountain and lots of surrounding activity.

Don't forget your obligation to toss three coins over your left shoulder into the fountain to insure your return to Rome. Chances are, you'll hit someone else in the head because it's too damn crowded to get within throwing range of the fountain. We understand the fountain is under extensive renovation, so be prepared for disappointment—or at least a tougher toss. Then again, you might not even want to come back to Rome, so don't bother with the fountain at all

An easy stroll from the Fountain of Trevi is the **Pantheon**, one of the oldest buildings on your whole trip. It was started back in 27 B.C. (we're not sure which month). First built as a temple to the Roman gods, the Pantheon was later consecrated as an Episcopal Church, so it's probably destined to become a fashionable dance club soon.

Until about an hour before sunset (except on Monday), you can go inside the Pantheon and see a giant hole in the ceiling. Admission is free, but maybe they should charge money so they can afford to fix the roof.

The square just outside, the **Piazza della Rotonda**, is an idyllic setting for an outdoor drink or meal at night, and there are plenty of establishments that will provide suitable fare.

A bar near the Pantheon called **Miscellanea** at 110a via della Poste will have great appeal for the American college student abroad. Any U.S. university of any significance is represented with a plaque on the wall. Even some high schools that don't mean diddly are mentioned. It is therefore important that you go there, as a sort of ambassador of your school, and make sure it's represented. It's also a good place to meet fellow Americans on their semester abroad programs and Italians who want to meet American coeds. Beer is expensive, however (about $4.00 for a small glass).

A good place to eat nearby is **La Cave di Saint'Ignazio**, just off via de Seminario at 169 Piazza Saint'Ignazio. They offer excellent seafood and pasta dishes and lots of local charm.

Just a few minutes to the west from the Pantheon is **Piazza Navona**, another place to hang at night. The brightly lit fountains there attract people and street entertainers. It's a fun place, tucked away from traffic chaos.

Trastevere

This area is across the Tiber River and up the hill from the movie theater district. Cross the Tiber at the Garibaldi Bridge or Sisto Bridge.

The **Piazza S. Maria** in Trastevere is the center of gravity, a rather charming area of restaurants, *trattorie*, and art shops. There's a lot of outdoor seafood dining in this area at night, but get there early and snag a table. You have to knock the waiters over the head to get their attention, and the turn-over of tables is measured in geological time. Also, don't expect them to have a lot of patience translating the menu. So order something you can point to in a glass case or on someone else's plate, or you'll risk getting fish eyeball soup (served cold).

There are also a number of bars in this area that sprawl onto the streets. Notice wherever you go the men clutching their car radios like purses, as if to make a fashion statement. They certainly make it easy for a car radio thief carrying his goods.

Leaving Rome

You're pulling out of the *Stazione Termini*, bags stowed securely all over the seats to proclaim the compartment reserved. There's a faded picture of the Blessed Virgin on the wall, elegantly framed in a metallic holder screwed to the wall. "I think I've seen all there is to see of this country called Italy," you ponder. "Yes, I've had just about enough of the Roman way of life."

It's time to collect the memories of the day you've spent discovering the roots of Western civilization. It should all come back to you now as a surrealistic dream—or a few pages out of your Art 102 class (the Italian Renaissance unit that you blew on your final, remember?). If only you'd gone to Italy *before* you took that ridiculous class, you might have paid more attention. But then, it wouldn't have been possible to pay *less* attention.

What was it about Rome that makes you glad you're back on the train? The food was okay. So was the price of wine. Maybe it was all those gypsies that had you paranoid. Or those guys with AK47's slung over their shoulders, staring at your legs while you were trying to relax and eat. Whatever it was, you're content to look ahead to the next assault—Greece.

In the meantime, though, you might as well get into the train life again. It's a haul to Brindisi and these Italian trains are kind of slow (unless you compare them with Bulgarian trains).

But you've got to be careful on Italian trains. You can be ripped-off by the most innocent-looking people. There are a number of well-documented techniques, and you've heard a few war stories. One is the story of the guy who comes into your compartment late at night and wakes you up to offer mineral water. Just before that, someone else put a dead mouse in your mouth. So, when you are awakened, you gladly accept the water. And when you wake up next, you'll find that you've got a hell of a hangover and no more Eurailpass, passport, or cash.

Another technique: someone in an official-looking jacket asks to see your passport and tells you to follow him down the train. While he is "questioning" you, your compartment is being cleaned out.

The best advice is to kill anyone who enters your compartment and throw him off the train. Otherwise, you're taking a big chance.

Corfu & Athens

Greece is a very, very old country. How old is it, you ask? It's so old that an ordinary American—who considers a black-and-white TV an "antique" —can have a tough time getting a grip on the numbers. So we turned to that fine newspaper, USA Today, and asked the folks there who write the "Asinine Statistics for Boring People" boxes to help us out. Their report is as follows:

Gather all the moldy tomatoes and zucchini in the bottom of every refrigerator in America and add their total age. Add that number to the percentage of White Males who bowl Tuesdays. Subtract the White Females who believe Elvis is alive. This gives us a working number of 5,320. Fine. Divide that by the fraction of college students who have tried pot and believe that walking on sidewalk cracks is unlucky. Finally, depending on whether you add or subtract the percentage of Retired Americans who own a handgun and suffer from lower back pain, you come out with a number in the 1900-1700 B.C. ballpark. (By the way, 8% of all working Americans drive past a ballpark going to and from work each day.)

So Greece is a pretty old place. (32% of Americans think the spelling of "old" should be changed to "olde.")

On a slightly more serious note, Greece presents a problem for the Let's Blow traveler. Since a lot of the fun in Greece happens on the islands, you need more time than we've alloted to really see anything. If you're really rushed, spend a few days on an island and then head into Athens for a day or so. If you have more time, the most popular islands to visit are **Mykonos**, **Ios**, and **Santorini**.

If we stick with our goal of telling you how to experience everything worthwhile in Europe in two weeks, there just isn't time to visit a series of Greek islands. There is time, however, for a stop on the island of Corfu. Besides, some say the Greek islands are like Chuck Norris movies—if you've seen one, you've seen 'em all.

Getting There
Via Brindisi

For folks with a Eurailpass, the most popular route to Greece has always been the ferry from Brindisi, Italy to Patras on the west coast of Greece. With a ticket to Patras, you can stop over in Corfu.

The huge popularity of this ferry route has nothing to do with the quality of the service or the cleanliness of the ships. (In fact, 53% of all male passengers with receding hairlines thought that the restrooms could be cleaner.) It's because the crossing is FREE if you have a Eurailpass. Be warned: the ferry can be a real zoo during the summer. The ships are more crowded than the after-Christmas sale at Wal-Mart.

The crossing can be worth it just for the opportunity to meet fellow Americans on their way to Greece. On the top deck, there are swarms of them facing the Greek coast, trying to memorize the glossary of Greek words from their *Let's Go*: "Hey Tim, pah-rah-kah-LO. Tee O-ra Fev-yo-me? Pou-EE-ne A-m-e-r-i-c-a-n E-x-p-r-e-s-s? Dhen mee-LAO el-leen-ee-KA? Oh, hell. This is all god-damn Greek to me, man."

Via Yugoslavia

An alternative route to Greece is via one of the ships that come down the Yugoslavian coast, starting from the port of **Rijeka** on the Italian border. You can reach Rijeka via buses from the Italian city of Trieste (where, incidentally, James Joyce is buried, but see the chapter on Dublin).

The ferry ride down the Yugoslavian coast is spectacular, and the boats stop at several islands on the way. If one catches your fancy, you can hop off and catch the next boat a few days later to continue to Greece. (In particular, we recommend a stopover on the islands of **Rab**, **Hvar**, or **Korcula**.)

If you decide to take this route, be sure to stop in **Dubrovnik**, a beautiful walled city on the Yugoslavian coast. It's a lot of fun and inexpensive.

At press time, Yougoslavia was embroiled in a nasty civil war.

By the time you read this, they might have blown themselves to smithereens or kissed and made up. We have no idea what will happen, so you'll have to judge for yourself whether a trip down the Yugoslav coast is worth it—or even possible.

Corfu

If you've arrived on the Brindisi ferry, you'll make landfall on Corfu at the New Port. Find your way into the city and go to the **Spianada**, a kind of big garden with lots of cafes and restaurants. There you'll find the Tourist Office (**GNTO**), where all the folks speak English and will provide you with lots of advice and an island map. From the port, walk away from the water on Napoleontos Street and hang a left onto I. Theotaki. Then find G. Theotaki Street.

Wait a minute. Weren't we just on Theotaki Street? Well, you've just discovered one of the big problems with Corfu: all the streets are named after one family. They're probably swell folks, but the Theotakis can make your visit complicated. For help, be sure to get a copy of *Corfu News* from the Tourist Office.

West of the Spianada is the main attraction in Corfu Town: the remains of a huge, old fortress built by the Venetians, of all people. Don't ask us why. We're still confused by the Theotaki family. The fortress—or the **Paleo Frouri**, as we Theotakis call it—was built in the 14th century and was one of the best defended fortresses in Europe until the British blew it up in the 1860's. (Very destructive people, the British.) The fortress is worth a look, and there's a sound and light show during the summer from Tuesdays to Fridays.

On your right as you leave the fortress, the **Palace of St. Michael and St. George** "houses an exquisite collection of Japanese and Indian ceramics, silk screens, and wood carvings. No visitor will want to miss the breath-taking collection of mosaics from the Byzantine basilica at Paleopolis." Thanks, but we'll save our money for a trip to The Yarn and Knitting Needles Museum.

Eating in Corfu Town

The best place to start looking for food is in the area around N. Theotaki Street. (There's that name again.) Of the scores of restaurants, we tried **To Nautikon** at #150, mostly because we wanted to hear people practice the Greek they learned from *Let's Go*. The best pizza is at **Pizza Pete** at 19 Arseniou Street.

Evening Entertainment

Nothing really happens in Corfu until late in the evening. The time-honored way to pass the early evening is to wander the Spianada and maybe stop for a drink at one of the cafes. Later, you can head for one of the discos on the port road north of town. The **Hippodrome** is a good place to meet people; it even has a swimming pool.

Even more entertaining is to head down the coast to the village of **Benitses**, which has become a vacation ghetto for the British working class. Here you can mingle with " *'undreds of blokes wot came to get a bleedin' tan and maybe a bit a wot you fancy, y'know wot I mean, John?"* Darned if we do, actually. However, if you didn't completely clog your arteries in London with fried animal by-products, you can stop at the **Olde King George Grill** for fish 'n chips and a warm Watneys.

Afterwards, head over to **Spiros On the Beach**, where you can engage in repartee with your new British mates: *"I don't like you, I don't. I sarw you making eyes at my mot's tits, didn't I? I mean, it stands to reason that a bloke can only take so much, you know wot I mean, John? Wot I mean is like I fink it's all a load of bollocks, like. 'Nother pint of Watneys there, mate?"*

West of Corfu Town

Although Corfu Town and the area around it can be interesting when you first arrive in Greece, folks with a little more time on their hands may want to head to the west of the island to the town of **Agios Gordios**. This village is one of those oases in Europe where there are more American college students in one **place than Theotakis in Corfu.**

On one hand, it's easy to see why people go to the west of the island. The scenery is spectacular, and you get beautiful sunsets. On the other hand, most of the college kids aren't sober enough to notice. They're in town strictly for the four famous S's—sun, sand, sex, and suds.

The village of Agios Gordios is about ten miles west of Corfu Town. You can take a cab there, or you can bum a ride at the ferry. Several hotels meet the international ferries and try to entice people to come to their establishment. If you agree to take a look at the hotel, you can usually get a free ride across the island.

Once in the village, many tourists stay at the **Pink Palace**, a dump of a hotel on the beach. Anyone with class and taste avoids this place. Therefore, it's full of young men in clothes too gay-looking for a Brazilian hairdresser, who refer to each other only as "Bud" or "Dude," and who spend their days tossing footballs to each other on the beach. You've probably recognized your fraternity brothers by now. The hotel attracts its share of women, too, and it's well worth spending a few days there.

Further down the beach, the slightly better **Hotel International** is owned by the cousin of the Pink Palace owner and absorbs the overflow from the Palace. Guests at either hotel may use the facilities of the other.

Most of the action in Agios Gordios takes place on the beach, and there's lots to do: water skiing, jet skiing, parasailing, wind surfing, scuba diving, etc. Divers should ask around for Andreas Dukakis, a local P.E. teacher who operates a dive shop from a restaurant on the beach.

Of the restaurants on the beach and in the little village, we give high grades to **The Seabreeze**, located right on the beach.

Be sure to rent a moped while on the west side of the island. It's by far the quickest and cheapest way to get around. Be careful, though, because the roads are twisty and narrow, and the natives drive as if they're delivering transplant organs to the nearest hospital. Add spectacular scenery and the donkey sitting in the middle of the road around the next bend, and you can see why driving is hazardous.

Places you should consider visiting from Agios Gorgios include the village of **Pelekas**, which sits high on a hill overlooking **Glyfada beach**. The beach is a nice place to relax for a few hours and take a swim to wash all the bugs out of your teeth (another hazard of mopeds). Another beautiful beach, **Myrtiotissa**, is further north, and you can try nude sunbathing there if you're anxious for your privates to get skin cancer, too. But remember: riding 20km back to your hotel with a third degree burn on an erogenous zone can ruin your whole day.

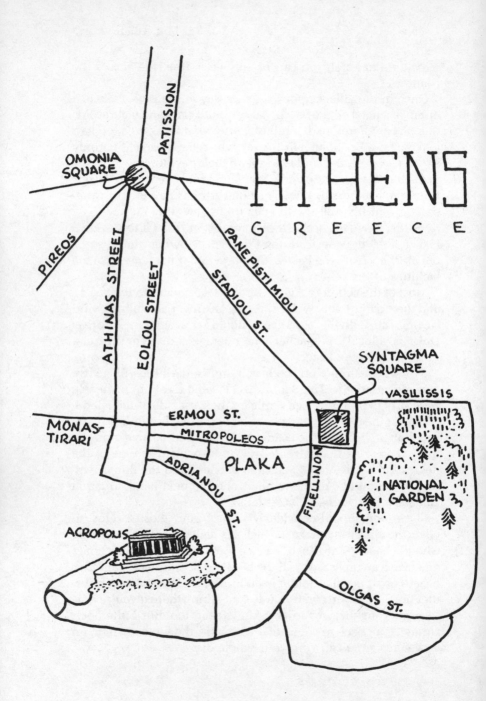

Athens

If you've arrived on the Brindisi-Patras ferry, the train will come into the Peloponnese station. From there, get to **Omonia Square**, which is close to most of the action in Athens. Cabs are cheap, so if don't want to lug that fake statue of *David* you bought in Italy, grab a taxi.

If you've arrived on a ferry that came down the coast of Yugoslavia, chances are you'll need shrapnel removed from your body, so go to the hospital.

Lots of cheap hotels surround Omonia Square. Cheap, in this context, means about $25 a night for a double room. In particular, head for the area around the food market near City Hall. If you can stand the smell of rotting olives and rancid feta cheese and the sight of skinned sheep heads and octopus, then this is the area for you.

Look at the little map of Athens we've provided. There are basically two squares—Omonia and Syntagma (also known as Constitution), the flea market area of the city (known as Plaka), and the Acropolis. Everything important to the *Let's Blow* occurs around these landmarks.

Details

The unit of currency in Greece is the *drachma*, and there are about 160 to the dollar, which means one *drachma* is worth about two-thirds of a cent. One of the big advantages of Greece is that all restaurant prices contain the tax and gratuity. Therefore, at least in theory, what you see on the menu is what will appear on the bill. More on this later.

American Express is located at 2 Ermou St., Syntagma Square, and it is air-conditioned.

On the cooler days in summer, the temperature in Athens is unbearable. On the warm days, it's somewhat hotter. Also, the city fathers have thoughtfully provided 24-hour smog, so visitors from Los Angeles can feel right at home.

The traffic is equally impressive. A city ordinance in Athens requires each driver to test his horn every ten seconds during the day, more frequently after 11:00pm. Cabs have a special horn that blares continuously.

Air Tickets

Athens remains one of the best cities in Europe for getting cheap airfares, either back to the U.S., or, if you have a taste for lamb served in somewhat dangerous surroundings, to the Middle East. The **USIT** office near Syntagma Square is reliable, but hundreds of travel agents are scattered all over the city, particularly around **Filellinon Street**.

However, bear in mind that you get what you pay for. Consider, for example, a visit by Mark and Jill to the Miami Travel Shop, where Costos Papadopolous, the owner, greets them:

Costos: "Hello, my friends. May I help you?"

Mark: "We're interested in a cheap flight back to Chicago."

Costos: "Chicago! My own brother, Dimitris, lives in Chicago! I'll give you very special price—$400."

Jill: "We were hoping for something cheaper. We're, like, a little low on cash."

Costos: "Where you from, baby?"

Jill: "New York."

Costos: "New York?! My cousin Spiro lives in New York—Spiro's Subs and Pizza. You know it?"

Jill: "Actually, I'm from outside New York, more like New Jersey."

Costos: "Spiro gets his pepperoni from New Jersey! Best pepperoni in America comes from New Jersey, Spiro says. How much do you want to spend?"

Mark: "We hoped about $250 each."

Costos: "That's a tough one kid, but maybe I can help you. You mind making a couple of changes?"

Jill: "No."

Costos: "I can get you two seats on a plane to Riyadh."

Mark: "Is that in Canada?"

Costos: "You're a funny guy, I like you. No, it's in Saudi Arabia, but it's very nice—all air-conditioned. You need a visa, but my friend Andreas can fix it real quick. Five bucks each. The only other problem is that your beautiful girlfriend needs a veil for her face."

Jill: "Why?"

Costos: "Uh, well, it keeps out the dust. It's no problem. My wife is a dressmaker. She can make you a nice veil and a nice black dress to cover your legs. You can use this dress again for disco in Chicago. Very fashionable. All for $15 American."

Mark: "How long do we have to stay in Saudi Arabia?"

Costos: "One day, it depends . . . "

Jill: "On what?"

Costos: "On whether the airport in Beirut is open."

Jill and Mark: "*Beirut?!*"

Costos: "It's no problem, all very safe."

Mark: "But Americans aren't safe in Beirut."

Costos: "You won't be Americans then! My friend Georgio does some, er, business with people in Swiss Embassy. He get you two nice passports. But I need pictures. If you don't have any, I got a Polaroid. I'll throw them in for free."

Mark: "How long? . . . "

Costos: "In Beirut? Two hours. But you can catch a museum. I think there's still one left, or at least part of one. Then it's *kijowohworskiwolski!*, as they say in Poland."

Jill: "Poland?"

Costos: "You'll love it there! Friendly people, big monuments. The Poles can do things with concrete you won't believe. Pack a few meals, though. Food's a bit short there. My neighbor, Constantine, runs a snack bar. He can pack you something. Six bucks American each, plus eight bucks American each for the Polish visa."

Mark: "Then do we fly . . . ?"

Costos: "To America? You betcha, buddy! Chicago, Windy City, White Sox, deep-dish pizza, Sears Tower, delays at O'Hare."

Mark: "I don't know. It sounds like a lot could go wrong."

Costos: "Okay, I give you written guarantee. If you have any problem, just call me."

Jill: "It *is* cheap, Mark."

Mark: "Okay, we'll take it."

Costos: "Great! You pay now. Cash only, small bills, okay? Hey, you kids want to buy some t-shirts?"

Eating in Greece

Greek food is distinguished by the fact that it contains more oil than Jed Clampett's former backyard.

The most popular dish in Greece is *moussaka*, and it's served almost everywhere, although the quality varies considerably. *Moussaka* consists of baked hamburger or lamb cooked with vegetables, usually eggplant, often topped with mashed potatoes and cheese. It's flavored, as is most food in Greece, with oregano. Generally, it's pretty tasty, although at times you'll get some that's a few days old and hasn't been refrigerated very well. In that case, order a *choriatiki*, a big tomato and cucumber salad, also served almost everywhere.

Another Greek specialty is *dolmothakia*, which consists of ground meat and rice wrapped in grape leaves. "*Grape leaves?!*" you say. "Haven't these people ever heard of hamburger buns?" Actually, it tastes good, but it doesn't remind you of Welches Grape Jelly. You could also try *souvlaki*, which is shish kebabs of lamb, chicken, or pork.

The Greeks favor a beverage called *retsina*, a wine with pine tree sap. You can impress your friends with your mastery of Greek culinary arts and make this wine at home. Just buy a bottle of cheap wine and add a cup of drain cleaner. *Retsina* does make a good paint remover, but be careful not to spill it on exposed flesh.

The famous Greek aperitif is *ouzo*, a licorice-flavored liqueur which turns milky white when diluted with water. *Ouzo* makes Noxzema taste great. Fortunately, Heineken, Löwenbräu, and Amstel are widely available and rarely cost more than a buck.

Be wary in restaurants, because many Greek waiters have poor math skills. (Must be the public schools.) They're especially weak in addition. If your own command of math extends only to knowing that 230+470+520 *drachma* equals a lot of *drachma*, then resign yourself to paying a little more than you should. Also, be careful that the waiter doesn't add a service charge to the bill, because the prices include a 13% gratuity. You'll note that all menus give two prices for everything. The price on the left is the actual cost of the item, and the price on the right includes service and tax (it's what you end up paying).

The Acropolis

On a hill overlooking Athens, **The Acropolis** contains the ruins of several temples and theaters and was the center of activity in ancient Greece. Wait until the temperature drops into the low 90's, and head up for a look. You go from the Plaka region of the city, or take bus #5 or #9 from the Museum of Archaeology in the center of town. Admission to the Acropolis is about $4.00 ($2.00 if you have a student ID card).

Stroll up to the **Parthenon**. The center of the Acropolis, it's a temple built, oh, eons ago, for the goddess Athena. It was under repair when we were there, but it's a nice building to get photographed against. Since the walls are white, you should wear something colorful so your friends don't have to play "Where's Missy in the Photo?"

From the Acropolis, you can survey modern Athens, shimmering in a cloud of smog. Millions of TV antennas point proudly skyward, and thousands of ugly apartment buildings provide a concrete counterpart to the grandeur of the ancient city. If only Plato and those guys could see what progress has brought!

While you're on the hill, you may want to check out the **Acropolis Museum**, sort of behind the Parthenon and down the hill a little ways. It contains lots of bits and pieces of broken statues that fell off the buildings or were dug up during renovations.

Seriously, folks, the Acropolis is one of the few sights in Greece that is truly moving. Even if you hated Philosophy 101 and think Socrates deserved all the hemlock he could drink, the Acropolis is the birthplace of democracy and Western civilization, and you can't help but be a little awed. America—and its philosophy of individual freedom, civil rights, open debate, God, guns, and guts—exists because of the ancient Greeks, and you're standing where it all started.

At night, the Acropolis is floodlit, and if you got a hotel room where we told you to, you should have a great view of the hill—especially if your hotel provides access to the roof.

Every night during the summer, the Acropolis features a sound and light show highlighting the ruins. The only exception to this rule is when there is a full moon. Check before schlepping up there. The cheapest seats cost about $2.20 for students. The whole shooting match lasts only an hour. So what happens? Well, they light up the buildings on the Acropolis hill and play music and stuff. It's a little like describing the best home run you ever saw or the Genesis concert with lasers. You have to be there.

Shopping

Athens is a great place to shop for a few specific items: leather goods, loose wool sweaters, and ceramics. Of course, there are plenty of trashy tourist treats, like a tiny plastic Parthenon you can buy for people you don't like.

If you have some money to spare and want to pick up a nice leather purse, head for the area known as the **Flea Market** in the Plaka near the Monastiraki subway stop. Just start exploring the side streets. There's a huge number of shops to browse, and most stay open until 11:00pm. Walk around before dinner, check out the prices, and return just before closing time for the kill. Often, of course, it's not clear who's hunting whom:

Stavros: "Hello, little lady. May I help you?"

Kim: "Hi, I'm sorta interested in a leather bag."

Stavros: "I give you special price because you are American. Look at this bag, genuine calf leather, finest quality. Soft as a woman's teet."

Kim: "What's a teet?"

Stavros: "Boobs, titties, knockers, gumbies, you know. For you, special price—10,000 *drachma*."

Kim: "That's kind of high, but it is a nice bag, I guess."

Stavros: "Best quality! This calf was only fed fresh grass. The leather was coaxed off. 10,000 *drachma*."

Kim: "How about 4,000 *drachma*?"

Stavros: "Hey, you make funny jokes, little lady! Feel the leather. Lick it. Okay, so my children go hungry tonight. No problem. For you, *9,500 drachma*."

Kim: "4,500 *drachma*."

Stavros: "Oh, so you want to insult me now? Okay, my wife can beg on the streets for money so my daughter can have the operation that will save her life so her blind grandmother can see her one last time before they lock her up for stealing money to help my cousin Constantine get help for his alcohol problem. But, for you, okay, 8,000 *drachma*."

Kim: "6,000 *drachma*."

Stavros: "Okay, you've got a deal, lady. Boy, you really beat me down in price. I'm not making anything on this sale."

One of the stores where we got a good deal (only after negotiations so protracted that we could have eliminated an entire class of nuclear missiles) is **Petropoulos and Kourbelas** at 109 Andrianou Street in the Plaka. Just be persistent!

Nightlife

The best place to eat in the evening is along the **Plaka**. This is not for the quality or the price of food—indeed, prices will be higher than elsewhere in the city. However, the action's in the Plaka at night, and you can easily spend an entire evening there.

Start with an apéritif and some olives to nibble to take away the taste of the *retsina*. As the sun goes down and the air cools, the streets of the Plaka become crowded with natives and tourists. Take your time, stroll around, and note restaurants you may want to try later.

It's a good time to look at the leather shops in the area. Nobody seems to eat until at least 9:30pm, so don't allow yourself to be hustled by the "hosts" who block your path on every street in the Plaka and try to persuade you to enter their restaurant. Many of these guys could build successful careers in the U.S. selling used Pintos.

We won't pretend to have tried even a fraction of the restaurants in the Plaka. (And anyway, choosing a restaurant is like choosing a bowling ball—someone else just can't do it for you.) A place we did enjoy was **The Moon** on Adrianou Street, which serves unexceptional food but is run by friendly people. Another famous guidebook mentions The Moon, so be prepared for a wait in line with fellow Americans.

We've always believed that the average vegetarian isn't suffering from anything that a good meatball sub wouldn't cure, but we were impressed with **Eden**, a famous vegetarian (it's "famous" because you-know-who from Harvard recommends it) restaurant at 3 Flessa Street. Try to sit on their nice little terrace. They serve a really delicious dish called *bureki*, a sort of pie with potatoes, cheese, and lots of mint. While we thought bologna or at least some bacon bits on top would improve it, it's pretty good as is.

Also, check out eateries on Panos Street, a small street with some so-so restaurants—many with great views of the Acropolis from their outside tables. The only problem in eating at, say, **Taverna Poulokis** on this street is there are more stray cats than Japanese tourists. It's tough to swallow your grape leaves stuffed with whatever they stuff grape leaves with (cats, perhaps?), while emaciated cats surround your table and stare at you with pitiful, hungry eyes. The view, however, makes up for the guilt.

Other places to try in the Plaka: **O Kostis** (18 Kithadineon), which is right in the middle of the pedestrian traffic swarming through the area. The food is fine but nothing special. **Platanos** at 4 Diogenous has better food. Order the roast chicken—it's worth coming to Greece for.

After dinner, take the time to stroll around the streets again. Do Greeks ever go to bed? You could maybe visit one of the hokey Greek cabarets found all over the place. We saw the type of people who were going in—maybe your parents?—and decided to give it a miss, but if you like that kind of thing . . .

Dublin

A well-known student travel book once described Dublin as a city where "literature hangs in the smokey air." Of course, this begs the question of why Tolstoy wasn't born in Detroit.

A more accurate description: Dublin is a pleasant, run-down city and, though it doesn't have the attractions of London, Paris, or Munich, it's a pretty nice place to spend a few days, maybe at the end of your big Two Week Trip. And, if you're from Boston College, Notre Dame, Loyola, or any other Catholic school, a trip to Dublin assumes the importance of Columbia students heading to Israel (which we will tackle in our book *Israel in a Weekend*, coming out next year).

Getting There

You can get to Ireland easily from London by taking the combination of a train and a ferry. You pick up the boat-train (or, as it's affectionately known to the Irish, the "cattle boat") at **London's Euston Station**; there's both a day and a night departure.

The night sailing can be unpleasant, since throughout the train ride (and possibly stormy ferry crossing) you'll be in the company of hundreds of drunk Irish migrant workers intent on guzzling their I.Q.'s in pints of beer. If you're a fan of fraternity parties, this may sound awesome, but be warned that you'll probably leave the ferry *wearing* several pints of regurgitated Guinness. To each his own.

If you've taken the day sailing, you'll arrive in **Dun Laoghaire** (the port where the ferry docks) in the early evening. You can pick up a bus or a train into the city.

The train will drop you at **Pearse Station**—a good area to find a bed-and-breakfast. Irish B&B's are an institution in themselves.

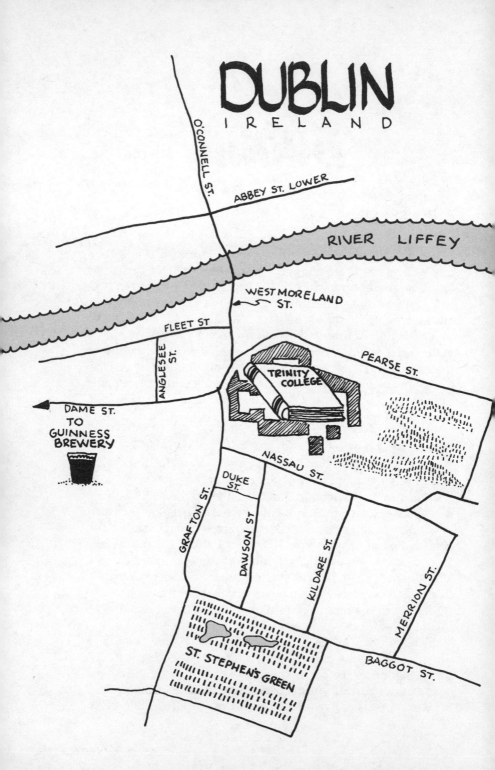

They generally have names more suitable to a Catholic girls' school than a flophouse: "St. Contracepta's" or "St. Pious the Martyred."

By the way, for you young lovers who brought your hormones along, a visit to Dublin may be your chance to experience first-hand the Rewards of Celibacy. Things are changing in Ireland, but not very fast, and Irish landladies have a reputation for not allowing their sheets to be besmirched, if you'll pardon the expression, with the joyous issuances of youth. Claiming to be brother and sister may work, though not, we hasten to add, if your name is O'Mahoney and your girlfriend is a dead ringer for LaToya Jackson.

Your Fellow Travelers

There are two types of young people who visit Ireland. First, there are the pseudo-intellectuals from colleges in New York and Boston who pretend to have read James Joyce and are in Dublin to catch a little authentic flavor.

Second, there are the legions of big, cheerful guys and gals from B.C. and Notre Dame with names like Shannon O'Shea, Shaun O'Malley, or, horror of horrors, Erin Flanagan. These folks think Joyce is a nice girl's name. They're in Dublin to "like, discover my roots" and to have stories to tell at the local Ancient Order of Hibernians when they get home.

Money

Irish money, called the punt (think of football), is sort of like British money but a lot prettier. Irish coins are the most attractive in Europe, with all sorts of neat animals on them (think of Animal Crackers).

The **American Express** office is at 116 Grafton Street, and it's about as spacious and comfortable as a temporary dorm room, except there's nowhere for you and your girlfriend to stretch out.

Another useful place to know about is **USIT**, an Irish student travel agency and one of the best of its kind in Europe. Unlike many "student" travel agencies in Europe (especially in London, Amsterdam, and Athens), USIT is completely legitimate—it's part of the Student's Union of Ireland. USIT is at 19-21 Aston Quay, on the south side of the river near O'Connell Bridge (phone 778-117). They offer great deals on airfare, the ferry/train to London, and even reduced-price theater tickets. While you're in the neighborhood, check out the huge Virgin store next door. USIT also has an excellent branch in London near Victoria Station.

Things To See

Dublin is a small, rather sad city. A lot of it is being knocked down to make way for office blocks that look like dorm buildings at a state school. It does have a certain charm, however, and the people are very friendly. Best of all, you can understand them (after a fashion), since they speak English (also after a fashion).

Your first stop should be Trinity College, a beautiful old school founded in 1594 and just across the river from where you're probably staying. It's one of the few schools that uses carbon-dating technology to determine the graduation date of its older alumni. Unfortunately, hardly any Irish students will be around in the summer, because they're all working illegally in the U.S. However, you will find many of your fellow countrymen and -women around, all pursuing their quest for knowledge of Joyce. See if you can identify the following two major species:

Type A: Short, New York, Woody-Allen-without-the-clarinet-looking students trying to finish their thesis at NYU and desperately scratching for evidence that Joyce, in his quest for the allegorical subconscious, was attracted to his mother's view of the essential synthesis of catharsis in the metaphysical. Also, they're hoping to get laid.

Type B: Regular-looking people who thought that being in Ireland for a semester would be neat, and, while they haven't actually cracked their copy of Ulysses yet, they keep meaning to. Next year, they may spend a semester at the University of Kenya, because that might be neat, too, and because that way they could get to meet, you know, real black people.

Walk around Trinity and gape at all the old buildings. The library contains the **Book of Kells**, a famous copy of the New Testament drawn by monks in the middle ages (the period after eight-tracks but before compact discs). You know, it's nice to see a book that old with its cover intact, but the colors aren't exactly Day-Glo. Plus, the book is locked in a glass case, so you can't exactly flip through the pages to find the good parts. They turn over only one new page each day, so it would take as long to see the whole thing as reading a Henry James novel or writing a Ph.D in chemistry or something. Oh, did we forget to mention that the whole thing is in *Latin*? Real mass-market appeal.

If you're in Dublin in late August or early September, you may have the chance to see a **hurling match**, perhaps even a championship game. Hurling, a kind of legalized rioting, consists of a group of men with sticks trying to beat the hell out of a small ball, while another group of men with sticks tries to stop them. There are goalposts at both ends of the field, and the official objective is to get the ball into or over the goalposts, but that ignores half the fun and all the violence.

Hurling is fun to watch, and it's the closest thing to *American Gladiators* they have in Ireland. It looks really dangerous (and, for insurance purposes, our publisher insists we warn you not to try hurling at home), but it is pretty darn exciting. Irish people will tell you it's not half as dangerous as it looks. They're lying.

For a really bizarre experience, take a trip to **St. Michan's Church** on Church St. (now there's *real* urban-planning for you). The vaults of this small church contain a collection of mummified bodies that for some reason have been preserved by the atmosphere. If the guide is in a good mood, he'll even let you shake the hand of a 700-year-old Crusader. ("But didn't The Crusaders release an album in 1989?") It costs about $2 to go into the crypts, and hours are Monday-Friday 10:00am-4:30pm, closed for lunch 12:45pm-2:00pm (mummies have to eat, too).

Dublin has some of the least expensive **theaters** in Europe. We know—the only theater you've attended has 15 screens with *Friday the 13th, Part 6* playing on 12 of them. Well, this is different. This kind of theater has live actors, sort of like *Masterpiece Theatre* on TV but without Alistair Cooke.

"How do they do car chases in a live theater?" you ask.

"They don't," we reply.

"Sounds boring," you grumble.

"It's not!" we retort quickly. The language and drama of the theater can have unparalled tension and excitement. Wait'll you see a live Shakespeare play! There, in front of your eyes, are the foibles and failures of humanity, the interplay of emotion and desire and idealism, the marriage of wit and pathos.

"Not even a quick car chase?" you ask. "How about shootings or explosions? Any of that?"

"No," we say. In the theater, *language alone* has the power to mutilate, to rend lives into wretched scraps of battered flesh, to detonate evil and explode wickedness. Language alone!

But we're losing you. If you want to take in a play, you can usually get cheap ($10-$20), last-minute tickets by showing your student ID at any of the main theaters. The most famous is the **Abbey Theatre** (26 Lower Abbey St., phone 787-222), but also check the **Gate Theatre** (Cavendish Row, Parnell Square; phone 744-045), the **Gaiety Theatre** (S. King St., phone 771-717), and the **Olympia Theatre** (Dame St., phone 777-744). Remember, there won't be scenes from upcoming plays, and people don't usually bring a trough of popcorn, 96-ounce sodas, and moose-size M&M boxes inside.

Food

After this intellectual overload, you're going to need sustenance. Irish food is all-too-similar to the food you enjoyed in England. Like the English, the Irish will deep-fry anything—unless, of course, they can boil it to mush.

In a country where the four basic food groups have long been beef, pork, lamb, and french fries, and where frying is considered a sacrament, the concept of healthy eating has had about the same appeal as seeing the Pope cruise around town on a moped. Nonetheless, the Irish have recently discovered you can reduce your intake of animal fat to half your body-weight per day without ill-effect. For the Dublin equivalent of health food, visit **The Coffee Bean**, a small restaurant above a vegetable shop at 4 Nassau St. called The Runner Bean. They have great salads— something hard to find in Dublin—and a wide selection of pseudo-vegetarian dishes and good desserts. It gets very crowded at lunch, and there's also the little Irish problem of incessant smoking, so go early or late.

There are a few other interesting places to check out, too. What used to be fun but is now getting a little run-down is a strange place called **The Bad Ass Cafe**, whose motto "Always a Nice Pizza Ass" is available on t-shirts. The restaurant, located in an old warehouse between the river and the huge, ugly Central Bank building, is directly inland from the Ha'penny Bridge, a famous footbridge across the Liffey River. (The street address is Crown Alley, but ask anyone where the Ha'penny Bridge is, get on the south side of it, and you can't go wrong.) The Bad Ass Cafe is painted in violent shades of red, which gives it the air of an abandoned firehouse, and it features creaking wooden floors, mediocre but edible pizza, and pretty good soup. The staff is young and friendly in an off-hand, don't-blame-us-we-just-work-here way. The walls are papered with U.S. memorabilia and posters of upcoming events in Dublin, so you can plan your evening while having dinner.

Another pretty good place to eat is a new but built-to-look-old restaurant called **Casper and Gambini's** on Suffolk Street. It features a piano player, lots of dark corners, and reasonable food. Very crowded at lunch. They even serve things that aren't deep-fried (the salads, for instance). And—be still your heart!—they serve Schlitz and Bud.

If you can afford an angioplasty when you get home, you might want to indulge in fish 'n chips, as popular in Ireland as in England. By far the best place to sample them is **Beshoff's** at 14 Westmoreland St., pretty close to American Express. (They also have a branch at 7 O'Connell St.) On an average day, they'll have 20 kinds of fish they'll fry fresh for you. Go on—go for it. Zits give your face character.

One of the best places to eat in Dublin is the self-service cafe/restaurant of the **Kilkenny Design Center** on Nassau St. The KDC is a neat shop selling a huge range of ceramics, pottery, woolens, jewelry, etc., all designed and made in Kilkenny (about 70 miles from Dublin). The store itself is worth visiting, though it's not cheap. However, they also have a small restaurant upstairs with salads, soups, homemade breads, cheeses, and several hot dishes at lunchtime. It's best to go at odd times because of the lines. A nice treat is to have a mid-morning coffee there (and definitely a piece of their shortbread). Read the paper and watch the cricket players mincing around on the lawns of Trinity across the street. (Cricket is a sport that makes prostate surgery seem like a fun way to spend the afternoon.) The Kilkenny shop is in constant danger of going out of business, so let's hope they're around when you and your prostate are.

Finally, an institution in Dublin is the chain of **Bewley's Oriental Cafes**, which have been around longer than California. You can find Bewley's scattered around the center of the city, and they serve both lunch and breakfast. Lunch is not recommended, but their breakfast is pretty good if you like the Irish tradition of eating six kinds of fried meat before 9:00am. Our friend Frank had a big breakfast there the morning of his wedding, and he swears it was the only thing that got him through the ceremony. They do serve excellent coffee and awesome pastries in an old-world atmosphere. Bewley's used to be big student hangouts, especially the ones on Grafton St. and Westmoreland St., but they've become overpriced for the student market in recent years. Also, the branch on Westmoreland St. has a little museum upstairs. Whoops! Scratch that! What are we advocating here, *education*?!

Language

Some advice on the language in Ireland will be useful.

Until recently ("recently" in Ireland being anytime after the birth of Christ), the Irish spoke their own language, called "Irish" by the natives and "Gaelic" by American linguistics professors. From about 1700 on, the Irish were persuaded by their British rulers to speak English. The Irish learned English quickly, thanks mainly to the innovative teaching methods used at the time: beatings, deportation, and starvation. (And you thought Spanish 101 was tough.)

To make a long story short, most people in Ireland ended up speaking English, except for some parts of western Ireland where the civilizing influence of the Brits never penetrated.

Since the independence of Ireland, the Irish government has made a valiant effort to teach children the ancient language of their forefathers. The teaching methods are very innovative: beatings, deportation, and school cafeteria food.

The result of all this concern for the cultural soul of the Irish people has been to leave most of the people confused. They speak English most of the time, but, with persuasion, they'll admit to knowing a little Irish. The extent of this knowledge consists of singing the national anthem in Irish—arms wrapped around each other, blind drunk—whenever Ireland beats any other country at anything, be it soccer, cycling, or fire-walking. For your reference, Irish sounds a lot like your Polish (or Russian, or Ukrainian) grandmother muttering the rosary.

Your only contact with the Irish language will be in trying to figure out where the buses go. The bus destinations are written in Irish in large letters, with the English translation underneath in print fine enough to go on the bottom of a "Waterfront property in Florida for $10 an acre and NO MONEY DOWN" contract. You'll find the Irish place names about as useful as if they were written in Thai, but here's a good tip: Any bus with "An Lar" as its destination will go near or on O'Connell Street.

The F-Word

Since we're on the subject of language, the Irish have another interesting characteristic that most of the snobbier guidebooks gloss over: The Irish are the most elegantly profane people speaking English today. They have a special fondness for the word "fuck," and even well-educated people will insert the f-word into every other sentence.

The first thing to notice is that the Irish use the word "fuck" as a noun, verb, adjective, and adverb. True masters of the genre will use the word in several different contexts in a single sentence. Here are several examples:

Sean: "Hey Mick, want to fucking play soccer?"

Mick: "Would ye ever fuck off of that. I have to fuck on down to the superfuckingmarket to get some fucking fags for the fucking auld' wan.

A rough translation of Mick's words would be, "I'm afraid that your suggestion, while having much merit, is impractical. I am committed to strolling to the food emporium to purchase some cigarettes for my dear Mama."

Note in the above example that the true expert will insert the f-word into the *center* of a word without breaking pace in the slightest. We thank Paul Neenan of Dublin for this interesting observation.

Another peculiarity of English as spoken by the Irish is the way the Irish greet each other, using language that would get you expelled from any small Christian school in the U.S. Consider a reunion of two old pals Joe and Frank:

Joe: "Frank, you fucking bollocks! Where've you been, you dirty whore?"

Frank: "Joe, you scaldy arsed bastard! How're they hanging?"

Literary Dublin

The Irish, as those of Irish extraction know, write English better than anyone else, which is why all the Joyce fans go to Dublin in the first place. Some Irish short story writers are especially famous. If you have a sober moment, look for the work of Frank O'Connor, Liam O'Flaherty, or (more modern) William Trevor.

The best place to look for paperbacks is **Easons** on O'Connell St. They also have a discount store on Abbey St. (go out the side exit of the O'Connell St. store, and it's right across the street). Two other good bookstores are **Fred Hannas'** and **The Greene Bookstore**, both on Nassau St. (beside Trinity). The employees at Hannas' are really prissy (failed short-story writers, many of them), but The Greene Bookstore is a neat, turn-of-the-century place with lots of nooks and crannies. Be sure to check out the upstairs.

By now you know that Dublin is a big-time literary city. In normal circumstances, this alone would be enough to disqualify the town from *Let's Blow*. What can we say? Dublin seems like a genuinely friendly place, where people love to talk. Plus, Ireland is one of the few countries in Europe that still welcomes Americans (or at least tolerates them, with a certain degree of amusement).

Pubs and Pub Culture

As you can imagine, there are more pubs in Dublin than nerds at MIT. Most pubs are rather ordinary places where locals go to drink. Contrary to popular belief, most of these places are quiet, without music, where people chat and gossip.

Most Irish pubs are named after their current or former owner, unlike the English custom of naming pubs in an evocative way. For example, "Murphy's" in Dublin would be called "The Royal Cat in the Microwave" in London.

Below is a list of some pubs to try:

The Bailey (South Anne St.). Trendy place, mainly inhabited by fashionable young office workers. Very few students.

John Kehoe's (up the street from The Bailey). Much like The Bailey in character, but a little more down-market. No place for anyone with respiratory troubles. Los Angeles imports much of its smog from this pub.

The Pink Elephant (Leinster St.). A dark, youngish bar. David Bowie once stopped in after a Dublin concert. According to informed sources, he did not have a drink. (It's still a pretty neat story though, huh? I mean, you and David sort of like walking in each other's footsteps and stuff. . .) There's a disco downstairs. The Elephant is somewhat unique in being one of the few pubs in Dublin that offers happy hours with free munchies.

Hartigan's (near the corner of Leeson St. and St. Stephen's Green). A big student hangout, especially during term time. Popular with med school students from Earlsfort Terrace across the street.

O'Donoghue's (15 Merrion Row, near Baggot St.). A great place to hear free Irish music. But watch out for the legions of middle-aged American tourists from the Shelbourne Hotel up the street. You can recognize them as follows: The couples will be wearing matching "fisherman's sweaters." He's got a bright green cap, at what he thinks is a rakish angle, while she's clutching a plastic Handi-Hat (so popular with middle-aged housewives abroad) and murmuring "Wonerful, wonerful" at every break. Also watch out for the legions of *Lets Go'*ers who infest this place like roaches. O'Donoghue's gets so crowded with this lot that the management often makes them to check their big, orange books at the front desk. Make sure to venture upstairs. (To do this, go back onto the street and go in the other door.) There's always music upstairs, and it's not quite so crowded.

Toner's (down the street from O'Donoghue's). Pub in the front and a music club at the back. U2 used to play here before every sophomore at Univ. of Illinois decided U2 was really cool. Less Irish folk music here and more rock.

The Wexford Inn (Wexford St., near the west side of St. Stephen's Green). A real working class nightspot. Gets many good Irish folk groups, but also a lot of real crap. Ask around before you go. Very few tourists here, so keep it to yourself.

McGrath's (corner of Wexford and Kevin Sts.). Another working class bar, but also attracts students from the nearby technical college.

The Stag's Head (1 Dame Court). This is difficult to find, but it's a cozy bar and, depending on whom you believe, the oldest operating pub in Dublin. Here's how to get there: Get onto Dame St. and, with your back to the huge Central Bank building, look across the street and 100 yards to your right. There's a narrow passageway between two buildings. Cross the street and go through the passageway (hold your nose). The Stag's Head is in front of you.

The Students' Club (University College). This bar, unfortunately, requires a bus ride. Take the #10 bus from O'Connell Street. Make sure it's going in the right direction. It should say "Belfield" on the front, and you need to be on the opposite side of the street from Eason's Bookstore. Belfield is the site of the new campus of the National University of Ireland (University College Dublin). The campus itself looks like it was designed by someone who wasn't very good at building housing projects in Bulgaria, but it's worth a look around anyway. During the term, the Students' Club is standing room only, but you'll manage to meet a few natives, especially if you get really loud and obnoxious.

Meeting the Natives

Since this is one of the few countries you'll visit where you can understand the natives to some degree, you might want to chat with some Real Irish People in the pubs. There are some general guidelines to learn so you don't stand out like an oil sheik at a bar-mitzvah:

Suppose you're sitting in a pub and want to strike up a conversation with the guy on the next stool. The first thing to do is make some kind of eye-contact. Then, chances are, you'll receive that peculiar Irish greeting of a twitch of the head and a "How ye."

In pubs frequented by rural folk, this greeting may instead be "How's she cutting?" —a phrase derived from some agricultural activity in the misty past. Do not misconstrue the greeting by turning to see if there's someone with a chainsaw in the corner. Instead, take a long pause (five minutes is not excessive for a man or woman to gather his/her thoughts) and give a nod that speaks well of your skill in gathering the crops before the rains come. The critical point to remember is that you must *ease* into the conversation. This is not a frat party, where everybody is anxious to get upstairs ASAP.

After a half hour or so of silence, drain your glass with a satisfied sigh, say something like "Well, tide seems to be out on this one," and call for another by saying "Another pint, Mick." (99% of all Irish barmen are Mick or Paddy). This might be a good chance to say something to your would-be-conversationee like "Ye look as dry as the inside of a fertilizer bag. Will ye have a pint?"

Thus begins the friendship dance. Murty (as you subsequently discover is his name) will be compelled to make a vigorous show of refusing your hospitality, uttering things like "Ah, aren't ye an awful man to be tempting me like that. I have to go away home for me dinner." You: "Ah, ye'll have one pint before ye go?" Murty: "I won't now. Sure it would be the death of me."

After a decent interval, you can deliver the killer blow by using one of two lines: "I'll be hurt now if ye don't" or "Isn't it a terrible day when an Irishman will turn down a drink." Murty will accede gracefully.

By the way, before you settle down to chat with your new friend, look over your shoulder and make sure the whole exchange isn't being taped by a Celtic Studies professor from Harvard to use for his book *Structural Features of Cadence in the Irish Oral Tradition.* You'll spot him by the fact that he's wearing a white plastic belt and white shoes with his tweeds.

As you begin your chat, bear in mind that the average Irishman has a limited interest in, and knowledge of, the Jeep Cherokee, R.E.M., Hoosiers basketball, or the problem of non-English-speaking teaching assistants in physics class back home. You can always try to discuss the situation in Northern Ireland, which the Irish describe as "The Troubles" with the same understatement that would lead them to call World War III "The Unpleasantness." However, you'll find the Irish have about the same interest in the northern conflict as the average American has in the Law of the Sea Treaty.

Guinness Brewery Tour

We've already discussed in detail the delightful way of passing the evening in the company of new Irish friends, discussing the merits of the wishbone offense and sinking pints of Guinness. Well, if you really become enamored of this black brew, you should visit the brewery itself.

While they no longer allow tours of the interior, there's a nice visitor's center off Thomas St. As at any Budweiser brewery in the U.S., they first torture you with a short video that's as exciting as watching crackers turn stale. However, you can actually bypass the film and head straight to the little bar in the back, where large ladies will be happy to administer creamy crucibles of comfort. Over all, the Guinness visitor's center is a fun thing to do in Dublin and well worth the time.

Glendalough

About 30 minutes southwest of Dublin are the remains of an ancient monastic settlement called **Glendalough**. Now, before you all yell "WE DON'T DO ANCIENT MONASTIC SETTLE- MENTS!", hear us out. This one is really neat, and it's also a romantic place for a side trip with that special (or not-so-special) person you picked-up at the pub in Dublin last night.

To get there, go to St. Stephen's Green (the side closest to and parallel with Grafton St.). With any luck, you'll find a bus stop for the "St. Kevin's Bus Service," whose blue buses are as ancient as the monasteries. From there, it's only 30 minutes and $5.00 to Glendalough.

The place consists of two old stone towers, lots of ivy-covered ruins, beautiful hills rising from the bus stop, and a wonderful waterfall. Try to bring a picnic lunch for you and the someone special, because, as your mother told you, you can't live on love alone, and there isn't much to eat there. Watch out for nerds ("Would you like to peruse my *Sodomizer's and Schmidt's Extremely Detailed Guide to the Antiquities of Western Europe?*" "No, but I'll take a look at *Sports Illustrated* if you've got it.") on the bus and also that middle-aged couple from O'Donoghue's last night ("Isn't Glendalough just *wonerful*, hon?").

St. Stephen's Green

St. Stephen's Green, or "The Green" as it's known to the natives, is a famous landmark in the center of Dublin at the top of Grafton St. It can be a pleasant place to wander on the rare occasions when the weather is sunny. Sit awhile and write in your journal. Don't snicker—how do you think Thoreau got his big break?

The park is home to flocks of wild birds and herds of man-eating, stick-wielding, whistle-blowing wardens. They execute tourists who desecrate the lawns with their Reeboks. Nonetheless, on the occasional warm day, thousands of pale office workers descend on the park and cover every scrap of grass. The wardens kill many, but enough survive to ensure the survival of the species. Yes folks, nature is both cruel and beautiful.

One of the more interesting sights in the park is the young

women who dispense with their shirts and catch a little sun clad only in a bra. Indeed, many an Irish tax return has been botched by a young accountant whose nerves were shattered by the sight of a thousand shimmering Playtexes.

Shopping for Sweaters

Without a doubt, shopping for sweaters is an important ritual for the visitor to Ireland. You know the kind—big, off-white "fisherman's sweaters" that make you look like the guy in the Irish Spring commercial (or is it the Lucky Charms commercial?).

The sweater-hunter has a few good choices in Dublin. If you're hefting Dad's Gold Amex Card, check out **Brown Thomas** (Grafton St.). B.T.'s, as we travel experts call it, is the fanciest department store in Dublin. A visit there will also give you a chance to rub shoulders with what passes for yuppies in Ireland. You can recognize them because all the women have faces like horses and have names like Fiona and Finnoula, and the guys all wear turtlenecks with expensive tweed jackets. You probably saw them earlier at The Bailey.

Other good stores to check on Grafton St. (the main pedestrian drag between O'Connell and St. Stephen's Green) include **Switzer's** and **Arnott's**.

The very best place to look for sweaters, though, is called **Dublin Woollen Mills**, on the north side of the Ha'penny Bridge, facing the water. This store is interesting for several reasons. First, it has a huge selection of sweaters arranged in a wonderful, no-two-are-the-same way on long tables. If you find one you like and it's too small, forget it, because they won't have it in any other size. But there's always some new treasure at the bottom of the pile. You can get some good deals there, but it's not cheap—expect to pay $100 for a good, heavyweight sweater.

The other interesting thing about the Dublin Woollen Mills is that James Joyce was briefly an agent for the company back in the early 1900's. So, busloads of American tourists descend there every hour on the half hour, seeking a double dose of culture and cross-stitch ("Oh hi! Weren't you kids on the *wonerful* bus to Glendalough yesterday? Wasn't it just *wonerful*? Isn't Dublin just *wonerful*?")

Finally, you could pay a visit to the **Blarney Woollen Mills** on Nassau St. It's smaller in scope, but sometimes it has good sales.

Then again, maybe it's just time to head for home.

Epilogue:
Leaving Europe

While the 20-year-old charter plane is still climbing at a 45-degree angle in heavy turbulence, you fight your way out of your seat, and, ignoring the cries of the cabin staff, you make it to the toilet in time to throw up the residual wine, beer, ouzo, schnapps, and plum brandy you didn't expel in the airport bathroom. Your head feels as if a fleet of ocean-going tankers is being riveted in your brain. The inside of your mouth could qualify for federal toxic dump clean-up funds. You think you might feel better if you shaved your tongue.

You stagger back to your seat, wondering if the damn plane is ever going to level out, and then you realize it's you that's at an angle. You lurch over the two nuns in the aisle and center seats. You remember you've been wearing the same clothes since yesterday morning, but, for several frightening moments, you forget what city you're flying to. You try to take a nap, but your seat companions start saying a loud rosary for the salvation of your soul.

You manage to doze lightly, but you're shaken awake by the drill sergeant stewardess who offers you a choice of Beef Surprise or Chicken Surprise. You barely make it back to the toilet in time.

When you return, the nuns have departed to a section of the plane where the pastures are greener salvation-wise, and you can finally stretch out and sleep.

You awake somewhere over the Atlantic, feeling much better. Things start to come back to you about that last crazy night in

Munich, where you and your buddies decided to find out exactly how many kinds of alcoholic beverages were available in the city. You smile as you recall your last glimpse of Joe, hanging by his fingertips from the bridge over some river. And you can still hear the echoes of Todd's screamed obscenities as the Munich-to-Moscow train pulled out of the station with him handcuffed to a seat. He's probably testing the limits of *glasnost* just about now, you think.

"Jeez," you mutter, "this has been one hell of a trip." You sift through the memories, trying hard not to invoke any that involve food. You remember how proud you felt, after two days on the road in London, when you saw a poster for an upcoming concert by the Grateful Dead. *Hey, I know that band!* you thought to yourself. *Wow. Imagine them being in London the same exact time as me!*

And you think of the time in Amsterdam (or maybe it was Paris) when you and Dexter found a bar that actually had Bud on tap! What a night that was! You guys stayed there until 2:00am trying to explain the rules to Thumper and Quarters to two Swedish girls. God, it just doesn't get any better than that, does it?

But there were some sad times, too—like when Scott called his girlfriend back home, and Bubba, his Brother in the pledge class, answered the phone. What a bummer! A lot can happen back home when a guy is out there On The Road; that's the way it is. A guy really finds himself that way. But it turned out okay, because Scott scored bigtime with a girl in Rome two days later!

Thinking about Scott reminds you that the shit is going to hit the fan when you see your own girlfriend, because you sent her only one postcard and didn't call her once. You start to rehearse your lines: "Oh, *of course* I missed you, sweetheart. I just needed time to, like, grow and be alone with my thoughts." *At least,* you think to yourself, *I bought those sexy French undies to give her.* But then you get a vague recollection of wearing them on your head at a beer hall last night. You hastily search through the flight magazine for the perfume section of the Duty Free Shopping Guide.

You decide to review the crib sheet a friend prepared for you last week, because you realize you'll be seeing your grandparents at the airport in about two hours—the same grandparents who financed this educational journey through Europe. Let's see: "Ah, Paris. The treasures of the Louvre, the glories of Notre Dame. I was overcome with emotion by the astounding collection at the Musee d'Orsay. And the stained glass at Ste-Chapelle, well, what can I say . . . " (Meanwhile, you're thinking, *Stained glass? If it's stained, why don't they just clean it?*)

By now your plane is over land and heading down the coast of Canada, and you try to remember how many bottles of booze you tucked away in your backpack. And how about those "art" magazines you picked up in Amsterdam? Plus, will the Customs people buy your story about how you brought 15 heavy wool sweaters with you when you flew over last July? "Yes, sir," you'll say, "I brought those sweaters with me because I read an outdated travel guide that said that Italy was, like, near Iceland and cold in the summer. But I guess it's changed a lot, what with global warming and all, you know?"

The memories of the trip now come flooding back. You chuckle as you recollect the places, the people, the feelings. You remember a wet night in London, huddling around a fire in a smokey pub, quaffing pints of bitter and trying to dry your clothes from the soaking you got from one of those famous English summer showers (which lasted two weeks). You savored the musty, almost unpleasant smell of the pub, until you realized that the odor came from your sweatshirt, last washed in New Jersey three weeks before.

You remember Paris, strolling down the Champs with your nose full of the aroma of coffee and croissants. *That's where I'm going to settle*, you think. *As soon as I get my degree in Sports Sociology, I'm going back to live in Paris. Maybe I'll write a little, do some teaching, a little consulting. I wonder if I need to learn French?*

But not all your memories are so pleasant. You remember one day, after you had been on the road for several weeks, when you had a cold, you lost your passport, and nobody spoke English. You were so homesick you called the long distance operator in the U.S. just so you could hear a familiar, nasal voice ask, "What city, please?"

You remember meeting so many young people from tons of different places—some of them you'd never heard of before, like Fargo and Casper. You recall a long evening spent around the table at a bar, discussing the deep issues that young people everywhere discuss when they get together—sex, rock music, and sex.

Occasionally, the conversation would shift to politics, and you found yourself for the first time defending your country's values and ideals. You learned about other cultures and how to debate the advantages and problems of the U.S. Of course, if the going got too tough, you could always yell "USA #1! All you foreigners suck the big one!"

Sometimes you came across other Americans at these debates. They had been in Europe too long, and they were cutting down the U.S. in an attempt to suck up to these socialist-loving foreigners. One time, you had to tell some guy from an artsy-fartsy school in Massachusetts, "Hey, why don't you go back to Moscow, Boris?!" Yeah, this trip had certainly made a patriot out of you, and you were glad to be returning to the Land of the Free.

Your stomach has calmed down a little, so you start to think about what you'll eat first when you get home. A really good pizza with pepperoni? Or maybe some decent Chinese take-out, or some hot nachos? No more foreign food for you for a while. It's going to be great to get a really cold beer again that tastes the way beer should taste—good and clean and foamy, with none of that malty taste foreign beers have. And white bread! You can almost taste it sticking to the roof of your mouth so you have to scrape it off with your tongue.

As the plane descends into New York, you begin humming the beginning of *God Bless America*. A young woman behind you picks up the refrain, and a very drunk nun on the far side of the plane starts to conduct the impromptu chorus. Slowly the music swells, and before you know it, the plane fills with a ragged rendition of the song. You feel the tears start to cloud your vision as the plane swoops over Brooklyn until, finally, the wheels kiss the earth and the pilot throws the engines into reverse. You burst into tears as you croak out the last line: " . . . and the hoooome of the braaaave."

You are home again, and on this silly, totally contrived note, we bring the European section of this book to a close.

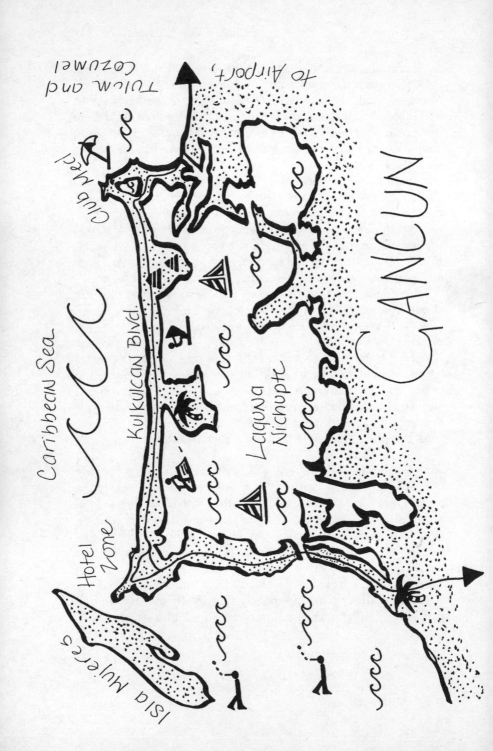

Cancun

Your plane banks steeply along the beachfront skyline as the stewardess hastily grabs the gin-and-tonics from your hands. You gaze at the pristine sand gleaming below and wonder if you'll be too conspicuous at the airport because (a) you're carrying a ski jacket, (b) you're still wearing snow boots from your trek across the tundra of Long Term Parking at Buffalo Airport, and (c) you're white enough to be a poster child for the KKK.

The guys in the front seat are yelping like dogs in heat. You get a mild rush as you realize you've arrived. YES! The excitement makes you remember you need to tap your faucet (five gin-and-tonics between 6:30am and 10:00am), but the stewardess is now shouting for everyone to SIT BACK DOWN! Then you recall the sight and smell of the bathroom in the back of the 30-year-old charter plane, its sink foaming with vacationers' partly digested breakfasts. You decide the G&T's can remain on board a little while longer.

The plane levels out, comes in low over the palm trees, and drops with a thump onto the broiling tarmac. "I'm here!" you say to yourself (or, if you've done a little student theater, you say it out loud). "At last! I'm here in Cancun! **YES! Cancun!**"

Why Cancun?

Hey, wait a minute! you, the alert reader, are thinking. *I thought this book was about Europe, not New Mexico.* It is, but let's do a little comparison between, say, Paris on the one hand and, say, Cancun, on the other.

Both places have funny foreign languages that you don't know how to speak and don't care about anyway. Both places offer a chance to escape parental control for several weeks, eat strange, intestine-disturbing food, and sample exotic alcoholic concoctions. Both places require a plane ride to reach, but, while Paris is many, many hours away, Cancun—**YES! Cancun!**—is just a hop, skip, and a jump away, and you can fly there cheaply.

Consider further: Cancun does not have the Louvre, old smelly cathedrals, boring museums, or guys named Roger (pronounced "Ro-jherrrr") who wear black turtlenecks, smoke clove cigarettes, wet their pants laughing about Jerry Lewis, and try to steal your girlfriend. Instead, all Cancun can offer is miles of great beaches, a peso that has less value than a paperclip, and Spring Break.

Paris vs. Cancun? Cancun vs. Paris? Hmmmm. No contest! **YES! Cancun!**

So we decided—with your best interests at heart, of course—to offer our unique insights and expertise into this most interesting of American playgrounds. (Okay, okay—we needed the tax write-off, too.) And besides, those Harvard dweebs include Malta, Morocco, Turkey, and probably South Carolina by now in *Let's Go Europe*, so we figured Cancun isn't stretching it all that bad.

No, Really—Why Cancun?

We believe the best approach is to go to Cancun for Spring Break, just to get your feet wet, and then whine incessantly until your parents subsidize a summer trip to Europe. Think of your trip to Cancun as Stanley Kaplan for the GRE (Grand Race thru Europe) ahead.

There are several reasons to consider Cancun during the off-season (that is, Spring Break, when you're still several months away from Europe). Foremost, of course, is the **tanning factor.** You can't beat the white beaches and bright sun of Cancun for activating those pigments. (No, pigments are not small Mexican beach bandits.) Just be sure you acquire a good base at a tanning salon before your trip, so as not to waste precious time or, God forbid, arrive all chalky and pale. You *do* want to hit the bars on the first night looking sensational, don't you?

Secondly, there are **no laws** in Mexico—at least no laws that impede fun as we know it. The drinking age may be, oh, 8 or 9 in Cancun, but we didn't see anyone get carded. Plus, for all of you who always wanted to scuba dive but didn't want to bother with scuba classes, Cancun is the place. You won't be turned away even if you're asthmatic, a mediocre swimmer, or cognizant of water pressure only as it relates to your bathtub. You could even have an allergy to compressed air—all you have to do is sign a waiver and flash your credit card. Oh, and a string bikini won't hurt, either.

Last, but not least, Cancun is a total **Ciudad Party**. It was carved out of a jungle just 20 years ago, so you won't feel compelled to read about the area's history—there isn't any (with all due respect to you Mayan Literature majors out there). The town is a cornucopia of late night bars that cater to the young (underage) and restless (horny). Of course, we'll elaborate on the particulars later.

Where To Stay

There are basically two options here. You can stay in the beach area (**Hotel Zone**) or in town.

The beach has undeniable advantages:

1. You can scope the opposite sex from your balcony.
2. You are close to the water and the daytime action.
3. If you discover that a combination of body surfing, four Coronas, bean dip, and two margaritas isn't sitting well in your stomach, you can stagger to your room for an emergency pit stop.

Staying in town, on the other hand, has a charm all its own. The best thing: it's pretty close to the nightlife, an important consideration at 3:30am when you're trying to get a non-existent taxi home. The hotels in town are generally much cheaper, too.

If you want specific hotel recommendations, check with the package tour operators or your travel agent. (Do you really think we'd waste our time in Cancun investigating which hotels provide the nicest black velvet paintings in the rooms?) Generally, anything with the words "Americana," "Fiesta," "Oasis," or "Beach" in the name are fine. Be warned that this covers 95% of Cancun hotels.

Getting Started

Assuming you've made it from the plane to your hotel with your ski jacket and boots stuffed up your t-shirt to avoid getting laughed at, and you've checked-in and changed into your hot pink beach gear, what do you do next?

Well, first thing might be to **explore the beach**, either the one in front of your own Fiesta Beach Americana Hotel or the beach next door at the Hotel Americana Fiesta Beach. It really doesn't matter too much. The beaches in Cancun are pretty awesome and will banish any ideas of the Jersey Shore or Venice Beach from your mind forever. So slip on your swimsuit, cover all exposed skin with two inches of partly hydrogenated coconut oil, don the Ray-Bans, and hit the sand. On the way, pick up a few Coronas or drinks with silly umbrellas in them from a poolside bar. Snag a prime piece of oceanfront real estate, and settle in.

Now, take a good look around you. If you arrive at the right time (late February-April), it will be the height of Spring Break season, and you'll be surrounded by 30,000 American college students—average age 19, average I.Q. some small multiple of 19. A guffawing group of 300-pound Neanderthals with baseball caps on backwards are playing a game called Toss the Squealing Coed from the Univ. of Texas at Austin. Cruising down the beach are two iron-pumpers from Queens, whose bikini bathing suits can only be seen from the rear, the fronts obscured by bulging beer guts. "Fuckin' babes everywhere, huh Vinnie?" one of them says in his inimitable way, all 50 neurons firing simultaneously.

To get some peace and quiet, you may need to pack up your stuff and move to the intellectual end of the beach, where it's Judith Krantz Day. There you'll be surrounded by 200 nervous sociology majors, twisting and turning on their towels as they race to the end of I'll Take Wednesday. Will the beautiful, passionate, and temperamental Wednesday O'Donnell Berkowitz wrest control of her father's perfume empire from her evil twin Blaise? Will she find happiness with the swashbuckling plastic surgeon/airline captain/gun runner, or (turn page) is she fated to fall into the clutches of the evil Baron Von Braü, who has already (turn over, apply oil to back of legs) fathered an illegitimate daughter by Wednesday's lovely but weak mother? The plot twists and turns as Wednesday's lips are crushed beneath the searing, needy kisses of her gun runner/airline captain/plastic surgeon, where he succeeds in touching her very core (ouch!), where he transports her to ecstatic heights and plunges her to depraved depths that she never knew existed within her own secret self, where . . .

Well, you get the picture. We have to go towel off now. This is fun, but its time to move on to the organized activities available to you and your dad's Gold Card.

Things To Do

A popular daytime activity includes getting one hour of instruction in a swimming pool and signing a Spanish document that could be either 1. a contract to purchase a time-share in the Oasis Fiesta Beach development, 2. the instructor's dry cleaning receipt, or 3. a consent form for **scuba diving**. Then, you take scratched-up, 10-year-old scuba gear, go a half-mile offshore, and dive 40-feet down in barracuda-infested, violently churning water so you can see fish that look just like the ones in the tank in your dentist's office, where you aren't 40-feet down in barracuda-infested, violently churning water.

Cancun has many dive shops that offer this exciting service. Don't worry—nothing bad can happen to you. You're on vacation!

Another possibility is renting a **jet-ski** for $40 an hour plus gas. Or how about **windsurfing**? For half the price of a jet-ski, you can flop and flounder around as you try to stay upright for an hour.

Better yet, there's the thrilling experience of **parasailing**. There's no need to be frightened, as you were last summer when Scott made you go bungee-jumping at Great Adventure. For one thing, you'll be amazed at all the assistance the ground crew will give you when you land. Literally dozens of hands will grasp your buttocks, thighs, torso, buttocks, and thighs to guide you gently to the ground. The friendliness and concern of these people is really quite impressive.

By late afternoon, it's the tradition in proper Cancun Spring Break Society to repair to your room. If you've come with a bunch of *compadres* (hey, your Spanish is coming along nicely!) and are housed six to a room, feel free to spend the next few hours fighting over the shower. If you've come with a special someone, you don't need any advice from us. Suffice to say that by sundown you should put your clothes back on and get ready to tackle the extensive evening entertainment.

Nightlife

Most of the nightlife in Cancun involves going to dinner and then trying to get into one of the hot bars of the moment (see below). To get to any bar or restaurant or combination of the two, grab a cab or bus along **Kukulcan Blvd.**, the strip along the Hotel Zone. The buses are about one-tenth the price of a cab, but if there are ten of you, you might as well all pile in a taxi.

For dinner, it's quite helpful if you like Mexican food. Don't expect to find gourmet Mexican fare—Cancun caters strictly to the tourist trade. But if Taco Bell is your idea of an exotic eating experience, then you'll find Cancun *muy delicioso*, as we Mayans say. The most reasonable restaurant is **The Captain's Table**, of which there are two branches, the better one being across the street from the Oasis and Omni Hotels. The lines can be terrible, so bring something to read (*The Collected Works of Judith Krantz* is probably about the right weight and intellectual level) while you wait.

The Captain's Cove has good buffet breakfasts (with excellent fruit). It's a good idea to get in line right after dinner if you want to have breakfast there.

In the downtown area, two places to check out are **Frijoles** at 33 Tulum Ave., which has live mariachi music during the high season. Also consider **Mi Ranchito** down the street (15-16 Tulum Ave.).

Note that the bill at a Mexican restaurant includes tax but not tip. Be careful of an endearing local habit of adding tax to the bill as a separate item. The waiters will back down immediately if you call them on it, but you'll notice this little scam several times during your stay.

After dinner, stroll Tulum Avenue and wait to see if dinner stays put or if you'll be catching the Kaopectate Express back to your hotel. Assuming everything is okay digestion-wise, it's time to head to the bars and interface with other Young College Kids on Spring Break.

Most of the bar scene takes place on the strip connecting the downtown area with the hotel strip (**Kukulcan Blvd.**). The current popular favorites are a set of look-alike places with a beat-up Friday's/Bennigan's decor, all part of some chain probably controlled by a company in an office park in Maryland with a name like Global Leisure Concepts, Inc. These include **Carlos** 'n **Charlie's**, offering dockside dancing (marker km 5.5); **Señor Frogs** (next door), with live reggae bands but slightly claustrophobic; and **La Mama de Tarzan** (opposite Aristos Hotel, marker km 9.5), a big place with dockside tables to dance on. All three feature Corona and a "slammer girl," Cancun's version of the German *barfrau*.

Another thing you'll notice in most Cancun nightspots: everyone tries to climb onto something much higher than the floor—tables, railings, rafters, etc. Occasionally, someone gets decapitated by a ceiling fan, but it's a great sight, and everyone just yelps and keeps dancing.

Everybody goes to these places, and there are long lines to get in. Once you get inside, you can practice the Primal Scream exercises your therapist prescribed, and no one will think you're weird. Probably, no one will even hear you. That's why these bars are such good places to meet people:

You: "Hi!"

Girl: "What?"

You: "I said, 'Hi!'"

Girl: "Who?"

You: "I SAID, 'HI!' What's your name?"

Girl: "I still can't hear you, and anyway you look really stupid in that shirt. It looks like something my father—no, my grandfather—would wear."

You: "Your t-shirt. Hard Rock Cafe—Boston. I go to Boston College. I SAID, 'I GO TO BOSTON COLLEGE!'"

Girl: "Could you go there *now* and maybe take your gross friend with you? If he wants to look down my shirt, why doesn't he stand on the bar? He's going to damage his eyes. On second thought, maybe I'll damage his eyes."

You: "ALRIGHT! IT'S WILD HERE, ISN'T IT? WE'VE BEEN HERE SINCE THURSDAY. Pretty awesome place! I SAID, 'PRETTY AWESOME PLACE!'"

Girl: "How long have you and your friend been walking upright?"

You: "THIS IS MY FRIEND HURL. MY FRIEND HURL! We call him Hurl 'cause when he's really smashed he hurls a lot! I SAID, 'HE HURLS A LOT!'"

Girl: "Excuse me, I think I see my friend waiting for me."

You: "Would you like . . . Uh, WOULD YOU LIKE TO SLAM DANCE WITH HURL LATER? HE DOESN'T GET OUT MUCH."

Later, tell your friends about the really cool girl you met and about the hot conversation you two had at the bar and how you made plans to get together back in Boston.

Other places to check out at night include **The Boat** at San Marino Center (again in the Hotel Zone), which claims to be the reggae capital of Cancun. It's a good place to hang out and listen to music. Because part of the bar is outside, it's also a good place to have a fight with your boyfriend and have some assurance that he can hear the names you're calling him. Finally, of course, there's a **Hard Rock Cafe** (where *isn't* there one these days?), where you can pick up a t-shirt to add to your collection, you dork.

Those of you who participate only in organized events should look into the **Pirate's Night Cruise**, held on a very unauthentic pirate ship that doubles as a dive boat during the day. For about $40, you get to eat from a mediocre buffet, drink at an open bar, dance to disco music, and throw up over the sides. (You may want to Hi-lite the last sentence with your yellow Hi-liter so you do things in the right order.) The boat leaves from **Playa Langosta dock** daily (except Sunday) at 6:00pm. Anyone with a sense of irony may appreciate this last fact—a pirate ship with a printed schedule:

"Ahoy, ladies and gentlemen! The 6:00pm departure of our Pirate's Night Cruise will be attacking *The Fantasy* of the Carnival Lines, off Santa Domingo. We will be on board *The Fantasy* for approximately three hours, and you may burn, rape, and pillage at will. Be sure to join us on the pool deck at 11:00pm, when Kathie Lee Gifford will be stripped, lashed, forced to walk the plank, and then eaten by sharks. We expect to be back in port by midnight.

"Let me take this opportunity to thank you for sailing with *The Pirate's Ship*. The Captain has requested that you keep your seat belts fastened until the seat belt sign has been turned off. As this will be a raid of less than six hours, federal regulations prohibit the smoking of cigarettes, pipes, or cigars. For your comfort and safety, smoke detectors have been installed in the lavatories. . ."

Mayan Ruins

All the literature you'll pick up around Cancun urges you to see the fabulous Mayan Ruins, either at **Tulum** or the bigger pile of rubble at **Chichén Itzá**. In an effort to save you the trouble, we took a trip out to Chichén Itzá, and believe us, it wasn't pretty. Here is our report:

An integral part of any trip to Chichén Itzá is the need to hit the road about the same time you've returned from an extensive exploration of the nightly cultural opportunities along Kukulcan Blvd. Just as you're pretty sure there's nothing left in your stomach and you're lying on your bed in the peaceful twilight that marks the transition between feeling you could die and thinking that you might, in fact, be okay if you get some sleep, the phone rings. It's Pedro from Cancun Discovery Tours, calling to remind you that the bus to whisk you in un-air-conditioned comfort to the famous Chichén Itzá is waiting downstairs and that all the other happy tourists are aboard and anxious to get going. You explain that you've changed your mind because you're planning to die in the next few minutes and therefore you're not available.

Pedro, who earlier in the day (Or was it the day before? It's all a blur) had hustled you into parting with your Visa Card number with a command of English that would give William F. Buckley a run for his money, has become Señor No Comprendo. The next thing you know, Pedro and his driver Miguel are banging on your door and soon they've dressed you, combed your hair, and packed you onto the bus. Since you're the last to arrive, you get to sit beside a 400-pound German woman of an uncertain age who has been up for hours reading about Der Ruines.

The bus lurches off, and before you know it, you've gone two miles, with only another 123 to go. Sleep is impossible, because every time you doze off and slip a little sideways, your seatmate elbows your ribs with such force it could have brought down the Berlin Wall with one knock.

A mere four hours later, you arrive in Chichén Itzá. *Hah,* you think, *I'll let everybody else check out the rubble, and I'll catch a few zzzz's on the bus.* Wrong again, gringo. It seems that Miguel, your driver, has some ideas that involve the bus, himself, and a local hostess, so you are pitched into the balmy heat of the late morning. Miguel, one hand on the steering wheel, one hand unbuttoning his pants, promises to be back in five hours.

The moment your feet hit the ground, a new set of problems appears: packs of urchins selling crap—a sight you've seen in every movie set in the Third World, except that in this case you don't have Robert Redford to yell at them in Aztec or whatever they speak in Chichén Itzá. Instead, they surround you like gnats, wanting to sell you postcards, candy, guidebooks, cigarettes, their sisters, their brothers. To escape this band of cutthroats-with-training-wheels, you pay the admission and stagger around the ruins.

The ruins are in ruins all right. You wonder why they don't take the trouble to fix them. It's obvious to you that both the Mayans and the Egyptians were inspired by extraterrestrials, who taught them how to make rubble and half-collapsed buildings. The sun beats down, you can't find anything to drink, and you need to go to the bathroom. Bad.

You hook up with the rest of your party and follow a guide around. He's explaining that Chichén Itzá was mysteriously abandoned about the middle of some century and nobody knows why. But you know why instantly: there's no air-conditioning. The Mayans probably just moved to Cancun, where at least they've got AC.

Late in the afternoon, you discover the difference between a trip to Chichén Itzá and a barium enema. After a barium enema, you don't have to take a four-hour bus ride home.

Shopping

In downtown Cancun (right off Tulum Ave.), there's a large **Crafts Market**, where you might want to spend a few hours shopping for goods you won't find at Wal-Mart. These souvenirs will delight your folks and enrich your own personal life. Not.

There are several types of pottery to buy, and, let's face it, you can never have enough containers to hold your spare pennies until you find time in your busy schedule to roll them, right? Or how about a nice earthenware pitcher decorated with festive, lead-based glazes for someone you're not real crazy about? You can enjoy watching him slowly turn into goulash: "Still drooling profusely, huh, Bobby? Here, let me get you a nice big glass of orange juice. Oh, I see you're using that pitcher I brought back from Cancun for you . . ." You'll also find good buys on leather goods, especially sandals and whips. (Hey, what you do in the privacy of your own love pad is up to you, but, off the record, tell us—have you been a bad boy again? Do you need to be punished by Mommy?)

Haggling with the natives is certainly acceptable, and, after you hear the opening prices for anything, your inhibitions about bargaining will disappear quickly. Most of these stall owners worked for defense contractors in the days when the Pentagon gladly spent $2,000 for a toothpick holder. Because of military budget cuts, the stall owners are now forced to make a living off visiting college students.

Kelly: "Scott, look at these cute sandals! Aren't they just the neatest things you have ever seen! I've just got to have them. Do you think that this guy understands American?"

Scott: "Probably a little. I'll try to talk to him, even though I flunked Spanish in high school. I wish I knew the Spanish word for 'sandals.'"

Kelly: "Isn't it *sandalista*?"

Scott: "Yeah! Um, excuso me, Pedro. How mucho dollars Americano fora thesa sandalistas, por favor?"

Stall Owner: "Ninety bucks."

Kelly: "Ohmigod, Scott, he understands you! Can you try bargaining with him a little. Ninety dollars is a lot. After all, this *is* Mexico."

Scott: "Ninety dollars mucho por Americano collego studento. Ten dollars, por favor?"

Stall Owner: "Ninety bucks."

Kelly: "It's not working, Scott. Maybe I should try."

Scott: "C'mon, Kelly, you don't speak Spanish. Let me try one more time. Por favor, sandalistas mucho, er, good. How mucho dollars?"

Stall Owner: "Ninety bucks, and I'll throw in a box for free."

Kelly: "It's working! You made him compromise. Keep going Scott! Don't stop now! Please don't stop now!"

Scott: "Kelly, you know I hate it when you pressure me to perform."

Kelly (thinking to herself wistfully): *Bill could always perform. I never should have dumped him.*

Scott: "Itsa stilla grande mucho, señor, por favor."

Stall Owner: "Ninety bucks, plus I'll throw in the box and a coupon for half off the next pair you buy when you come back to Cancun."

Kelly: "We'll take it!"

Scott: "Kelly, I think I can get him to go lower. I have him where I want him now."

Kelly: "Let's not push our luck. Anyway, it's only ninety dollars in pesos. How much is that in American money?"

Scott and Stall Owner together: "Ninety dollars."

Kelly: "Really? Are you sure?"

Time to head for the airport.

About the Authors

Thomas Neenan was raised in Ireland and grew up confused while watching *Dallas* and *The Waltons*. Graduate school in the U.S. did not help. After two years at Harvard, he managed to get a grown-up job in New Jersey, where he is now trying to break into professional bowling. He doesn't watch *Dallas* anymore.

Greg Hancock spent 23 years of soul-searching in school while accumulating over 4,552 credits (but still lacking 2 required P.E. credits). It took getting an MBA from a really huge state university to land him a job in a really big corporation in New Jersey. Now he has the money but only two weeks a year in which to travel.

More Great Travel Books
from Mustang Publishing

Europe on 10 Salads a Day by Mary Jane & Greg Edwards. A must for the health-conscious traveler! From gourmet Indian cuisine in Spain to terrific take-out pizza in Italy, this book describes over 200 health food/vegetarian restaurants throughout Europe. *"Don't go to Europe without it"* —*Vegetarian Times*. **$9.95**

Europe for Free by Brian Butler. If you're on a tight budget—or if you just love a bargain—this is the book for you! With descriptions of thousands of things to do and see for free all over Europe, you'll save lots of lira, francs, and pfennigs. *"Well-organized and packed with ideas"* —*Modern Maturity*. **$8.95**

Also in this series:
London for Free by Brian Butler. **$7.95**
DC for Free by Brian Butler. **$6.95**
Hawaii for Free by Frances Carter. **$6.95**

The Nepal Trekker's Handbook by Amy R. Kaplan. This book guides trekkers through every aspect of planning and enjoying a trek through Nepal—one of the world's most magnificent adventures. From medical advice to cultural *faux-pas*, it's an essential guide. *"A must"* — *Midwest Book Review*. **$9.95**

Australia: Where the Fun Is by Goodyear & Skinner. From the best pubs in Sydney to the cheapest motels in Darwin to the greatest hikes in Tasmania, this guide by two recent Yale grads details all the fun stuff Down Under—on and off the beaten path. *"Indispensable"* —*Library Journal*. **$12.95**

Festival Europe! Fairs and Celebrations throughout Europe by Margaret M. Johnson. What's the best—and least expensive—way to interact with Europeans and their cultures? Attend their myriad festivals, celebrations, fairs, and parades, most of which are free! From the somber Holy Blood Procession in Bruges to the wild Oktoberfest in Munich, this guide will help any traveler have a terrific, festive time in Europe. *"An excellent book for the serious traveler."* — *Bookviews*. **$10.95**

France on the TGV: How to Use the World's Fastest Train to Get the Most out of France by Mark Beffart. Imagine boarding a train in Paris in the morning and arriving in Nice—almost 700 miles away—in time to get a suntan! With the TGV, the world's fastest train, it's easy, and this book describes everything you need to know about this *magnifique* rail network. With walking tours of over 50 French towns served by the TGV, **France on the TGV** will help you get the most out of your trip to France. *"An exceptionally useful guide"* — *Atlanta Journal-Constitution*. **$12.95**

Northern Italy: A Taste of Trattoria by Christina Baglivi. For the most delicious, most authentic, and least expensive meals in Italy, head straight for *trattorie*, the small, unassuming cafes known only to locals. This guide, describing over 80 *trattorie* from Rome to Chatillon, is a must for the hungry traveler. *"A tasty tidbit of a tour guide"* —*Quick Trips Travel Letter*. **$9.95**

Mustang books should be available at your local bookstore. If not, send a check or money order for the price of the book, plus $1.50 postage per book, to Mustang Publishing, P.O. Box 3004, Memphis, TN 38173, USA.

Allow three weeks for delivery. For one-week delivery, add $3.00 to the total. *International orders*: Please pay in U.S. funds, and add $5.00 to the total for Air Mail.

For a catalog of Mustang books, send $1.00 and a stamped, self-addressed, business size envelope to Catalog Request, Mustang Publishing, P.O. Box 3004, Memphis, TN 38173.